The Work of Graham Sutherland

# The Work of Graham Sutherland

Text by Douglas Cooper

Lund Humphries 12 Bedford Square London WCI

For K.F.S. and K.M.C. Supporters and Friends

First edition, Autumn 1961
Reprinted, Spring 1962

Made and printed in Great Britain
by Percy Lund, Humphries & Co. Ltd
London and Bradford

# Contents

# Author's Foreword

The firm of Lund Humphries has distinguished itself in the
post-war years by publishing a succession of lavishly illustrated
monographs on the work of living British artists. The idea for this
series originated with the firm's chairman, the late Mr E. C. Gregory,
one of the leading supporters of the modern art movement in England,
and it was essentially his personal interest in and enthusiasm for the
project which kept it alive and expanding. Eric Gregory spared no pains
or pennies in his attempt to produce the best possible book, that is to
say one which would do most honour to the artist and help to make his
work better and more widely appreciated. Gregory it was who first
thought of adding a volume on the work of Graham Sutherland to his
series, and during many conversations that we had together before he
died I learnt how keen he was both on seeing it materialize and on
knowing that nothing was being neglected which would enable the
artist and the author to achieve their ideal presentation. Few publishers
can have been as generous or co-operative to work with and, speaking
personally, I would not wish this occasion to pass without due
recognition of how much this volume in its final form owes to
Eric Gregory's sense of perfectionism and sympathetic understanding.
Fortunately, his successor, Mr Anthony Bell, is imbued with much of
the same spirit and so carried on with this publication in like manner
after the death of his chief.
My own share of the responsibility for compiling this monograph was
defined early on when Eric Gregory and Graham Sutherland asked me
if I would write the introductory text and assume, in conjunction with
themselves, a general editorial responsibility. This I willingly agreed to
do, but the more closely I studied Sutherland's work the more I
realized that I could not ultimately content myself with writing a
conventionally non-committal, gently explanatory, brief prefatory essay.
Gradually I found that nothing less than a full-length critical and
biographical study would suffice to explain what I had discovered as I
probed more deeply into the personality of Sutherland the man and the
original pictorial imagery through which he expresses his reactions to
the world within and around him. After studying Sutherland's works,

however, and arriving at certain conclusions, I was still faced with many problems of interpretation. And so, wanting to test my ideas and learn more, I had no alternative but to resort to the process of direct question and answer. This meant, of course, that I had to persuade both the artist and Mrs Sutherland, who has shared his life, kept written records of events, and listened to all his most intimate thoughts for the last thirty-five years, to co-operate with me in a succession of long, intimate, and often difficult conversations. But because they understood the reasons for my curiosity and continually showed willingness to reply to provocative questionnaires, to answer innumerable awkward and often indiscreet questions, and to check and re-check facts and dates, I was able to make this book more comprehensive, more authoritative, and more fully documented than it otherwise could have been. Accordingly, I take this opportunity of expressing to both Mr and Mrs Sutherland not merely my gratitude but also my sense of personal satisfaction that they bore with me so patiently and showed me along the way so many marks of friendship and affection.

For the rest, it remains only for me to thank Mr John Richardson for the stimulation and encouragement which I received from him while I was at work; also to express my gratitude to Sir Kenneth Clark, one of Sutherland's earliest patrons, for reading my text in manuscript and offering some helpful suggestions.

D.C.

## Publishers' Acknowledgements

The publishers acknowledge with thanks all those who have assisted in the preparation of this volume. Owners of works, wherever ascertained, are acknowledged individually in the list of plates; for special permission to reproduce certain paintings and drawings, thanks are due to: The Right Hon. Lord Beaverbrook, Dean Hussey of Chichester, Mr H. P. Juda, Sir Basil Spence, The Vicar of St Matthew's, Northampton, The Arts Council, The Birmingham City Museum and Art Gallery, The British Council, The Controller of H.M. Stationery Office, Imperial War Museum, The National Museum of Wales, The Tate Gallery.

The publishers also wish to thank the following: For editorial assistance and research: Mrs Lilian Somerville of The British Council, Jane Wade (for research assistance, particularly amongst the American Collections), Bernard Karpel of the Museum of Modern Art, New York, and Paul Rosenberg, New York. Deutsche Verlags-Anstalt, Stuttgart, for permission to use their colour plates for the portrait of Prince Fürstenberg; The British Council and Penguin Books Ltd for help in reproducing the colour plate 'Gorse on Sea Wall'; W. Churcher, A. C. Cooper, Felix Man, James Mortimer, John Underwood, for permission to reproduce photographs of works; N. R. Farbman and Time-Life International Ltd for permission to reproduce the portrait of Graham Sutherland which serves as the frontispiece; Curwen Press Ltd for their work in connexion with the proofing and printing of Graham Sutherland's design for the binding.

## I. Concerning Graham Sutherland's Artistic Personality and Achievements

Graham Sutherland is the most distinguished and the most original English artist of the mid-20th century. Fifteen years ago this statement would have seemed surprising. Admittedly Sutherland was already recognized then as a leading personality, but he had not reached maturity nor transcended the limitations and provincialism of most English art. For this reason his pictures did not have the deeply affective and imaginative quality of those which he paints today. During the last ten years Sutherland has developed a more penetrating vision, his handling has become more sure and his colours clearer and more brilliant. In short, he has overcome the weaknesses which bedevil painters of the English school and has emerged as a painter of international standing. Sutherland owes much of his remarkable gain in strength as an artist to what he has learnt from the best contemporary art produced in Europe. But he does not shamelessly borrow from other painters any more than he tries to imitate successful European styles. He does not need to do so because he has the capacity to transform anything which he takes over in such a way that it becomes part of his personality and is fully absorbed into his own English manner of painting. That has been one of the secrets of his development into a painter with an international reputation. For Graham Sutherland has now taken his place among the leading artists of Europe and is contributing something of his own to their tradition. And it is this achievement which has recently received official recognition by the award of the Order of Merit. Today, no other English painter can compare with Sutherland in the subtlety of his vision, in the forcefulness of his imagery and in the sureness of his touch. Also there is none whose sensibility and inspiration are so unmistakably and naturally English, yet whose handling and technical approach are so authoritative, modern and European.

During the last seventy-five years repeated efforts have been made by English painters with an awareness of contemporary developments elsewhere to overturn the English tradition of painting 'by the light of nature' in favour of a tougher style related to that of European masters. But when one thinks of the members of the New English Art Club practising a debased impressionistic idiom, of the members of the Camden Town Group and Duncan Grant trying to make something of their own out of Gauguin and Cézanne, of Nevinson and Wyndham Lewis aping the Futurists and Cubists, of Matthew Smith trying to be a Fauve, or of Paul Nash's flirtation with Surrealism, it becomes abundantly clear that these efforts were vain. As strictly English painters some of them had undoubted merits, but none forced his way into the main stream of European art and made there a significant individual contribution. In order to do so, they would have needed far more passion, concentration, and technical ability, as well as insight into the sources of inspiration and motivating forces which had produced the various European styles. Lacking these they could not achieve a viable and creative fusion between an English vision and a European practice of art, so the pictures which they produced were mannered, genteel, inelegant hybrids.

Sutherland, on the other hand, has succeeded where his predecessors failed, for he has established a cunning and convincing balance between these two elements, the English and the European. In true English fashion he persists in looking for inspiration in nature, in the objective world around him, yet he has never shirked his duty as an artist to transcend and transform the evidence of his eyes through pictorial science in order to arrive at a more effective image. To this end he has familiarized himself with the pictorial language of a Matisse, a Picasso, a Kandinsky, a Miró or a Max Ernst and, because he has understood, he is able to apply their procedures to his own work without affectation or plagiarism. Sutherland's pictures transmit characteristically English feelings: an attitude to nature which is ambivalent in its reverence, suggesting at once fascination, awe, and horror; a certain fear of vast open spaces and of the peculiarities of natural formations and growth; a love of luxuriance and of the mystery surrounding the impenetrable; a pantheistic acceptance of the cycle of growth, fruition and decay. Yet these feelings are formulated in terms of the language current among contemporary European artists. Moreover, Sutherland is an exception among English artists in that his works do not make one feel that their content could have been more satisfactorily expressed in words. But then, unlike most English painters, Graham Sutherland is aware that observable facts must take precedence over extraneous ideas, because the true painter should have 'no need of a remoter charm, by thought supplied, nor any interest unborrowed from the eye'.[1] This is particularly evident in the series of psychological portraits with which he has been increasingly concerned during the last ten years. There is no bravura in these, no false flattery, no tendency to present a sitter as he might see himself, no cheating with the truth. These portraits are essentially honest, realistic character studies and result from the artist's understanding of his sitter after persistent observation and personal contact. What Sutherland sees is, of course, only a part of the whole truth, but the merit of his portraits is that they contain nothing which has not been obtained by visual or psychological observation. Moreover, the necessity to build up on canvas an image of another human being which is instinct with life demands a special degree of technical control from the artist. Thus the discipline of portraiture has also contributed greatly to Sutherland's growing

[1] *vide* Wordsworth's *Tintern Abbey*.

mastery. Such are the qualities which constitute his originality and his importance and which make of him – in European as well as purely English terms – a painter of the front rank.

If, however, one tries to situate the work of Graham Sutherland in relation to the English pictorial tradition and to contemporary European art in general, one immediately becomes aware of the ways in which it is singular and surprising. None of the familiar stylistic labels can be attached to it absolutely: Graham Sutherland's painting is neither expressionist, nor realist, nor surrealist, nor cubist. Nor is it abstract or decorative. It is an amalgam, in varying degrees of strength, of them all. This has proved a stumbling-block for most critics – especially in England, where the unconventionality of Sutherland's outlook is not understood – and has delayed recognition of his personality abroad.

'An artist like Sutherland is not, is *essentially* not, a humanist,' writes Sir Herbert Read. 'Sutherland is a landscapist, like so many of his English predecessors.'[1] No judgment could be more misleading. This attempt to limit the range of Sutherland's interests and to deny him any concern with human affairs is contrary to the truth, because it ignores Sutherland's portraits, his studies of insects and animals, his religious paintings, his still lifes and his designs for fabrics and tapestries. Admittedly landscape once provided Sutherland with the principal source of his inspiration, but for a long time now it has been no more than an occasional subject. And even when he was strictly a landscapist, Sutherland never showed himself to be 'like so many of his English predecessors'; indeed his attitude was very different. Sutherland never subscribed to the typical English view that when God made the world he intended it to be a beautiful, fruitful and wonderful habitation for Man. Nor will the view of the world reflected in his pictures please Sir Kenneth Clark's average Englishman who 'looks to nature as an unequalled source of consolation and joy'.[2] Quite the contrary. Sutherland refrains from a broad, rapturous or sensuous view of nature. In fact he avoids both the awe-inspiring panorama and the type of landscape in which the diverseness of the constituent elements is used by the artist to underline the excellence of God's handiwork. Instead, he has contracted his vision to focus on individual natural phenomena which have a special significance for himself.

So much for the ways in which Sutherland's view of nature differs from that of other English painters. Instead of describing him as a landscapist, I would suggest that it is more accurate to describe him as a nature painter, though even this description demands immediate qualification, because Sutherland does not paint nature for its own sake – as a matter of fact he is apt to look at it askance – but for what it has to offer

[1] Introduction to the Catalogue of the Sutherland Exhibition at the Tate Gallery, May 1953.
[2] *Landscape into Art* (London, 1949), p. 133.

him in the way of images relating to human beings. In his eyes, nature is not a friendly force which exists to be 'fruitful and profitable for man'.[1] He inclines to see in it a repertory of forms which are in part reflections, in part caricatures, in part adversaries of man. The predatory gorse clambering up the sea wall[2] has long bony fingers like a miser or, if we read the image in another way, the plant appears to be crowning the featureless head of a mannequin; two barren oak-trees in association[3] suggest tragi-comic characters in a costume play; a thorn-bush formation becomes a head in which are expressed all the agonies of a Crucifixion;[4] a palm palisade calls to mind a phalanx of fixed bayonets.[5] A concern with life and with human beings – hence his easy transition to portraiture – underlies all Sutherland's imagery, and his attitude was well summed up by Sir Kenneth Clark when he wrote: 'Sutherland does not, like the "abstract" artist, give up imitation in favour of a new pictorial reality; on the contrary, he seems to imitate objects with the most literal accuracy; only these objects have no material existence. And yet they convince us that they could exist. This is due partly to the moment of vision in which they were identified, and partly to his skill in endowing them with the structure and articulation of living things.' And the same writer concluded, significantly, that 'there are signs in Sutherland's later work that his creatures are trying to claim full human status'.[6]

From a European standpoint, the very fact of Sutherland being concerned nowadays with the painting of nature appears anachronistic and proclaims his Englishness.[7] So does his animistic tendency. In Sutherland's pictures things are what they seem to be, but in a dimension of super-reality. For the artist has filtered and sharpened his original experiences while working towards a more immediate and convincing image of them in visual-emotional terms. Yet he does not have recourse to irrationality or the double-image technique beloved of the Surrealists. On the other hand, Sutherland does depend for achieving his effects on the pictorial science which he has progressively acquired from studying modern European idioms. Undoubtedly, Sutherland has an innate personal sense

[1] Myles Coverdale in *The Olde Fayth* (1547).
[2] Plate 18.
[3] Plates 24, 25.
[4] Plates 83, 84, 111.
[5] Plates 92, 93, 94.
[6] Introduction to the Catalogue of the Sutherland Exhibition at the Tate Gallery, May 1953.
[7] Bonnard, among French painters, is an obvious exception to this generalization, but his paintings, being essentially concerned with 'the good life', with sunlight and with the colourfulness of nature, are not in the least like those of Sutherland. Nor are those of Masson, another nature painter, whose imagery is of a literary kind. Sutherland has, however, European counterparts in two German painters, Paul Klee and Max Ernst. Paul Klee is comparable with Sutherland in his obsessive concern with organic growth and vegetable and animal life, but unlike him in so far as his pictures are scientifically organized and have a disconcerting fairy-tale quality. Max Ernst and Sutherland are more closely related through dark, romantic sentiments, a cult of *genius loci* and mysteriousness, and a preoccupation with the disagreeable and frightening in animals, birds, and natural objects. But Max Ernst relies on all the tricks and textural devices (*frottage, collage,* irrationalism) of Surrealism to make his paintings more telling, and in this way diverges from Sutherland.

of the decorative propensities of colour, but he is not unaware of the subtle creative use made of them by artists such as Bonnard, Braque, Matisse or Miró. Equally, Sutherland has developed a stronger and more original sense of composition through observing the practice of Picasso, Matisse and many other modern artists. In particular, he says of Matisse that he has taught him 'a lot as to the distribution of objects in space'.[1] From the Expressionist painters, too, Sutherland has learnt something of the emotive possibilities of colour, of the character-giving property of line and of what can be achieved with exaggeration or distortion. Then he has experienced the arresting effect of mysterious 'presences' such as Picasso, Miró and de Chirico employ in their pictures, and these have affected Sutherland's own conception of what constitutes, in pictorial terms, an 'atmosphere'.

Thus Sutherland has drawn to his best advantage on a variety of European sources in the course of forming his own style and elaborating his imagery, but the final result is strictly personal. However, Sutherland only arrived at this state of creative independence after a long evolutionary process during which his original English vision and understanding of the art of painting were sublimated through exposure to foreign influences. And when he emerged in the post-war years it was as an artist of international stature with an outlook which had increased breadth and a new orientation. One of his outstanding later achievements, it seems to me, is to have bridged the gap which today separates the English from the European conception of painting. Yet Sutherland has remained at heart and in fact an English painter. Therein lies his strength, his artistic integrity and consequently his importance for the future. Because so long as he maintains intact a link with his artistic origins[2] he will continue to be proof against transient considerations of taste or fashion and will not succumb to the temptation of assuming a false identity.

## II. The Landscape Years: 1921–45
### (i) The Etcher and Engraver: 1921–31
Graham Sutherland was born in London on 24th August 1903. He grew up at Merton Park, Surrey and at Rustington in Sussex before going first to school at Sutton (1912), and then on to Epsom College in 1914. In 1919 – by which time his artistic inclinations were already manifesting themselves and he had spontaneously begun to draw – Sutherland went to serve an apprenticeship in the engineering branch of the Midland Railway works at Derby, where an uncle worked. But he soon found that having

[1] Letter to the author of December 1959.
[2] *vide* G. Sutherland, 'A Trend in English Draughtsmanship' in *Signature,* No.3, July 1936, p.11, where he quotes Jean Cocteau: 'The more a poet sings in his genealogical tree, the more his singing is in tune'.

to respect strict mathematical calculations and draw precise linear forms was contrary to his temperament. He realized that he had chosen the wrong career. After a year, therefore, Sutherland left Derby and went to London to study to become a painter. Accordingly, he enrolled at The Goldsmiths' College School of Art in 1921 and continued to work there until 1926. During these formative years Graham Sutherland proved himself to be a diligent and earnest student; he profited by every aspect of the teaching which the school had to offer – drawing from casts, ornament, modelling, life class and so on. At the same time he began to make frequent excursions into the country, to Kent and Sussex, because what appealed to him particularly was drawing from nature. But far from turning into a painter, Sutherland began to adopt the engraving techniques (which were taught at the school by Malcolm Osborne and Stanley Anderson) as his medium of expression. He appears to have had an innate gift for handling these and before long was showing that he could obtain a wide range of effects.[1] Then Sutherland had the good fortune to attract the attention of a master technician, F. L. Griggs, who generously offered him much useful advice of a technical kind and helped him to sharpen his engraver's vision. Moreover, a real bond of friendship was established between the two men when Griggs found that Sutherland was becoming enthusiastic about the work of Samuel Palmer and his circle of Shoreham friends.

If we look at the *Barn Interior*[2] of 1922 or the *Mill Interior*[3] of the following year we see at once the sort of subject which Sutherland originally favoured while he was an art student. There is nothing old-world, picturesque or sentimental about these works, and they are executed with an extraordinary sureness. Both are characterized by brilliant and dramatic light effects, by a clever disposition of objects within the picture space, and by an emphasis on the lines of the composition. In the former, human beings play a minor role, but in the latter they have disappeared and Sutherland shows a more modern interest in machinery, a feature more striking when, profiting by hindsight, one finds that this interest recurs not only in his wartime canvases but also in many that he has painted since 1952–53.[4] Turn now to *Cray Fields*[5] of 1925 or *Lammas*[6] of 1926 and we find that a profound change, both of mood and of technical approach, has occurred in Sutherland's work in a very short space of time. These new engravings are less rigid, more consciously artistic and remind

[1] In 1925 Sutherland was an unsuccessful Prix de Rome finalist as an engraver. One of the set-pieces for this competition was a Biblical subject, hence his two Biblical etchings *Adam and Eve* and *Cain and Abel*. All the others, except *The Philosophers*, are landscape subjects.
[2] Plate 2a.
[3] Plate 2b. No edition was issued of these two plates.
[4] e.g. plates 43, 44, 48, 128, 134c.
[5] Plate 3b.
[6] Plate 3d.

one even of Bewick or Reynolds Stone. They are of course also unmistakably Palmerish, that is to say picturesque, pastoral, weather-conscious, rather sentimental, and a little too full of 'the felicity of Olde England'. In them, Sutherland has turned away from frank statements about objects in order to cram into a few square inches an elegiac rendering of 'a universe of beauty and suggestion'.[1] And in this respect these sheets form an episode in the development of his work and bear little relation to the subject-matter or style of his subsequent drawings and paintings. It should, however, be said that when Sutherland came under the influence of Palmer at this stage, he did so because he believed that it would help to free him both from the servitude of copying nature and from the dullness of an academic approach to engraving. As he says himself: '. . . my feeling for this was partly a bid for independence from the stereotyped Seymour Haden etc. engraving tradition of the school, which caused in me a bias towards heavily worked plates – partly also, since I liked Palmer drawings of the early few years . . . because as a young man I was drawn to a strongly romantic and, so it seemed, independent approach to nature from which I was always drawing'.[2] Obviously, Sutherland had a conscious desire to stimulate his imagination through a romantic view of nature,[3] and he maintains that Palmer provided him with the means to this end because he felt him to be 'a sort of English van Gogh'.

At first this statement seems surprising because we are more aware of the obvious differences between Palmer and van Gogh: the one a tranquil visionary, a quietist content to work with subdued colours, the other an *illuminé*, a passionate personality whose colour, line and brushwork could hardly be more exalted and expressive;[4] the one virtually a miniaturist compressing all he knows and feels into the smallest space, the other bursting with excitement and frenziedly pouring out his sensations and visual experiences over untold areas of canvas or paper for fear that something vital might escape being recorded. But if we think again, we can discover many resemblances between these two artists: both excelled at painting cornfields and night, both were subject to the spell of the sun and the moon, both revelled in the opulence of nature, both were inspired by religious sentiments and both relied greatly on symbolism in their pictures. What is curious, however, is that Sutherland should have instinctively sensed these parallels and yet have been content to remain one of 'the Ancients'. For this awareness of van Gogh should have urged

[1] Palmer.
[2] Letter to the author of December 1959.
[3] cf. Blake's: 'You have only to work up imagination to the state of vision, and the thing is done'. Also, Palmer's: 'In proportion as we enjoy and improve in imaginative art we shall love the material works of God more and more'. (Both quotations from G. Grigson, *Samuel Palmer* (London, 1947), pp.22–3.)
[4] Blake advised Palmer that 'he who does not imagine in stronger and better lineaments, and in stronger and better light, than his perishing mortal eye can see, does not imagine at all'. (Quoted by G. Grigson, *op. cit.*, p.23.)

him towards expressing himself more freely, on a broader scale and in a more modern idiom; whereas, in fact, because the reactionary influence of Palmer prevailed, Sutherland's development was retarded for over five years. Between the ages of 22 and 27, vital years of activity in the evolution of young European artists,[1] Sutherland plodded on and showed no tendency to escape from well-trodden paths or to discover anything significant on his own. In this respect, his development is typically that of an English artist. Not until 1930, indeed, in an etching such as *Pastoral*,[2] is it possible to say that Sutherland has outgrown Palmer and begun to display something of a personal vision. There, the gnarled hollow stump in the right foreground, like the bare bent tree-trunks on the left, fore-shadow much that appears in his paintings during the following ten years.[3]

As a result of two exhibitions at the Twenty-One Gallery in London in 1925 and 1928, Graham Sutherland established a considerable reputation for himself as a young engraver. His work was greatly praised by critics; in professional circles he was regarded with respect; he showed at the Royal Academy in London, as well as in exhibitions at Glasgow, Liverpool, Stockholm, Buenos Aires, and New York; and his etchings were eagerly sought after both by English and foreign collectors as well as by museums.[4] Nevertheless, he was unable to live by the sale of his prints alone[5] and had to take up teaching to increase his means of livelihood. First of all, he accepted a job at an art school in Kingston (1927), then, in 1928, he was invited to assume the greater responsibility of teaching engraving at the Chelsea School of Art. Thus, after a relatively short period on his own in London, it seemed to Sutherland as if he could look to the future with equanimity. It was at this point that he decided to marry Kathleen Barry,[6] a girl whom he had met at The Goldsmiths' College School. After their marriage they set up house at Farningham in Kent. But their hopes of a settled existence were soon dashed, because, in 1930, as a consequence of the financial crash in America, the market for etchings in England collapsed and Sutherland had to cast around for other ways of earning his living.

Thus it was that he gave up engraving and set about becoming a painter; that between 1931 and 1939 he accepted commissions to design posters

[1] By the age of 27, for example, Monet had painted his *Déjeuner sur l'herbe,* the first pure impressionist picture, while Braque and Picasso had painted their first cubist pictures.
[2] Plate 4b.
[3] e.g. plates 9b, 12c, 22, 23, 25, 32, 33.
[4] Including the British Museum, the Victoria and Albert Museum, and the Boston Museum of Fine Arts.
[5] In all, between 1923 and 1930, Sutherland made about thirty etchings. From 1925 on these were mostly issued in an edition of seventy-seven copies; about three new plates appeared per year, and brought in a total sum of approximately £900.
[6] Mrs Sutherland abandoned her intention of pursuing an artistic career independently to devote herself entirely to the needs of her husband. But her artistic training has enabled her to keep in touch with the evolution of his work and to understand his many technical and aesthetic problems. Thus at all times she has been able to give him moral support and assistance, and these have proved one of his greatest sources of inspiration and encouragement.

Fig. 1
**Dorset Farm**  1932 Oil on hardboard
Private collection 23⅞ × 19¾ in.

for the Orient Line, the London Passenger Transport Board, the Post Office and the Shell-Mex Company; and also that during the same years he began to make designs for fabrics, ceramics and other decorative articles. In consequence of this great shift in his interests, Sutherland gave up teaching engraving at Chelsea and in 1932 agreed to teach Composition and Book Illustration instead. This he went on doing until the outbreak of war in 1939. Now one of the best ways of gaining a real insight into a subject is to teach it, and the expansion of Sutherland's vision and the increasing boldness which he showed in his paintings throughout the 1930's are surely fruits of this new activity. In the same way, the fact that he was suddenly obliged to make allowances for considerations of taste and to cultivate whatever decorative sense he had, forced Sutherland to enlarge his understanding of art and to release instincts which he might otherwise have suppressed. But the effort was rewarded, for the experience that Sutherland gained in the fields of design and decoration during the pre-war years has proved of use[1] and actively influences his ideas of composition and colouring even today.

[1] In the last twenty years Sutherland has designed many fabrics, also book-jackets, carpets and table-tops. In 1949 he designed a tapestry for the Edinburgh Tapestry Company (repr. in R. Melville, *Graham Sutherland* (London, 1950), plates 23, 62, 63). Since 1952 he has been at work designing and supervising the execution of a vast tapestry for Coventry Cathedral, *vide* Plates 158–160, also Chapter IV(i).

## (ii) The Painter: 1931–45

Sutherland did not, as it might seem, give up engraving altogether in-voluntarily. By 1931, when he had etched his last plate, he already felt that he had said all he 'wanted to say within the Palmer tradition'.[1] The time had come 'to revitalize' his work and Sutherland knew that unless he could shake off 'the habit' of confining his vision within 'a narrow field' he ran the risk of imprisoning his art in a *cul-de-sac*. It is, anyway, difficult for an artist to expand his field of vision and broaden his handling at will, but in Sutherland's case this process was further complicated by the fact that he had decided to turn to another and, for him, unwonted medium: painting. Not unnaturally he had some misgivings and his development up till 1940 was to be both painful and slow. He had spent the previous ten years compressing his complex visual experiences of nature on to surfaces often smaller than that of a post-card, with only black and white to supply the tonal effects. All of a sudden he was confronted by the much larger surface of a canvas and an infinite array of different colours. What should he paint? And, more important, what manner of representing things did he find most appropriate? First he had to learn a new discipline, and for this reason Sutherland began, as he says, 'to paint painstakingly and objectively from the *motif* in nature', literally copying what he saw and matching, tone by tone, the colours on his canvas with those in an actual scene. At the same time he had to face up to the relationship between colour and light as an active pictorial element. In order to make the necessary effort to free himself from the constrictions of the past, Sutherland felt that he had for a while to get away from Kent, which was too closely associated in his mind with Palmer and a type of art against which he was reacting. Accordingly, he went to work in Dorset, a county which he had first visited as a child, and which seemed to him to offer many pictorial possibilities.

We know virtually nothing about the paintings which Sutherland made between 1931 and 1934 because in his eyes they were failures and, with one exception,[2] were subsequently destroyed. Suffice it to say that they were not imaginative works but conscientious exercises in the hand-ling of a medium for which Sutherland still had to discover how much natural facility he possessed. Yet for all that he was striving to master the art of painting, Sutherland did not neglect to cultivate his imaginative vision. He continued, as in the past, to draw regularly from nature, but in these smaller drawings and water-colours[3] he permitted himself to treat natural appearances in a freer and altogether more conceptual manner.

[1] The information in the following pages has been mainly gathered during conversations with the artist, although many quotations are also taken from letters to the author.
[2] Fig. 1.
[3] Plate 5, a, b, c and d.

They are somewhat tentative and, from a stylistic point of view, lack homogeneity. But there are certain features about them which deserve to be noticed, in particular the disregard of naturalism, the rejection of scientific perspective, the use of line to create rhythm and the careful choice of a few colours which are used not to describe things but to evoke sensations. They also have a documentary interest since they are the first works which reveal Sutherland's preoccupation with the process of organic growth.

The year 1934 marks a vital point of departure in Sutherland's evolution. In the spring of 1934, he made the first of many visits to Wales,[1] found himself at last as a painter and had the courage to begin transposing his imaginative sketches from black and white into colour. These pictures were the first which he felt to be serious creative works, and those that have survived constitute the foundation of his *œuvre*. They are landscape visions of a bare, dramatic, strongly romantic sort and their spirit is unmistakably English. How indeed could they be otherwise, since at that time Graham Sutherland's pictorial inspiration had been nourished exclusively from English sources, he had not yet visited Europe and knew no more of contemporary European art than he had been able to see in a few poorly stocked galleries at the Tate?[2] Admittedly, he was directly exposed to the impact of European art when, in June 1936, he allowed two of his paintings[3] to be exhibited in the company of works by Arp, Chirico, Dali, Duchamp, Ernst, Klee, Miró, Picasso and many others at the International Surrealist Exhibition in London. But so far as his own work was concerned, the experience of seeing this exhibition produced no immediate change, although Sutherland admits that he was greatly impressed by some of Picasso's paintings, and that he was fascinated by the Mirós because he 'seemed to see in them a kind of parallel with the forms' that he himself was 'finding in nature'. The truth is, of course, not only that Sutherland's work was out of place in this exhibition,[4] because he shared none of the preoccupations of the true surrealist painters, but more particularly that he was not yet ready to turn to account anything he might learn from European painting. At this stage of his development Sutherland was in the truest sense an English landscape painter, concerned above all with investigating the structure of the natural scene, with the

[1] Plates 4a, 6, 7, 8, 9. The scene was Pembrokeshire.
[2] Sutherland remembers well the attempts of Clive Gardiner, in about 1922, to interest him in the work of Cézanne, Matisse and other modern French painters, but all to no avail. He did not like what he saw. Incidentally, Sutherland was one of two students from the Goldsmiths' College School employed by Clive Gardiner in 1923–4 to help execute his large modernist decorations for the Wembley International Exhibition.
[3] *Thunder Sounding*; and *Mobile Mask* (repr. Melville, *op. cit.*, Fig.1).
[4] 'Invited by Penrose. Thought it rather a compliment. Talked to him about light in painting and was witheringly dismissed' (Letter to the author).

play of light and with the evocation of space. This emerges clearly, for example, in his sketches of *Solva* and *Valley above Porthclais*,[1] also in a painting such as *Welsh Landscape with Roads*.[2]

In an article in the periodical *Signature*,[3] published in 1936, Sutherland referred to works by various English artists which he felt were particularly akin to his own type of vision and which had obviously helped him in developing his personal vision and forming his style. Palmer naturally figures prominently among them. Surprisingly however – since figure compositions played no part in his work at the time – Sutherland also lists Blake's water-colour illustrations for Dante. Yet if we study the purely landscape elements in, for example, *The Pit of Disease, The Primeval Giants sunk in the soil* or *The Laborious Passage along the Rocks*[4] it is difficult not to be struck by certain resemblances – in the boldly simplified handling of the hills and rocks, in the swirling rhythms, in the concentration on incidental details, and in the emphasis on surface qualities – to passages which occur in Sutherland's paintings even as late as the mid-1940's.[5] Then, too, Sutherland mentions the later paintings of Turner,[6] the one colourist among his favourites; the drawings of Henry Moore, whose imagery was then based on an interplay between the forms in nature and parts of the human body; and finally Paul Nash's illustrations for an edition of Sir Thomas Browne's *Urne Buriall* and *The Garden of Cyrus*,[7] which Sutherland described as 'a poetic and imaginative achievement without equal today in this country'. He was, of course, also acquainted with Nash's oil paintings and water-colours executed between 1933 and 1936 in Wiltshire and Dorset,[8] and it was these in particular which gave him confidence to disregard English pictorial conventions and go ahead in his own way painting partial aspects of, or excerpts from, the natural scene if for him they had emotional and visual significance. That Sutherland should have needed this sort of encouragement may seem strange now that we are used to the compelling strength of his vision. But in 1936 modern European art was not merely laughed at in England, it was also resented and opposed. So it is hardly surprising that Sutherland should have ventured into the field hesitantly and that, as he says, he was grateful to Nash for leading him 'to think of certain objects in nature as being sanctioned as fit and possible subjects for a picture'.

[1] Plate 6a.
[2] Plate 9a.
[3] No.3, July 1936, pp.7–13, G. Sutherland, 'A Trend in English Draughtsmanship'.
[4] *vide* M. Butlin, *Catalogue of Works by Blake in the Tate Gallery*, London, 1957, Plates 35 and 37.
[5] e.g. Plates 20, 29, 34a, 47c, 65.
[6] Particularly *Sunrise with Sea Monster* in the Tate Gallery. 'I did very much admire at the time certain late Turners, and the Monster itself, technically and otherwise, I have always felt remarkable.' (Letter to the author.)
[7] Published by Cassell (London) in 1932; *vide* M. Eates and others, *Paul Nash: A Memorial Volume* (London, 1948), Plates 62–66.
[8] *vide* M. Eates, *op. cit.*, Plates 70–79.

Fig.2
**Swan** 1935 Pen and wash drawing 5½×9 in.
Collection: the Artist

Nevertheless, Sutherland was by nature an independent painter. He could assimilate ideas from others but he never lost sight of those personal experiences to which he wanted to give expression. He was thus able to persist and, after a considerable struggle, evolve an art of his own. He never wanted, for example, to make poetic pictures like Paul Nash by relating natural objects to each other in a sort of surrealistic association.[1] For Sutherland, organic structure and character counted above everything else. A *Blasted Tree* or an *objet trouvé* such as a *Lobster Claw*[2] could be studied objectively and as an entity in itself without the artist feeling impelled to imagine it in relation to an invisible whole or in some fantastic context where it would appear more interesting. In the same way, when Sutherland looked at a landscape his eye gradually rejected its 'scenic' value in order to concentrate on a few features which he found vitally expressive. We can follow the workings of this process by looking, for example, first at the panoramic *Sand Hills, Dorset*[3] of 1932–33, then turning to the simplified *Landscape, Green, Pink and Brown*[4] of 1937 and the boldly generalized studies of interlocking stones in a landscape[5] of 1939, and finally to the extraordinary *Mountain Road with Boulder*[6] of 1940 where, for all that he has not broken the essential link with nature, Sutherland attains a degree of artistic freedom comparable with that of Kandinsky in 1911–12.

Now this type of selective vision is characteristic of Sutherland's approach to nature throughout the decade 1935–45[7] and in order to understand it we must familiarize ourselves with his subjective but nevertheless humanistic outlook on the world. For Sutherland regards man and nature in conjunction and sees both as being at the mercy of the same formative forces. He has therefore made it his artistic purpose to isolate and make visible the workings of that common principle of growth and decay through which they are related. Also, Sutherland is 'highly conscious of the "figurative" element in landscape', by which he means that when he is confronted with the 'confusion of shapes and movements' in nature his eye begins instinctively to select and simplify until the scene is reduced to a figuration which has the organic coherence of 'some extraordinary, huge figure'. Man is therefore at once his measure and his inspiration.

[1] Contrast *Men-an-Tol* (Plate 5b) or *Red Tree* (Plate 9b) with for example Nash's *Event on the Downs* (1933) or *Nocturnal Landscape* (1938) (repr. in M. Eates, *op. cit.*, Plates 72 and 77).
[2] Plates 5e and 11.
[3] Plate 5a.
[4] Plate 10a.
[5] Plate 21.
[6] Colour Plate III.
[7] These years constitute the second period in Sutherland's work as a whole and the first phase of his work as a painter. The stylistic unity of the period is, of course, broken for a while by the series of war pictures, but the second group of Welsh landscapes painted in 1943, 1944 and 1945 repeat earlier *motifs* and continue the pre-war manner. A change of style only occurs in 1945–46 with the *Crucifixion*, the *Thorn Heads* and the *Chimeras; vide* Chapter IV(ii).

13

A figure in Sutherland's eyes is a self-sufficient entity which can be divorced from any context and represented so completely within the confines of a canvas that the idea of its having extensions, in whatever direction, beyond what is shown will not occur to the mind. Sutherland sees landscape in these same terms, which accounts for his chopping up (as it were) the natural scene and also his way of articulating the forms in his pictures organically. His eye did not pick on objects or forms because they were in themselves curious or might appear to have a special degree of permanence. It found its way gradually through to a set of shapes which seemed linked together by a process of growth. These he then lifted out of context to make his picture. So one finds a detached section, enlarged and shown with all its informality, surface coruscations and rugosities instead of, as in a panoramic landscape by Turner, for example, a greatly compressed whole which has gained in richness and formal precision during the process of reduction. This attitude does not amount to a denial on Sutherland's part of the continuity, the expanse, of the natural scene as it appears to the eye: he merely focuses on those elements, or a particular set of relationships, which determine for him the *genius loci* and seem to be most fitted for translation into pictorial terms.[1] But he represents these elements in a simplified form, because he found that when he paraphrased what he saw he had captured more of 'the essence or the *gesture* of reality' and could project into it more of his own emotion.

In 1936-37 Graham Sutherland wrote a remarkable description of a Yorkshire site[2] which he had visited. This text gives us such a vivid insight into his emotional response to the relationship between man and nature, as well as into the working of his eye and of his intuitive pictorial sense, that it deserves to be quoted from at length:[3]

'It is a primitive environment. A wide plain surrounds us. It is redeemed from emptiness by the road which curves across it. The attention becomes drawn to an irregularity of contour on the horizon. Lit by the effulgent figure of the sun, which hangs low behind, innumerable sharp forms cut brightly into the sky. Their outlines, devoid of order or rhythm, confuse the eye as the crazy cacophony of village church bells confuses the ear.

'This confusion clarifies; we are approaching a vast congregation of rock forms. Passing through the outer stones the road is soon joined by another, which, running straight like an arrow, leads us to the centre of the area . . .

[1] 'My aim is always to catch and pin down the essence of that aspect of reality which moves me – to fix and mark out the shape of my sensation.' Sutherland quoted by J. T. Soby in *Contemporary Painters* (New York, 1948), p.139.
[2] Brimham Rocks in Nidderdale, N.W. of Harrogate. Sutherland visited this site in the autumn of 1935 at the suggestion of Jack Beddington, who wanted it to figure as one of a series of Shell posters (Fig. 3).
[3] Graham Sutherland, 'An English Stone Landmark', in *The Painter's Object*, ed. M. Evans (London, 1937), pp.91–92.

Fig.3
**Brimham Rock** 1937
Lorry Bill for Shell-Mex & BP   30 × 40 in.

'The rocks lie in every direction . . . Yet now the whole effect seems to form a single entity. Each intricate grouping unfolds the limit of another. Every space establishes that interval which gives to each form its significance.

'The dismal privacy which these forms impose is at the highest point off-set by the intrusion of a house. This single evidence of the presence of man not only gives scale, but quickens by its implications and associations our apprehension of the strangeness of the scene . . .

'The largest stones lie near the house; many of them rise, like unmentionable bathers, from pools of water. Supporting on their backs small rocks like little slothful heads, they bend forward casting their huge shadows into the depths which half obscure their bulk . . .

'The setting sun, as it were precipitating new colours, turns the stone, rising from its undulating bed of bright green moss and blackened heather, yellow, pink and vermilion. The coloured patches which streak the surfaces give emphasis to the form and variety to the eye. These patches are warm, even in a cold light. But now they assume tones as of blood. In addition the surfaces are speckled with lichens. Some are yellow-red and sparkle unnaturally from the cool tones of the shadows, while others shading from white at their centres to blackish green evoke the texture and form that we associate with the uncontrolled blots on French marbled papers. Indeed, the pleasure derived from such textures is comparable with that produced by all decoration added to and not contained in a

15

material. Here it is as if, by a kind of prodigality of nature, the natural processes must add to the patterns inherent in matter.'[1]

When studied in relation to Sutherland's paintings of the period 1936–40 this text takes on so much meaning that its implications are worth closer examination. We can start with the importance of the setting sun and its power to create and transmute colours. Have we noticed how rare it is to find a midday brilliance in a picture of this date by Sutherland?[2] In some canvases strong sunlight (or so it seems) is filtered through and dampened by layers of intervening green foliage.[3] But nearly always in his paintings the hour is that of sunset, the light strikes surfaces from an oblique angle, the sun 'hangs low behind', the hills have gone dark, and the sky, like the foreground, is suffused with red, yellow or orange. In all of this we recognise the romantic and see again the influence of Palmer. Light effects contribute vitally to Sutherland's visual response to a scene, more especially when they enhance the suggestion of mystery: 'The quality of light here is magical and transforming', he writes about Wales. 'Watching from the gloom as the sun's rays strike the further bank, one has the sensation of the after-tranquillity of an *explosion* of light; or as if one had looked into the sun and had turned suddenly away.'[4] Now it is through colour that Sutherland transmits this kind of sensation, and so the colours in his pictures have an emotional as well as a descriptive significance. But as he himself tells us, colour also gives 'emphasis to the form and variety to the eye': that is to say he recognizes its expansive and decorative value. Line, on the other hand, is never mentioned by Sutherland. This seems surprising when we look into his pictures, for he uses line with great freedom as an expressive adjunct to give character, to set up a rhythm,[5] or in the form of U-shaped curves to create roundness. Sutherland's line is limp, not taut, and he rarely defines a form by precise drawing; instead he achieves definition by high-lighting some area of a surface and making it stand out in relief against deep shadows.

So much for his attitude towards line, colour, and light. Next we must note how, when Sutherland sees some features of a landscape in anthropomorphic terms – as when he likens a group of large stones with smaller ones on top of them to a group of 'unmentionable bathers . . . (with) little

---

[1] In this context it is instructive to contrast a passage from an essay by Paul Nash: 'Last summer, I walked in a field near Avebury where two rough monoliths stand up, sixteen feet high, miraculously patterned with black and orange lichen, remnants of the avenue of stones which led to the Great Circle. A mile away, a green pyramid casts a gigantic shadow. In the hedge at hand, the white trumpet of a convolvulus turns from its spiral stem, following the sun. In my art I would solve such an equation.' (From *Unit I*, ed. Herbert Read, (London, 1934) p.81). The similarities with Sutherland's description of a subject are at once apparent, but when Nash talks of solving 'an equation' we are conscious of the differences in approach between the two artists.
[2] Plate 27 is an exception.
[3] e.g. Plates 12c, 16, 22, 23c.
[4] 'Welsh Sketchbook' in *Horizon*, Vol.V, No.28, April 1942, p.234.
[5] e.g. Plates 11a and c, 12c, 19a, 21, 24, 27, 28c.

slothful heads' – he does so instinctively. He does not think up this sort of image as a means to achieving a curious effect. Sutherland cannot help himself from seeing things in this way, and that is why in so many of his pictures plants, bits of trees, foliage, animals, driftwood or insects assume an unmistakably human configuration.[1] Not that, as Mr Soby has wisely pointed out, he follows the practice of an artist like Arthur Rackham, 'whose discursive fantasy of mind led him to convert branches and twigs into a myriad of human visages'.[2] Nor does Sutherland have recourse to anthropomorphic images as a sort of surrealist device. He accepts his private vision and comes to terms with it pictorially in a way which he has described: 'It is not a question so much of a tree like a figure or a root like a figure – it is a question of bringing out the anonymous personality of these things; at the same time they must bear the mould of their ancestry. There is a duality: they can be themselves and something else at the same time. They are formal metaphors.' Thus what Sutherland puts down on paper or canvas has been or can be seen by us all and we can immediately recognize it for what it is. But athwart this image Sutherland reveals a 'hidden' identity which is perhaps not immediately apprehensible though we could all see it if we knew how to look. Here we encounter in Sutherland's work the first signs of his spontaneous response to Picasso, for he was deeply moved and impressed by seeing *Guernica* and the large group of preparatory studies for it when they were exhibited in London[3] in October 1938. As he himself puts it: 'Picasso's *Guernica* drawings seemed to open up a philosophy and to point a way whereby – by a kind of para-phrase of appearances – things could be made to look more vital and real. The forms I saw in this series pointed to a passionate involvement in the *character* of the subject whereby the feeling for it was trapped and made concrete. Like the subject and yet unlike. Everything I saw at this time seemed to exhort me to a greater freedom . . . Only Picasso, however, seemed to have the true idea of metamorphosis whereby things found a new form through feeling.' These few phrases give us an unexpected insight into the working of the expressionistic element in Sutherland's painting.

Lastly, something must be said about the roads and lanes which seem to have an emotional significance for Sutherland, although they frequently serve as little more than a useful compositional device. In the description of the Yorkshire scene from which I quoted above, Sutherland first mentions a road as redeeming 'a primitive environment' and 'a wide plain' from 'emptiness'. That is to say, the very existence of a road is evidence of the passage and potential presence of man. At the same time, Sutherland notes

[1] e.g. Colour Plate II, Plates 22, 23, 25, 33, 51.
[2] J. T. Soby, *Contemporary Painters*, New York, 1948, p.136.
[3] New Burlington Galleries.

that the road runs 'straight like an arrow' and directs the eye 'to the centre of the area', that is to say he sees it as a guide-line. Now Sutherland has more to say about the compositional and other purposes which a road fulfils in some notes of 1941–42 dealing with his reactions to a Welsh landscape:[1] 'The astonishing fertility of these valleys and the complexity of the roads running through them is a delight to the eye. The roads form strong and mysterious arabesques as they rise in terraces, in sight, hidden, turning and splitting as they finally disappear into the sky. To see a solitary human figure descending such a road at the solemn moment of sunset is to realize the enveloping quality of the earth, which can create, as it does here, a mysterious space limit – a womb-like enclosure – which gives the human form an extraordinary focus and significance.' In this passage Sutherland's two attitudes to roads are blended. As a result, we are better able to understand how he effected the stylistic transformation from his more or less literal *Road with Rocks*[2] of 1936 to his freely imaginative *Mountain Road with Boulder*[3] of 1940. In the latter, the road has lost its identity as a highway and has assumed a limited pictorial meaning as a bold simplified form which contributes to the general rhythm, acts as a foil to the menacing boulder, turns and disappears over a precipice into the sky. But this passage also throws light on Sutherland's attempts to introduce a figure into landscape compositions such as *Road and Hills* of 1938[4] or *Triple-tiered Landscape*[5] of 1944. These early attempts, it seems to me, proved unsuccessful, for while Sutherland could, by means of paraphrases, exaggerations and formal metaphors, communicate something of human relevance which he had perceived in a natural object or a slice of landscape, when he introduced an actual figure the effect miscarried. The human element was not subjected to the same imaginative transformation as the rest of the picture. Also these figures, supposedly alive, were so drained of corporeal reality as to become mannequins or scarecrows which have not the power either to arouse our emotions or to interest us visually. We become acutely aware of this shortcoming if we turn to those more effective and often disturbing pictures by Sutherland which have for their subject a path through a wood or plantation, a covered estuary, a subterranean gallery or a corner of a garden where no figure appears but in which all his imaginative power and painter's apparatus have been brought to bear on evoking some mysterious 'presence' or 'event' which is out of sight. For if it is true that in one sense Sutherland pursues 'character' by cutting away overgrowth in order to find and reveal the simplest forms and most expressive outlines, it is no less true that

[1] *Horizon, op. cit.*
[2] Plate 8b.
[3] Colour Plate III.
[4] Colour Plate I.
[5] Plate 54c.

where smells, sounds or any emanations of 'atmosphere' are involved his cultivated sensitivity has led him to paint visually impenetrable but imaginatively suggestive pictures in which the subject is conjured up indirectly.

'I wish I could give some idea of the exultant strangeness of this place', Sutherland wrote in his 'Welsh Sketchbook' about a river estuary near Milford Haven,[1] 'for strange it certainly is; many people whom I know hate it, and I cannot but admit that it possesses an element of disquiet . . . The whole setting is one of exuberance – of darkness and light – of decay and life . . . The life-giving sound of the mechanical reaper is heard. Cattle crouch among the dark gorse. The mind wanders from contemplation of the living cattle to their ghosts. It is no uncommon sight to see a horse's skull or horns of cattle lying bleached on the sand. Neither do we feel that the black-green ribs of half-buried wrecks and the phantom tree-roots, bleached and washed by the waves, exist but to emphasize the extraordinary completeness of the scene.' Ambiguity, surprise and intuitive seeing form the basis of Sutherland's experiences and provide the emotions which inspire many of his early pictures. He is deeply fascinated by 'secret' or hidden places and by ambiguous natural formations. We can feel this fascination already latent in the romantic and deserted *Barn Interior*[2] of 1922, but eventually it assumes an explicit and emotional form in pictures such as *Entrance to Lane*[3] (1939 and 1945), *Tin Mine: a Declivity*[4] (1942), *Path through Plantation*[5] (1951) or *Dark Entrance*[6] (1959). Nevertheless, there is a constant interplay in Sutherland's work between a 'clear yet intricate construction' discovered in visible natural forms, and an 'emotional feeling of being on the brink of some drama'.[7] The latter belongs to the invisible and is suggested as much by the way in which his landscape forms are abruptly cut off against the sky, thus suggesting a precipice,[8] as by the way in which the eye is arrested on the threshold of the wood and prevented from following the path any further.

Only certain types of landscape, a certain type of *motif* – or nowadays even a certain type of human physiognomy – are likely to provide Sutherland with the impulse to start painting. To this extent his inspiration is subject to regional and personal limitations, for it is only aroused where nature has produced the sort of growths which will attract his eye and

---

[1] *Horizon, op. cit.*
[2] Plate 2a.
[3] Plates 17 and 54a.
[4] Plate 46a.
[5] Plate 109.
[6] Plate 153.
[7] Both quotations from *Horizon, op. cit.*
[8] *vide* 'An English Stone Landmark', *op. cit.*: 'A path leads us to the edge of the area and now we see that there is a limit to the plain. For here the ground itself is rock, which precipitates itself to the fields, three hundred feet below.'

when he senses in advance that a given place (or personality) is likely to be attuned to his emotional preoccupations. This has not, however, made of him a regional painter in any narrow sense. Of course, Sutherland has to return occasionally to the sites which have provided him with *motifs*, but the fact that his pictures are generalized images permits him to live and work where he likes.[1] Since the spring of 1936, for example, Sutherland has made his home at Trottiscliffe, near Maidstone in the Weald of Kent, where he does much of his painting. Yet it is exceptional for elements of the Kentish landscape to provide him with subjects for pictures. Similarly, although Sutherland lived for an entire year (1939–40) in Gloucestershire at the beginning of the Second World War, there is nothing in his paintings of the time which can obviously be identified with characteristic features or even with the colouring of that locality. Whenever he has been to Wales, the South of France or Venice, however, the effects are soon manifest in his work. The explanation of this lies in Sutherland's ability to carry ideas for paintings in his mind, and in his accurate visual memory for colours, which means that he can work on subjects found in any locality no matter where he happens to be.[2] While he is painting, Sutherland does not need to look again at the actual object or place where he originally found inspiration. 'I may have noticed a certain juxtaposition of forms at the side of a road', he has written,[3] 'but on passing the same place next time, I might look for them in vain.' We can understand, therefore, why, as a painter, Sutherland is happy to put a distance between himself and the thing perceived so that he can recollect his emotion in tranquillity.

'It was in this country that I began to learn painting', Sutherland wrote to a friend about the Pembrokeshire landscape around St Bride's Bay.[4] 'It seemed impossible here for me to sit down and make finished paintings "from nature". Indeed, there were no "ready-made" subjects to paint. The spaces and concentrations of this clearly constructed land were stuff for storing in the mind. Their essence was intellectual and emotional, if I may say so. I found that I could express what I felt only by paraphrasing what

[1] *vide* G. Sutherland, 'Thoughts on Painting' in *The Listener*, 6 September 1951, p.378: 'I have been asked: Is it necessary to live within the landscapes one paints? From a purely physical point of view it is a convenience. One has longer time to find the things one likes, a longer time to react and for voluptuous awareness: one has calm, no hurry, time to notice how an infinitely small form at the foot of a tree is reproducing, in miniature, the whole structure of the surrounding landscape. In fact, though staying long in one place does not necessarily help me, one must stay in a place a fair time before one starts to work. But I do not think it makes very much difference where one is. I happen to work better and more easily in the sun.'

[2] *vide* 'A Trend in English Draughtsmanship', *op. cit.*, where Sutherland writing of Blake says: 'During the earlier part of his life we find inconsistencies of style which mar the unity of his designs. More often than not his work was filled with incongruous elements . . . It must be assumed that these vagaries of style were due, not so much to his inability to draw out of his mind a unity of those forms which inhabited it, as to the fact that these forms themselves derived little nourishment from the natural world . . . He rarely refreshed his imagination by making studies from natural phenomena.'

[3] 'On Painting', Notes by the Artist, published as a preface to the Catalogue of the Sutherland Exhibition at the Tate Gallery, May 1953.

[4] *Horizon, op. cit.*

I saw.' And so, after a few unsuccessful attempts 'to make pictures on the spot', Sutherland decided to give up *looking for* subjects and to adopt a more contemporary attitude, that of allowing his 'inner vision' to take control. 'It became my habit to walk through, and soak myself in the country', he continues. 'At times I would make small sketches of ideas on the backs of envelopes and in a small sketch-book, or I would make drawings from nature of forms which interested me and which I might otherwise forget. The latter practice helped to nourish my ideas and to keep me on good terms with nature.' But it was not only a store of visual images that Sutherland brought back from his trips; his baggage also contained souvenirs of a more material sort, in the form of stones, shells, tree-roots and the like, casually picked up during his wanderings. And with this accumulation of material at his disposal, Graham Sutherland felt free from the pressure of immediacy, free to wait for a spontaneous upsurge of pictorial imagery, free ultimately to work out the arrangement of his pictures without reference to the facts of nature itself. 'In the studio I react afresh', Sutherland has said.[1] 'The original images dissolve, objects lose their normal environment and relationship. Then things seem to be drawn together and redefined in the mind's eye – in a new life and mould – there has been a substitution – a change. But the process of digestion must preserve in the substance of my material – paint and canvas – the sensation of the original presence in its new form.'

In this first period (1935–40), Sutherland's 'process of digestion' was laborious and the pictures that he produced by no means equally successful, because he did not at that time possess the pictorial science which he can draw on today, and therefore had to be largely self-reliant and to find his own way. This he did slowly but with growing success. His early landscape paintings glow, they are instinct with vitality and are satisfying to look at. Nature takes on a strange, subtle and often fiery tonality, with Venetian and erythrine red, vermilion, pink, violet, Prussian and cerulian blue, alizarin green, veridian, yellow ochre, orange chrome and orange cadmium offset against greys, whites and heavy, but nevertheless almost luminous, passages of black. Already Sutherland displayed a great gift for handling colour and a very personal sense of harmonious tonal relationships. 'Colour', Sutherland once remarked,[2] 'has two major functions. It is form and mood. That is to say that, by its warmth or coldness, it can create form; it can also create a mood; it is fascinating to make complete changes of colour in the background of a painting and see how the whole atmosphere changes. Colour can suggest depth and shallowness, heat and cold – it can even suggest sound. There is the story of the blind man who, when

[1] 'On Painting', *op. cit.*
[2] 'Thoughts on Painting', *op. cit.*

21

his companion described the effect of scarlet on the eye, exclaimed: "It must be like the sound of a trumpet".'

The linear and formal structure of the landscapes which Sutherland painted between 1935 and 1940 is perhaps not always as solid and forceful as the images and emotional experiences which they convey. But then we must remember that at the time Sutherland was still feeling his way as an artist. The view of nature which he offers is neither lovely nor entrancing, but it is a new view, personal and distinctly English. Part of this novelty resides in the fact that Sutherland is one of the few painters who has seen the English landscape in its actual proportions. That is to say, in his pictures everything is on a comparatively small scale and even hills and mountains, far from being grand, ominous or dominating, seem like miniature excrescences which could be picked up and held in the hand.

From the moment Sutherland first went to Wales, he revealed himself as a true painter. Paintings such as *Green Tree Form* (1939), *Cliff Road* (1941), *Red Landscape* (1942) and *Landscape with Pointed Rocks* (1944)[1] show that he had a penetrating eye, an independent outlook, plenty of originality and an understanding of how to express himself pictorially. But, as I have said, Sutherland's artistic development was extraordinarily slow – a characteristic of English artists – and at the age of 35 he had still not accomplished the first stage. Apart from a gradual gain in strength and a trend towards bolder, broader effects, there was no real stylistic development in his landscapes between 1936 and 1946. In 1940, however, the continuity of Sutherland's work was broken and his evolution hastened by the experience of working for five years (1940–45) as a war artist, a side of his *œuvre* which I shall discuss in the following chapter. Occasionally during this time, Sutherland was able to paint more Welsh landscapes, and they are closely related to those painted before 1940. For reasons of convenience, however, I have dealt with these in more detail in the section devoted to his later nature paintings. But it is important to make clear that in style and in spirit they belong with those of the pre-war years. The great stylistic change in Sutherland's work does not occur until 1946.

The first period of Sutherland's development as a painter runs from 1935 to 1945 and comprises landscapes and wartime scenes. In the post-war years he has emerged as a much more interesting, varied and impressive artist. For he has developed his vision, polished his handling and pressed on from being an unusual English landscape painter to his present position as the leading representative of the English School. And today Sutherland is almost more concerned in his work with Man than with Nature.

[1] Plates 22, 28b, 29, 52b; *vide* also E. Sackville-West, *Graham Sutherland* (London, 1943) Plate 9.

### III. The War Artist: 1940–45

In March 1917 the British Government decided to found a National War Museum.[1] Its purpose was to assemble a permanent collection of objects and records covering the history of the First World War, illustrating the military means by which it had been waged and commemorating the efforts and sacrifices made by the civilian population. The carrying out of this project was entrusted to the Department of Information,[2] upon which pressure was brought by a group of influential *cognoscenti*[3] to agree that artists' 'records', no matter how imaginative, should be allowed to take their place with the rest. Thus painters such as Eric Kennington, Wyndham Lewis, John Nash, Paul Nash, Gilbert Spencer and Richard Nevinson, who had already been on active service at the front, were commissioned to paint aspects of the war which had particular meaning for them, while others such as William Orpen, Augustus John, Muirhead Bone and John Lavery, were engaged to paint portraits of the heroes as well as of leading military and civilian personalities. Judged by strictly artistic standards, the great majority of works executed under this first War Artists scheme and acquired for the nation do not qualify even as moderately good paintings. But that is to a great extent immaterial, for they have a valid human and documentary value. Even a bad painter's view of his contemporaries and the life they lead can be of more significance than an album of photographs, while the fact that so much English art tends anyway to an illustrative or journalistic approach proved in the circumstances to be an asset. The first experiment with official War Artists was then on the whole successful, and between the two wars the collection of paintings in the Imperial War Museum came to be regarded as an integral part of the history of contemporary art in England.

Small wonder that, with this precedent, a later British Government decided in the winter of 1939–40 to commission similar records of the Second World War. Once again the Ministry of Information was charged with organizing a corps of War Artists, and to this end it set up a War Artists Advisory Committee under the Chairmanship of Sir Kenneth Clark.[4] On this second occasion, however, the official attitude towards art and artists was subtly different, for in the changed circumstances of 1939 it was recognized that the State had to assume some responsibility for preserving a continuity in the cultural life of the nation during the dark times ahead. So the British artists of 1939–40 found that, instead of having

---

[1] Re-christened Imperial War Museum by Act of Parliament in July 1920.
[2] John Buchan, later Lord Tweedsmuir, was then Director of Information.
[3] They included Eric Maclagan, Laurence Binyon, Edward Marsh, John Drinkwater, Roger Fry, William Rothenstein, Henry Tonks and Charles Holmes.
[4] At the time Director of the National Gallery.

to fight officialdom[1] for recognition of their usefulness, as the generation of 1914–15 had been obliged to do, they were allowed to carry on with their profession and serve the State at the same time. The types of artists whose co-operation was solicited varied considerably, as did the assignments they received, but, of course, between 1940 and 1944 they had to find paintable subjects for the most part within the limits of the British Isles, that is to say on the 'home' front. Some artists were commissioned for the duration of the war with a specific branch of the armed forces, while some were assigned to work for a specific Ministry; artists already serving in any branch of the armed forces were invited to submit works independently; others were employed on a short-term basis, to execute a limited number of pictures dealing with a single subject; and still others were not restricted in these ways but given an opportunity to decide their own subjects. The greater part of the work produced was, inevitably, reportage of one kind or another. Inevitably, too, a scheme of this sort encouraged a great deal of slick, if not downright bad, art. But the story is not one of failure, because even the most banal or illustrative works which the nation acquired have a permanent documentary value, while on the plane of serious artistic creation the second War Artists scheme has to its credit the imaginative paintings of aircraft by Paul Nash, the ship-building scenes of Stanley Spencer, and the striking group of works by Graham Sutherland which I now propose to discuss.

Soon after the beginning of the war, Sutherland moved from Kent, which had become virtually a militarized zone, to Tetbury in Gloucester-shire,[2] where his friend Sir Kenneth Clark[3] had offered him accommodation and the possibility of working undisturbed. For the first time in fifteen years he found himself without a regular employment, the Chelsea School having closed, and his financial situation was precarious. Sutherland had, therefore, to be content to work from such material as he had already assembled, and the canvases he produced at this time were elaborations[4] from notes made in sketchbooks during earlier trips to Wales. He exhibited these paintings, with considerable success, at his second one-man show which opened early in May 1940 at the Leicester Galleries in London. But almost immediately after this exhibition closed France fell and the 'Blitz'

[1] *vide* letter of 11 April 1916 from Lord Northcliffe to William Rothenstein: 'I heartily agree with you and have long ago suggested that we should copy the Germans (whom we always have to copy much as we dislike them) and send distinguished artists to the front. As for the British authorities, they are absolutely impossible people . . .' (Quoted in W. Rothenstein, *Men and Memories*, Vol.II, p.307, London, 1932).
[2] Upton House.
[3] The influence of Sir Kenneth on Sutherland's mind and artistic outlook has been primordial from this time onwards. He has helped him to broaden his culture, made available many works of art for him to study, talked to him about painting of all periods, and made him familiar with the world of the art historian, as well as having been his principal patron.
[4] e.g. Plates 23c, 31; also E. Sackville-West, *op. cit.* (1943 edn.), Plates 5,14,20. Sutherland, in fact, paid a short visit to Wales, to refresh his memory, over Christmas 1939.

on London began. At this juncture Sir Kenneth proposed to Sutherland that he should become an official War Artist and he immediately agreed.[1] Nevertheless both men were conscious of the risks they were running. Sutherland might have proved to be an artist so wedded to landscape or preoccupied with inter-relationships of form and colour that he could not bring off pictures dealing with human experiences instead of with inanimate things. Equally, for Sutherland there was the possibility that he would have to cheat, according to his own artistic standards, in order to deliver pictures which the Advisory Committee would find acceptable, or else acknowledge his failure to meet the challenge. In the event, however, Sutherland acquitted himself with dignity and success, thereby proving that when a truly imaginative contemporary artist has suddenly to wrestle with subjects which involve human endeavour and suffering his modern idiom enables him to express more than can his academic colleagues with their hide-bound approach and worn-out conventions. At this point Sutherland, for the first time, widened the scope of his art and modified his style. That is to say, he showed unmistakably in his war paintings that, so far as he was concerned, formal and aesthetic considerations were not primordial, that he responded emotionally to all sorts of human experiences, and that, instead of feeling handicapped by having themes or *motifs* supplied to him,[2] this stimulated his pictorial invention. Sutherland rose to the occasion splendidly and his are among the few war pictures which have real artistic value as well as being genuine records of our time. What makes them remarkable is that they are, simultaneously, imaginative evocations of generally shared experiences and also more or less factual records. The familiar everyday sight, the hideous incident, has been transformed into a symbol of a greater and more searing struggle.

Sutherland was employed for the duration of the war but was fortunate in that he was granted more liberty than most other war artists. Not that he was free to wander where he listed and paint what he liked, satisfying only his own artistic conscience. On the contrary, he was continually subject to direction from the War Artists Advisory Committee, which had the power to turn down any paintings it did not like.[3] But this body sensed the sort of subjects which would affect Sutherland visually and

[1] Sutherland's first productive assignment was to the bomb-damaged areas of Swansea in September 1940; *vide* Plate 36b. He had previously been sent to airfields in Wiltshire but had not found any subjects which interested him.
[2] Very few of the Committee's suggestions were turned down by Sutherland, although he did not find some of their assignments – for example, the open-cast coal mines – sympathetic to his temperament. He was sent on one occasion to the Gunnery School at Melton Mowbray to watch guns being tested, but could see nothing there out of which to make a picture.
[3] A distinction was made between 'salaried' artists, all of whose war work belonged *ipso facto* to the Committee, and 'artists working on commission', whose war paintings were acquired for the nation only 'on the Committee's recommendation'. Sutherland was employed in the latter category.

emotionally and therefore managed to keep his interest alert and his inspiration flowing. He did not have to confine himself to one type of subject and his mission was frequently changed. Hence the extraordinary range of subjects covered by Sutherland in these paintings, which include bombed dwellings in Swansea and elsewhere, burnt-out office buildings and factories in the City of London and the suburbs,[1] bomb-shattered streets in Canning Town and Silver Town,[2] open-cast coal-mines at Pwll-du near Abergavenny,[3] stone quarries near Buxton,[4] tin mines at Pendeen in Cornwall,[5] iron foundries near Cardiff,[6] the Woolwich Arsenal,[7] flying-bomb sites at St Leu,[8] and wrecked railway-trains at Trappes.[9] Wherever he was sent, Sutherland was, of course, given every facility to familiarize himself with his subject and left to select whichever aspect of it he felt most acutely. But his work had to be done under difficult conditions, whether amid the roar of machines or in the flame-ridden inferno of an armaments factory, whether in the darkness and gloom of a subterranean tunnel with scarcely a human being visible and only an acetylene lamp to assist him, or among the smouldering and smoking rubble of a devastated area which was still being cleared and extinguished by fire brigades, rescue parties and demolition services.

It was practically impossible for Sutherland to do any painting on the spot, indeed he could not hope to do more than gather a sheaf of rough sketches which he could work up later in the studio. Thus, as usual, his official pictures were executed away from the scenes which they represent. Yet by resorting much of the time to gouache and coloured chalks, easy media which allow an artist to work quickly, Sutherland was able to pre-serve more of the immediacy of what he had experienced than if he had tried to work in the slower medium of oil paint. Human beings appear rarely in these pictures, but when they do, as in the studies of steel-workers and miners,[10] they have the anxious and tense look of creatures in thrall to some monster. However, whether or not human figures are actually visible, there is in all Sutherland's paintings and drawings of the war an intense awareness of man and of his activities. These gutted buildings and contorted girders, these blast-furnaces and desperate diggings, which make up the artist's personal imagery of the wartime scene, all signify immediate-ly that they are man's handiwork. They may be grim and terrifying outward

Fig.4
**The City of London after an air-raid**  1941
Gouache and chalk 6×6 in.
Collection: the Artist

[1] Plates 36a, 37–40.
[2] Plate 41.
[3] Plates 47b and c.
[4] Plate 47a.
[5] Plate 46.
[6] Plate 43.
[7] Plate 44.
[8] Not far from Chantilly; Plate 48a.
[9] To the south of Versailles; Plates 48b, c, d, 49.
[10] Plates 44a and b, 45, 46.

manifestations of his passage, but everywhere we feel – even in his absence – the presence of man. Eric Newton wrote, at the time, that Sutherland's devastated buildings 'have a wild, crucified poignancy that gives the war a new meaning', while his *motifs* of crumpled steel and eviscerated machinery seemed to the same writer like poems 'wrung from the bowels of destruction'.[1] These last, I believe, are Sutherland's most eloquent records of the war, and they are especially notable for the way that he manages to convey a sense of unutterable havoc with a minimum of expressive means. On the other hand, Sutherland did allow his pent-up feelings to burst forth in one outstanding drawing at this time: a violently expressive *Blasted Oak*[2] which has, at one end, roots as vicious as a vulture's claw and, at the other, an open formation which at one moment suggests the fearsome beak of a bird about to tear at its prey, and at another a human head screaming in agony.

Stylistically, Sutherland's war paintings are more diverse than were the landscapes which preceded them, and they form a contrast with those which he painted at the same time. This war period thus has a dual aspect of progress and expansion. During these years Sutherland extended his range of feeling, added to his technical experience and started evolving towards the more humanly-inspired vision which is characteristic of his post-war output. But these are not the factors which make for the success of his war paintings. This depends primarily on his refusal to adopt facile solutions or to take refuge in a humorous, topographical or picturesque[3] vein. No less important was his willingness to refrain from imposing his own artistic personality on his material, in other words to refrain from turning every picture into an immediately recognizable Sutherland.[4] Because he recognized that each subject obviously required to be handled differently he did not try to compress all subjects and themes alike into some convenient formula. In pictures such as *Tapping a Steel Furnace*,[5] in his views of underground caverns and demoniac workshops, Sutherland appears to have been viewing the contemporary scene through his memories of Blake's illustrations to Dante.[6] In his views of bomb-destroyed streets

[1] Eric Newton, *In My View* (London, 1950), p.117 (article of December 1940).
[2] Plate 33.
[3] e.g. John Piper's scenic and romanticized paintings of bombed buildings; *vide* S. J. Woods, *John Piper* (London, 1955), Plates 63–66; also J. Betjeman, *John Piper* (London, 1944), Plates 7, 19, 25.
[4] In this respect there is an obvious contrast between the war 'records' of Sutherland and those of Henry Moore. Why do Moore's drawings of miners or of people in air-raid shelters lack the feeling of reality, the human element, which comes across so strongly in Sutherland's pictures? The answer would seem to be that Moore, unlike Sutherland, chose to play down the factual aspects and human implications of a scene in order to extract something that was art for art's sake. Stylistically, Moore projects his own personality first and treats the cowering and sleeping crowds in shelters as models from whom he abstracts ideas for new sculptures. *vide* H. Read, *Henry Moore*, Vol.I (4th edn., London, 1957), Plates 216–50; also H. Moore, *Shelter Sketch Book* (London, 1945).
[5] Plate 45; also E. Sackville-West, *op. cit.* Plate 29.
[6] cf. *The Simoniac Pope; Cerberus; The Devils by the side of the Pool.*

he has recourse for the first time to the dramatic device of sharply receding linear perspectives such as one finds in the early work of de Chirico. This enables him not only to suggest vastness, solitude and a sensation of pathetic melancholy, but more particularly helps him to convey the sense of lifelessness and total silence which descended on such areas after their inhabitants had departed. Whatever the solution adopted, however, Sutherland produced an image which was personal, as for example in *Burnt-out Paper Rolls*,[1] which after their destruction continue to evoke the log-piles from which they originally emerged.

His own past also played a role in shaping Sutherland's wartime pictures. Thus the prosaic and detailed manner which he adopted in his handling of buildings – these had not appeared in his work since 1930 – derived from an ingeniously simplified constructional drawing of St David's Cathedral in Pembrokeshire which he had made by way of experiment in 1937.[2] At the same time, one finds his early training as an engineer influencing Sutherland not only in his style of drawing – which suddenly becomes firmer, with an emphasis on the sharpness of angles, the regularity of curves and the symmetry of forms – but also in his choice of subject-matter. For when he chose to paint furnaces, hydraulic presses and disembowelled railway-engines he was looking back to the world of his apprentice period in Derby.

Sutherland is not entirely satisfied with his group of war paintings because he feels that, with more time at his disposal, he could have purged them of the element of directness and immediacy and arrived at a more detached – not a more abstract – pictorial treatment. He believes that if he could have reduced the degree of realism he would have painted better pictures. Myself, I am not convinced that his reasoning is correct. For the strength of these paintings as war pictures lies precisely in the fact that they were produced under the pressure of events, that they are clear and concrete, and that for this reason they communicate something of the reality of the time not only to ourselves who lived through it but to those who come after and will want to understand. It is one thing to be able to set a distance in time and place between oneself and events and to paint a grandiose imaginative composition such as a *Rout of San Romano*, a *Dos de Mayo en la Plaza del Sol*, a *La Grèce expirant sur les ruines de Missolonghi*, a *Partie de Cartes* or a *Guernica*.[3] But the picture elaborated with feeling from an immediate record of a scene by a true artist has only slightly less artistic validity than these, more especially since the very nature of war has

---

[1] Plate 40.

[2] This drawing was known to many of Sutherland's artist friends in the years before the war; his manner of painting buildings had a considerable influence on John Piper when he later embarked on these subjects.

[3] By Uccello, Goya, Delacroix, Léger and Picasso respectively.

changed from being slow-moving and a sort of dangerous sport to one of the swiftest, most violent and most inhuman of man's activities. Asked why his own images of the war were so powerfully convincing to those returning from the battlefields of Flanders in 1916–17, Paul Nash replied: 'I draw very frankly what I see, so that altho' my subject is, I suppose, coloured by my imagination it remains credible and real to other eyes'.[1] By the same token, the sights and sounds of wartime England between 1940 and 1945 have been communicated by Graham Sutherland in a manner no less 'credible and real'.

## IV. The Post-war Years

### (i) Religious Subjects: 1945–1960

In September 1944,[2] Graham Sutherland was invited by Canon Walter Hussey, now Dean of Chichester, to paint an *Agony in the Garden* for a wall in the south transept of St Matthew's Church in Northampton. Instinctively he hesitated before accepting, because Sutherland felt that present-day artists 'have got out of the habit of working for a specific place and for a patron, and this gives rise to complexes and psychological inhibitions'.[3] At the same time, encouraged by his wartime experiences, Sutherland realized that he was not temperamentally averse to commissions, provided he could retain a degree of personal control, particularly in regard to the choice of subject. He could not deny that, as an artist, he had profited from working for the War Artists Committee, because the challenge of having to adapt himself and his pictorial conceptions to a given subject had proved a salutary discipline. Yet for various reasons he had no inclination at this time to undertake an *Agony*. On the other hand, partly as a result of feelings roused in him by what he had seen of the war, Sutherland did want to attempt a *Crucifixion*. He therefore proposed this alternative subject and his suggestion was accepted.

Perhaps it seems surprising to find Sutherland embarking on a religious subject at all. It is certainly strange that, in his first religious painting, he should have wanted to tackle not just the difficult problem of representing a naked human body, which hitherto he had not attempted, but in particular the body of Christ expressing by its contortions the utmost degree of pathos and anguish. But Sutherland, be it noted, harbours a tortured soul and a passionate temperament beneath a seemingly tranquil appearance. He is also a conscientious and resourceful artist, and as the

[1] *vide* A. Bertram, *Paul Nash, The Portrait of an Artist* (London, 1955), p.98.
[2] On the occasion of the unveiling of the sculpture of *The Madonna and Child* by Henry Moore in the north transept of the same church.
[3] *vide* G. Sutherland, 'Thoughts on Painting', *op. cit.*, from which many statements in this chapter have been taken.

illustrations in this book show has never been afraid of branching out in a new direction. What is more important, Sutherland is a convinced Christian and a convert to the Roman Catholic faith. Also he recognizes that his personal philosophy, his general view of the world, and hence his artistic inspiration, are profoundly coloured by the mysteries of religious experience. That this is so becomes abundantly clear if we consider what he said a few years ago about the significance that the Crucifixion had for himself as a pictorial subject:[1] 'The Crucifixion idea interested me because it has a duality which has always fascinated me. It is the most tragic of all themes, yet inherent in it is the promise of salvation. It is the symbol of the precarious balanced moment, the hair's-breadth between black and white. It is that moment when the sky seems superbly blue – and when one feels it *is* only blue in that superb way because at any moment it could be black – there is the other side of the mirror – and on that point of balance one may fall into great gloom or rise to great happiness.' In other words, Sutherland's view is that, for all its visible horror and underlying threat of extinction, the Crucifixion carries a message of hope: that the flesh can suffer and perish matters little, because the spirit within, fortified by tribulation, can rise phoenix-like to far greater heights of achievement. Such a view is traditional and orthodox, but Sutherland, being a modern artist and feeling acutely about this theme in relation to his own time, wanted to give his picture an appearance of actuality. And this raised the stylistic difficulty of devising a *Crucifixion* which would acknowledge the traditional iconography, without being pseudo-traditional in style, would belong to the twentieth century and yet would still be acceptable to the Church.

Over the last 200 years the once harmonious relationship between the Christian Church, of whatever denomination, and the creative artist has developed into an uncomfortable stalemate. The Church, fearful of the creative artist's potential non-conformism, and running away no less from naturalism than from symbolical abstractions,[2] progressively took refuge behind the saccharine *bondieuseries* which desecrate almost every religious building one enters. Artists, therefore, even those with faith, looked less and less to the Church for employment, because they were made to feel that within its domain they would not be allowed to treat the Christian iconography according to their own feelings.[3] Thus the two have gradually learnt to live and do without each other, thereby cutting off

---

[1] 'Thoughts on Painting', *op. cit.*
[2] The same is not true of its attitude to modern architecture, and many famous architects of the *avant-garde* – Le Corbusier, Mies van der Rohe, Oskar Niemeyer, Marcel Breuer for example – have designed religious buildings in the last thirty years. Can the explanation be that the traditional requirements of ritual are more easily reconciled with a personal aesthetic and that whereas the Christian Church will allow a new décor for its age-old ceremonies it will not tolerate a rejuvenation of its age-old imagery?
[3] The refusal by the *curé* of Nizon in 1888 of Gauguin's *Vision after the Sermon* is a typical example.

Fig.5
**Study for a Head of Christ**  1945
Oil on hardboard 12 × 12 in.
Collection: the Artist

religious art from successive stylistic developments and bringing about a fatal division between a current and communally shared repertory of images and a personal aesthetic. A Matisse embarking today on the decoration of a nuns' chapel at Vence or a Sutherland committing himself to paint a *Crucifixion* for an English parish church must therefore be prepared to do far more preliminary thinking than a Fra Angelico, a Tintoretto, a Rubens, or even a Goya had to do in similar circumstances. They must first decide whether they will dare to leap the barriers and invent a contemporary stylistic formula for traditional Christian subjects, thereby perhaps giving them renewed life and actuality, or whether they feel obliged to try to reconcile their own vision with an accepted formula in the hope of being able to achieve an up-to-date compromise. Matisse, whose outlook was pagan – or at any rate that of an unbeliever – rather than Christian refused to sacrifice his artistic independence and chose the first method;[1] Sutherland, a believer, chose the second.

Sutherland spent over a year pondering on how to represent the Crucifixion before he actually began to paint.[2] During this time he made notes and several exploratory drawings without arriving at what seemed to him an acceptable solution. From the start he had to reckon with what he has called 'self-imposed restrictions', but it was not long before he discovered also that the setting for his painting in the church was 'only moderately sympathetic'. Unforeseen factors, personal as well as material, therefore continually intervened to force him to modify his original conception. But he felt strongly about the subject and was not prepared to be hurried.

Sutherland's vision of the crucified Christ was, as I have already said, inspired in part by his emotional reaction to the war and its consequences. Then, one day, he received a booklet containing lurid photographs of massacred corpses and semi-bestial, starving survivors found by the liberating Allied armies in the concentration camps of Nazi Germany.[3] Not only was Sutherland intensely moved by the sight of these photographs, but also they provided him with a clue to the sort of image for which he was groping, because instinctively they evoked memories of the emaciated and outraged body of Christ in *Crucifixions* by Grünewald.[4] Thus the form that Sutherland ultimately gave to his own figure of the crucified Christ was precipitated by a curious correspondence between a contemporary image and a much earlier portrayal. It would, nevertheless, be false to

[1] *vide* A. Barr, *Matisse: His Art and His Public* (New York, 1951), pp.279–88; also Plates 514–26.
[2] An early project is reproduced on Plate 76.
[3] Published by the United States Information Services. Photographs of Auschwitz, Belsen and Buchenwald.
[4] Sutherland, of course, knew the drawings made by Picasso in 1932 after Grünewald's Isenheim altar-piece and published in *Minotaure*, No.1, 1933. He only knew Grünewald's painting from reproductions at this time and did not see it in the original until 1957.

suggest that the impact for Sutherland's *Crucifixion* was provided exclusively by either Grünewald or Belsen.

More than six months elapsed before Sutherland settled down to executing this commission.[1] During this time he accomplished a vital stage in his own artistic evolution. Sutherland was constantly preoccupied with the theme of the Crucifixion, but one day, not long after seeing the photographs, he went for a country walk[2] and experienced what one can only call an artistic revelation. 'When one goes for a walk', he has written, 'there is everything around one, but one reacts to certain things only, as in response to some personal need of the nerves.'[3] Now in Sutherland's thoughts there often recurred 'the idea of thorns and wounds made by thorns' because he had come to regard the Crown of Thorns as the quintessential symbol of the cruelty involved in the act of crucifixion. All of a sudden he found himself beginning 'to notice thorn bushes and the structure of thorns which pierced the air in all directions, their points establishing limits of aerial space'. Then, as is his practice, Sutherland began to make drawings of thorn bushes, but as he did so he realized – and it is a striking example of the workings of his anthropomorphic vision – that 'a curious change took place. While preserving their normal life in space, the thorns rearranged themselves and became something else – a sort of paraphrase of a *Crucifixion* or a crucified head.'[4]

At an early stage, then, Sutherland temporarily sublimated his conception of the Crucifixion in a succession of *Thorn Trees* and *Thorn Heads* whose writhings and prickings imaginatively evoke the flagellation and painful indignities to which Christ's body was submitted.[5] But while these thorn bushes became in one sense private symbols, they did not lose their real identity, because they remain natural growths which have also fascinated the artist by virtue of some curious beauty that he has found there. To scan these *Thorns* in search of human features or to look for a double image built up in the manner of an Arcimboldi is therefore pointless. Some of the thorn formations which Sutherland discovered served him as pictorial metaphors to conjure up the contortions of an agonized human head.[6] Five years later, however, he returned to these *motifs* and transformed them into a series of *Thorn Heads* in which the pictorial metaphor has more verisimilitude and is presented in the guise of a monstrance.[7] Thereby Sutherland consummated pictorially his imaginative

[1] Spring 1946.
[2] Near Trottiscliffe in Kent. The *Thorn* studies were made in part in Kent, in part in Wales.
[3] *vide* 'On Painting', *op. cit.*
[4] 'Thoughts on Painting', *op. cit.* From a letter to the author: '. . . only the rhythms which I seemed to want were recorded and the rest left out. I shall never forget the thrill of seeing these 'heads' actually present.'
[5] Plates 78–85.
[6] e.g. Plates 83, 84.
[7] Plate 111.

progression, for he had turned the fragment of nature into a cult object.[1]

But there is another aspect of these *Thorns* which has to be considered: the role they played in Sutherland's transition from being a painter of nature to a painter of man. As in other respects his approach was devious and oblique.

Sutherland once described his *Thorn Trees* and *Thorn Heads* as '"stand-ins" for a Crucifixion and a crucified head'.[2] That is to say they are figurative equivocations which have been substituted for a real thing. As 'presences' which evoke the apparatus and sensations of cruelty[3] they are certainly effective. Particular interest attaches, however, to these *Thorns* because they are among the first examples of a substitution procedure which Sutherland has frequently employed in the post-war years.[4] Yet we must not regard them simply as evasions, because in fact they served a vital purpose in the gradual evolution of the *Crucifixion* itself. When Sutherland saw that these growths looked more fearsome by contrast with a benign setting of blue sky and green grass – and this was how he painted them – he was inspired to break with tradition and make his own version of the *Crucifixion* 'more powerfully horrifying' by painting it in full sunlight against a blue sky with a feeling of warmth. Unfortunately, he was never able to carry out this project because he sensed that it would conflict with the internal structure and decoration of the church itself, and eventually therefore he had to resign himself to accepting as a background 'a bluish royal purple traditionally a death colour'. Nevertheless, we are free to discover a hint of the scene as he originally conceived it in Sutherland's *Thorn* substitutes.

Having, as it were, worked through this vein of cruelty, Sutherland turned to the crucial problem of the figure on the cross. Would the solution he arrived at be realistic and figurative? Or schematic and invented? He made exploratory drawings and sketches of various kinds.[5] But as he progressed, Sutherland realized that if he were ever to achieve the poignantly expressive and generally intelligible image which he envisaged he would have to opt for some form of realism.[6] He could not help feeling that the

[1] A further elaboration of this 'Cruelty' theme occurs in the *Thorn Cross* paintings of 1954 and 1959, *vide* Plates 138, 150, Colour Plate XI; also Chapter IV(ii).

[2] 'Thoughts on Painting', *op. cit.*

[3] As with the *Thorn Heads* of 1949–50, so with the *Thorn Crosses* of 1954–59, in which the thorn as a symbol of cruelty is ceremonially presented; *vide* Plates 138, 150, Colour Plate XI. Another later version (1959) is reproduced (No.5) in the catalogue of Sutherland's exhibition at the Paul Rosenberg Gallery, New York, in November 1959.

[4] *vide* Section (ii) of this chapter.

[5] e.g. Plate 77. From a letter to the author: 'I did also do a number of 'essays' more schematic, as an exercise, and some of the drawings which exist might give evidence of my thoughts in that direction.'

[6] From the same letter: 'I would have liked to make a more "detached" less naturalistic rendering. But two things deterred me: (1) I felt, rightly or wrongly, that since I was designing for a Christian *"culte"* the final form must be immediately intelligible and within the tradition. (2) I felt that certain overtones might be lacking if my rendering approached a technical detachment.'

consequences of detaching himself too much, for art's sake, from the reality of the subject might be a sort of sign-language decipherable only by a few and without the power to communicate or inspire great emotions.[1] As a result, he decided to paint what Sir Kenneth Clark has called 'a corporeal' *Crucifixion*.

After a long period of gestation Sutherland's immense *Crucifixion*[2] was at last finished in the autumn of 1946. It proved to be a sincere and powerful representation of the event, rigorously composed on the basis of a series of repeated rectangles, aggressive in its starkness and awe-inspiring in its effect. Indeed, only one other professing Christian artist of this century, Rouault, has handled this great theme with as much skill and real feeling, though apart from the fact that both artists have shown more concern for its mystical and emotional potentialities than with stylistic invention their conceptions are totally different. There is no doubt that, for Sutherland, the struggle to find an appropriate idiom for a meaningful modern *Crucifixion* was more considerable than for Rouault, who never gave a thought to modernism. This accounts for the uncertainty and clumsinesses[3] apparent here and there in Sutherland's handling. Against this, however, one must set the fact that his *Crucifixion* is an intense and poignant image of suffering which is made the more telling by the almost tangible presence of the figure.[4] The wide outspread arms and the open hands with clutching fingers create a terrible feeling of pathos, while the way in which the weight of the sagging body tears at the shoulders and ribs fills us with horror.[5] The Cross itself[6] – the instrument of torture – is of unusually sturdy build and seems to break and devour the emaciated body of Christ,

[1] *vide* 'Thoughts on Painting', *op. cit.*, where this is further explained: 'I think that today the time has come to do more than to be content to put a line round our reactions. By that I mean that the tendency has been to modify the forms of reality emotionally and intellectually, and to keep them in fact non-optical – or rather, optical only in the sense that observation and reaction have produced a kind of visual shorthand, which intellectually and sensibly refers one back to their prototype in life, as in Picasso's *Guernica*.' A classic example of this procedure, of course, is the *Stations of the Cross* panel by Matisse in the chapel at Vence, which post-dates Sutherland's *Crucifixion* by three years.

[2] Plates 74b, 75. The painting was unveiled on 16 November 1946. Sutherland began work on the final canvas in June 1946.

[3] The lower part of the body and the legs, for example, are weak in contrast to the upper part, while the half-abstract indications of shadow are often arbitrary.

[4] I have deliberately refrained from comparing the Sutherland with Picasso's great and moving *modern* image of the *Crucifixion* (1930) because this is totally different (though no less valid) in kind. Picasso has distorted and made use of the Christian iconography not with devotional intentions but as a private symbolism to express some interior and emotional drama of his own, *vide* A. H. Barr, *Picasso: Fifty Years of His Art* (New York, 1946), p.167 repr. This painting and several drawings for it were, of course, known to Sutherland from reproductions.

[5] Some critics see a 'face' in the upper part of Christ's body and have read into this 'apparition' a vitally expressive symbolical meaning, e.g. E. Sackville-West, *op. cit.* (1955 edn.) p.11: 'Because the eyes of Christ are shut and the face adroop, the vigilance of the figure is established elsewhere – in the "face" formed by the nipples, the nose-like shape of the rib shadows, and the construction of the abdomen.' Also, R. Melville, *op. cit.*: 'And then there is the most remarkable effect of all . . . It is the looming forth of a grave animal face from the torso, and in this depiction of the steady, unblinking gaze of the flesh amidst its own disturbances he brings The Crucifixion into the orbit of his innate predilections.' Sutherland denies the existence of the 'face', which anyway would not accord with his intentions, and regards such statements as nonsensical.

[6] Note the change of the Cross during the working out of the composition, from a drooping rustic T shape to one which approaches a Y.

while ourselves, spectators or worshippers, are made silent witnesses of this ghastly scene in place of the conventional figures of the Magdalen and St John. Owing to its assertive presence, and to the flattened spaceless background against which it is displayed, we cannot pass by nor get round this *Crucifixion*. We must look, and yet we cannot approach too close for, as the artist explains, it has been roped off to keep us at a respectful distance. The corporeal reality of the figure is troubling, the symbolic X's chalked on the wall by some unknown hand bring the scene almost into our own ambience, we feel that this might be an individual tragedy which has occurred in our midst. Yet Sutherland has also succeeded in removing the scene outside of definable time and space so that he has made of it a universal monitory symbol. At one moment we feel personally involved, at the next overawed. That is Sutherland's achievement.

While working on the *Crucifixion*, Sutherland essayed other related New Testament subjects, notably a *Deposition*[1] and a *Christ Carrying the Cross*,[2] a composition of which he made a second more elaborate version in 1953. Like the *Crucifixion*, both are strongly expressionistic in idiom, though neither has comparable merits as a painting nor seems to be as strongly felt. At the moment of writing, Sutherland is working on two more religious pictures, both recently commissioned: a *Noli Me Tangere* (1960) for the Chapel of St Mary Magdalen in Chichester Cathedral,[3] and a second *Crucifixion* (1960–61) for St Aidan's Church, Acton. Thus the painting of scriptural themes – and Sutherland is no less emotionally drawn to the Old Testament than to the New – though a peripatetic occupation, has not lost its fascination for him after one great attempt and will surely continue to figure as part of his work. For Sutherland is now interested in the pictorial possibilities of action, in the transference of feeling and the interchange of forms which occurs when figures impinge upon one another. Also, he feels particularly drawn towards scenes whose mythological or doctrinal import has a direct relevance to ourselves and to the world of today.

There remains one last religious work of art which must be mentioned in this context, namely the vast (72 by 40 feet) tapestry for the new Cathedral at Coventry,[4] the design for which Sutherland has worked on and revised more than once since 1952. This, too, was a commission, but for once the artist had no say regarding the choice of subject – *Christ in Glory*

---

[1] Plate 73.
[2] Colour Plate VII; *vide* E. Sackville-West, *op. cit.*: 'Never can there have been a more unconventional setting for this Station – a sort of ruined veranda with palm fronds edging their way over the parapet. But since the Way of the Cross is repeated every day, all over the world, why not in the remains of an abandoned Mediterranean villa? . . . for all three figures, though drawn processionally from left to right, are not going to leave their veranda, which is the only thinkable place for them, their eternal habitat.'
[3] Canon Hussey has been translated and is now Dean of Chichester.
[4] Plates 158–60. The cartoon was reproduced in colour in *The Builder* (London), of 28 March 1958.

*in the Tetramorph* – and had to accept the requirements of the Chapter of the Cathedral. Again Sutherland had to decide whether to invent his own iconography and idiom or to accept a traditional formula, though on this occasion the problem was less acute since he had to weigh decorative considerations equally with the need to create a majestic, dominating image. In the event, Sutherland had recourse to an established convention, although he has taken certain personal liberties in its interpretation. His solemn and imposing figure of Christ, for example, immobile, silent and watching, owes its conception in part to Byzantine models, but also in part to Egyptian royal figures of the 4th and 5th Dynasties.[1] And this element of inspiration from the Eastern world is further maintained in the mandorla and the framework with compartments for the symbols of the four Evangelists. 'I had seen Egyptian "mummy" pictures', Sutherland writes,[2] 'bound by tape to the coffined figures and I set out to make boxes round the central figure bound to it, as it were, by brass tape. Out of these, and against an ambiguous background of scaffolding, break the four beasts.'[3] Other innovations on the part of the artist are the introduction on the right of the patron Saint of the Church, St Michael, overcoming the Devil; the small figure of Man between the feet of Christ, and beneath that a Chalice and Serpent; also the Crucifixion panel at the base which contains the Weeping Sun and the Moon as well as a waiting bier behind the Cross. In general the design follows a Romanesque pattern, although the realism with which the figures are treated is modern rather than traditional. But at this stage it is impossible to judge the decorative or devotional value of the tapestry, for its conception is monumental and no one can tell what effect it will ultimately make until it has been carried out on the vast scale which is intended.[4] In the last resort, everything will depend on the proportions of the different parts of the design having been correctly judged, on the telling properties and harmony of the colours, and on the ability of the whole to impose its majestic presence across the great interior space of the Cathedral. But however it turns out, no one can deny the courage of a contemporary artist who has tackled such an exceptional and ambitious project in a medium rarely used today and with the technicalities of which he was not at the time familiar.

*(ii) The Painter of Nature: 1945–60*

Sutherland's work as a war artist did not interrupt his development as a

---

[1] From a letter to the author: 'After much thought I felt I wanted to do a large figure like a Buddha or one of the Egyptian figures in the Valley of the Kings.'
[2] Letter to the author.
[3] The background is green; the 'brass tape' is yellow; Christ in white against a grey background; flashes of red in the different symbols of the Evangelists, which are on various backgrounds, grey, pale blue, brown.
[4] This tapestry is being woven by Pinton Frères in the Aubusson factories at Felletin. [Publishers' note: the tapestry was delivered to the Cathedral as this reprint went to press.]

landscapist as much as one might expect. For as things turned out, many of the subjects officially assigned to him were located in Wales,[1] and he therefore had several opportunities of revisiting those areas of Pembrokeshire which he knew so well. At the same time he made the discovery of the Gower Peninsula[2] and found new subjects there. This chance of renewed contacts, not only with nature but, in particular, with the Welsh landscape, was of great importance to Sutherland, because in Wales his imagination had been more stimulated than in any part of England and he felt he had still not exhausted its pictorial possibilities. On each occasion therefore he could refresh his visual memory and imagination, was impelled to take up again the landscape subjects which he had been obliged largely to abandon for his other work and could satisfy his personal need for the discipline of drawing from nature.[3] So these visits enabled Sutherland to maintain enough continuity in his work to go on trying to resolve earlier pictorial problems.

I do not want to suggest that Sutherland could not have found inspiration in other parts of the country. We must, however, take account of the fact that he is to some extent a victim of his inspirational processes. For Sutherland does not easily discover the characteristic and meaningful *motifs* which will start him off painting. First of all he needs time to familiarize himself absolutely with a locality, because it is only after he has succumbed visually and emotionally to the ambience that what he calls his 'voluptuous awareness'[4] comes into play and releases his pictorial inspiration. Moreover, having found a locality which appeals to him, Sutherland allows himself to be obsessed by it and goes back in order to try and 'pin down its essence' more exactly. For he is haunted by a desire that the forms, lines and colours in his pictures shall really conjure up 'the essence of the likeness' to that particular place. Given this aim, it is understandable that Sutherland finds it necessary to maintain 'a singleness of purpose over certain periods of time',[5] and that in consequence his development should proceed, as it were, in a series of cycles. He is adventurous in so far as he is always trying to break new ground and exposing himself to new experiences. But as he gains in technical accomplishment during the process the perfectionist in him is aroused and, becoming aware of the incompleteness of his earlier treatment of a *motif,* he turns back to redefine and enlarge on his original visual experience. A typical example of this procedure is *Entrance to Lane,*[6] a *motif* which Sutherland had explored very fully in 1939

---

[1] He was there in 1941, 1942, 1943, 1944, 1945.
[2] Plates 34, 50-55.
[3] *vide* letter to Mr Hans Juda repr. in R. Melville, *op. cit.*, between Plates 13 and 14.
[4] *vide* 'Thoughts on Painting', *op. cit.*
[5] *vide* 'Welsh Sketchbook' in *Horizon* (1942), *op. cit.*
[6] Plates 16, 17, 68.

but to which he returned in 1945 to extract from it a more complex, sinuous and suggestive composition.

Being a war artist was, for Sutherland, a more or less full-time occupation and a serious challenge to his imaginative vision. Moreover, he felt obliged, as I have already explained, to adopt for the purpose a different style of painting, at once more precise and descriptive. It would be surprising, therefore, if he had been able to concern himself much with landscape between 1940 and 1945 or if his handling of it had undergone any significant changes. Most of Sutherland's wartime landscapes are in gouache or water-colour and on a small scale because he had not the opportunity to work them up into larger oil paintings. Thematically and in manner they are an extension of the pre-1940 group of works, though in so far as they show a trend towards a bolder and more simplified conception they represent a gradual modification of his style. Many of the same *motifs* recur, but new ideas also make their appearance. His treatment of space becomes shallower, he begins to pile planes one above the other rising up the canvas, he tends to concentrate more on single objects. The key works of this period are paintings like *Folded Hills* (1943), *Triple-tiered Landscape* (1944), *Horned Forms* (1944), *Landscape with Pointed Rocks* (1945), *Thistles* (1945) and *Landscape with Fields* (1945).[1] Each of these contains stylistic features of which Sutherland was to make more elaborate use in his later nature paintings, and to this extent they form a link between the first (1935–40) and second (1947 onwards) phases of his evolution.

Yet for all his passionate preoccupation with the landscape of Wales – and even then only with a small bit of it – Sutherland felt, rather than knew, that he had to free himself from its thraldom. As he wrote in 1941: 'He who is over-discriminating becomes narrow in achievement'.[2] The time had come by 1945 when his vision was ready to expand and his style to be enhanced. However, the transition to what may be regarded as Sutherland's new manner of painting natural phenomena was not sudden and developed intuitively rather than by an effort of will. This change occupied a period of about four years (1944–48) and affected every aspect of his work – subject, colour, composition and handling. But from 1948 on, when it was completed, there is no mistaking the fact that Sutherland had reached maturity and become a major personality among contemporary artists. His handling is more assured, his manner of painting finer and subtler, and his vision sharper than in the past; also, he has forged a style which is suppler but no less his own.

We must envisage the transitional phase in Sutherland's work as

[1] Plates 52, 54c, 59, 53c, 57, 65.
[2] *Horizon, op. cit.*

starting towards the end of his time as a war artist (*c*.1944),[1] continuing through the years when he painted the *Thorn Trees* and the *Crucifixion* (1946–47), and coming to an end six months before he began the portrait of Somerset Maugham (February 1949). If we examine the pictures that he painted during this time we are struck by all sorts of innovations. Thus we find Sutherland extending his field of vision laterally and dealing with a bolder but more complex group of inter-related natural forms.[2] At the same time he gives up receding perspectives and brings these natural forms – hills, trees, rocks and so forth – closer to the eye and to the surface of the canvas.[3] The foreground of the picture is then seen at ground level, as it were, and the natural growths appear to be standing on a sort of table-top or platform. This device, greatly elaborated, appears constantly in Sutherland's pictures from now onwards, but generally it is used to achieve a deliberately artificial effect: that is to say, he uses a stand or platform as a means of isolating some natural specimen from its organic context. We have seen how the *Thorn Heads* are eventually presented as monstrances. On the same principle, Sutherland sets his *Thistles* and *Thorns* up on the ends of poles,[4] hangs *Maize Cobs* and *Datura Flowers* on a line,[5] displays a *Cigale,* a *Mantis* and some animal-like pieces of driftwood which are called *Turning Form* and *Articulated Form* on pedestals,[6] and finally sets up his *Standing Forms, Poised Forms* and imaginary *Heads* on bases like pieces of sculpture.[7] Now in all of these pictures the element of pictorial space is greatly flattened. Thus Sutherland's eye ceases to roam and he begins to 'peer',[8] as it might be through a microscope, at some plant or insect, tree-root or stone. And as he does so he becomes aware of seeing more and more; in groupings of small forms he reads not just an expression of some secret character but often a whole life story.

Other innovations which we find in Sutherland's pictures of this time are increasing references, direct as well as indirect, to man and his activities. Sutherland no longer paints wild, empty, untilled landscapes as he did before 1940. Instead, he notices 'the imprint of man' on nature and occasionally ventures to recognize man's presence.[9] Fields are tilled, the corn has been harvested and piled in stooks;[10] the lamp burns[11] and the logs

[1] *vide* Plate 52.
[2] e.g. Plates 47c, 67.
[3] e.g. Plates 52c and e, 54, 55, 60, 87.
[4] e.g. Plates 57, 80, 81.
[5] Plate 95; also R. Melville, *op. cit.* Plates 54, 56.
[6] Plates 98, 100a, 104, 106; also R. Melville, *op. cit.*, Plates 34, 49, 50.
[7] Plates 102, 103, 118, 119–21, 126, 129, Colour Plate VIII.
[8] *vide* J. T. Soby, *op. cit.*, p.138: '. . . he is at his best when he peers rather than scans'.
[9] *vide* 'Thoughts on Painting', *op. cit.*: '. . . landscape without the imprint of man, that is to say landscapes which are not gardens or tilled fields – grand landscape – can be awfully boring'.
[10] Plates 54d, 62, 64, 65.
[11] Plate 61.

are aflame in the grate;[1] the vine has been trained to make a pergola;[2] the palm-branches have been cut and used to make a roof or a palisade;[3] hedges and plants have been arranged to make an enclosed garden.[4] Then man himself appears, surveying his handiwork: figures wander through plantations or inspect the vines;[5] one woman picks vegetables, another, mysteriously smiling, sits in her garden, and a third eats an apple.[6] And as the artist takes up new subjects so he varies his treatment of them, adopting an idiom which is less complicated and on the whole more naturalistic. Where the matter of the *Fallens Tree* (1940) was limp and decaying, where the composition of *Tree Forms in an Estuary* (1940) was sprawling and uncertain,[7] in comparable later pictures such as *Woods and Estuary* (1945) or *Palm and Landscape* (1948) the forms are defined with lines, the organic matter has resilience and the composition is clear and coherent.[8]

This change in Sutherland's approach to nature and in his handling was also accompanied in 1945-46 by a change in his palette. His tonalities lightened and he began to use much brighter colours.[9] As a rule, developments of this sort correspond with a change of surroundings or are the result of some other outside influence which it is the critic's responsibility to identify. But in Sutherland's case the change of surroundings followed after the stylistic change, which seems to have been largely the result of an intuitive urge. He says himself that colour suddenly became important to him for its own sake at this time, and that he also discovered he could use it 'emotively and arbitrarily'. Nevertheless, 'the lightening of key' which occurs in Sutherland's paintings in 1945–46 suggests a clearer and more steady light than is usual in England and makes his move to the South of France in the spring of 1947 seem like the logical fulfilment of a spiritual need.

At this stage, Sutherland reveals himself as a vivid colourist with an original and personal sense of harmonies. He banishes the dark and heavy tones which he had used earlier, though he preserves the sharp black and white oppositions.[10] For the rest he has recourse to acid pinks and mauve,

[1] Plate 56c.
[2] Plates 88, 90, 91, 123b.
[3] Plates 92, 93.
[4] Plate 94c.
[5] Plates 88d, 89b, 101f, 108, 109.
[6] Plates 61, 63.
[7] Plates 28c, 31.
[8] Plates 66a, 92c.
[9] From a letter to the author: 'I do not attribute the increase of colour to seeing more contemporary art, but rather to the feeling of a need to clarify and lighten at that time. Colour gradually became important to me and I found I could use it emotively and arbitrarily.' *vide* also 'Thoughts on Painting', *op. cit.*: 'When I did start working in France in 1947, I must confess that I did wonder how I had come to anticipate, by this lightening of key, the clarity of the steady southern light'.
[10] *vide* 'Thoughts on Painting', *op. cit.*: 'In my earlier work I used colour very sparingly: often blacks and greys and one colour'.

light blue and orange, scarlet, emerald and chrome yellow, colours which he uses arbitrarily to create radiant, exquisite and pleasing effects. This transformation was, however, fraught with a certain danger. For when the pictorial space is flattened in the way Sutherland flattened it at this stage, when objects are elegantly and symmetrically displayed against an unbroken background plane, and when colour is used for effect not for structural purposes, the painting that results tends to be decorative. In 1947–48 Sutherland's work passed through such a decorative phase[1] before his involvement with sculptural *motifs* and portraiture obliged him again to grapple with three-dimensional reality.

In considering this transitional phase of Sutherland's work, one must not lose sight of the fact that while he felt an instinctive need to enlarge his range of artistic expression and embarked on challenging new subjects of various kinds, he was also exposed more acutely than before to powerful influences both at home and abroad. For example, he was at this time on terms of close friendship with Francis Bacon, an artist whom he had known for some ten years. Bacon has a considerable personality and can talk fervently and persuasively. He also has sensibility, a strong feeling for the technique of painting, and a good knowledge of many periods of art. When Sutherland began to work on his own *Crucifixion*, Bacon had just completed his *Three Studies for Figures at the base of a Crucifixion*[2] (1945), which are expressionistic and semi-human figurations not unrelated to Sutherland's *Chimère* and *Stone Head*[3] (both 1946–47). Again, in a painting such as *Men Walking*[4] (1950) one senses something of the gangsterish mystery that Bacon likes to cultivate. Though it might be an exaggeration to suggest that Bacon had exerted an overt influence on Sutherland, it is at any rate probable that Sutherland was receptive to some of his ideas and allowed him to open his eyes to various technical possibilities and refinements.

Where other artists are concerned, Sutherland has, on the whole, remained detached and pursued his own vision of nature and man in his own way. 'We are deceived if we work contrary to our inclinations', is one of his fundamental tenets.[5] This does not mean, however, that Sutherland closes his eyes to the achievements of other artists. On the contrary, he is greatly interested in seeing all he can, and in the immediate post-war years took advantage of his trips to Europe to visit as many galleries and museums as possible in order to look at the works of old as well as modern

[1] e.g. the series of *Vine Pergolas, Palm Palisades, Gourds* and *Pomegranates*.
[2] Now in the Tate Gallery.
[3] Plates 71 and 74a.
[4] Plate 108b.
[5] *vide* 'Thoughts on Painting', *op. cit.*

masters. But he is well able to resist the temptation to become an imitator or a false disciple. For instance, in 1947 he visited the Picasso Museum at Antibes and shortly afterwards painted from memory a *Landscape* whose formal organization corresponds with that of a *Pastorale* which he had seen there.[1] The subjects of the two pictures are, however, entirely different, and Sutherland's canvas is not even a variant of the original but a transposition or 'paraphrase' in strictly personal terms.

Had Sutherland been obliged to confine himself to the English scene at this vital stage in his career, it is unlikely that he could have escaped from the provincialism of his native school. Foreign travel was now to speed his development and enable him to increase his stature over the next ten years. As a rule, when an English (or any Nordic) artist[2] moves to France, particularly to the Mediterranean seaboard, the effect on his work is disastrous. But Sutherland is exceptional in so many ways that it does not seem surprising that with him the reverse should be true. He was, in fact, saved from stagnation by being able to leave the artistic backwater of his native land just at the time when he most needed to stimulate his visual and emotional responses and when, on another plane, he was ready to come to terms with the formal and expressive means used by contemporary artists in Europe. Yet even so he remained curiously unaffected by two major achievements in modern French painting. He was unable to appreciate, at this stage, the analytical and structural feats which Cézanne had performed with colour. Similarly, he remained unaffected by the consequences of the pictorial revolution effected by Cézanne's heirs, the cubist painters. The explanation of this lies in his single-minded concern with his own type of vision. Cézanne's colour[3] evoked no *emotional* response in Sutherland, and he had not yet begun to see the potentialities of colour as a structural element. On the other hand, though he had already begun to flatten his pictorial space and abandon linear perspective, he remained faithful to the convention of a single view-point. To this day, Sutherland approaches his subjects head-on and does not try to see around them, nor to twist them in order to show other sides, means by which the cubist painters succeeded in evoking volume and recession in a shallow pictorial space. For all the modernism of his idiom and the pictorial liberties which he has been prepared to take, Sutherland is in this sense a traditionalist.

[1] Plate 64c; *vide* for a reproduction of the Picasso, *Cahiers d'Art*, 1948, p.33.
[2] Van Gogh is an obvious exception to this generalization, but even he was glad to get back to the calmer atmosphere of the north of France.
[3] From a letter to the author: 'I reacted against what little I saw when I was a student. In the last five years (since 1954) I have begun to see very much more exactly what it is all about and I find myself drawing closer to his fragmentary analyses in recent subjects such as certain *Wood Interiors*.' (Plate 155). Familiarity with the landscape of Provence seems to have changed Sutherland's view of Cézanne.

The changes that began to occur in Sutherland's painting after 1944 were half-conscious premonitory signs of a temperamental need for new revelations.[1] These he experienced in the spring of 1947 when he first visited the Mediterranean seaboard and discovered in the flora and fauna of the department of the Alpes Maritimes[2] a new world. No natural scene could have contrasted more absolutely with that of his familiar wild and picturesque haunts. For the Riviera landscape is harsh, arid, spectacular, somewhat exotic, highly-coloured and marked in many different ways by the civilizing passage of man.[3] Moreover, the light there is steady and clear, and the scene is a visual challenge. This ambience, in which Sutherland gathered around him the elements of a novel pictorial universe with its own forms and colours, provided just the sort of imaginative stimulus that he needed, more particularly since it was free of romantic overtones and therefore assisted his efforts to clarify his style. Yet, as he was soon to discover, there lurks beneath the luxuriant and unruffled outward appearance of the place an acute struggle for survival. Nature's products are either swathed in protective covering or else defensively armed. Sutherland's eye was caught by the pomegranates bursting their tough skin,[4] the ripe maize cobs casting off their sheath of foliage, the delicate undulations of banana leaves,[5] the tough bottle-like gourds[6] and the sinuous vines tying themselves in curves to the framework of the pergola. At the same time, he did not overlook the spikes of the palm-branch, nor the prickly defences of the artichoke and the cactus,[7] nor yet the scaly armour and serrated legs of the cicada or the predatory attitudes of the mantis.

Since his first visit to the Riviera in the spring of 1947, Sutherland has spent several months of each year there and now owns a house at Menton. So great has been the hold of this countryside over him that, although much of his actual painting is still done in England, he finds virtually all his *motifs* there – more recently the Veneto has become a second source – and this has brought about a complete change in the subject of his nature

---

[1] The continued vitality of Sutherland's art is related to his practice of constantly looking to nature for visual and imaginative refreshment. The reverse case is that of an artist like Henry Moore who, for want of fresh and authentic experiences, repeats his own prototypes and allows his work to become bloodless and academic.

[2] 'I happen to work better and more easily in the sun.' *vide* 'Thoughts on Painting', *op. cit.*

[3] *ibid.*: '. . . unless one can reduce the objects of a landscape to such a size as one can hold in one's hand . . . If you were to take a piece of lichen from a rock in one of these gorges, or pick up a shaped stone, a drawing of these would seem to be more interesting, because man, after all, could have plucked the lichen off the rock and picked up the stone.'

[4] Plate 110c.

[5] Plates 99, 101.

[6] Plates 96, 101.

[7] Plates 97, 110.

Fig.6
**Owl, Bats and Hanging Form** 1955
Lithograph in three colours 20 × 25½ in.

paintings. He has more or less given up painting landscape as such:[1] 'Can you imagine anything more boring than painting mountain gorges?' Sutherland now asks.[2] We find him still, on occasion, being attracted to a mysterious or half-hidden place, as in the continuing series of paths leading into a wood. But for the most part he has turned his attention to still-life subjects,[3] to elaborating a mysterious imagery (deriving in part from things he saw during his term as a War Artist) in which organic elements are treated in quasi-mechanistic terms,[4] to building up inert fragments of natural growths into substitute living creatures,[5] and, since 1956, to the study of birds and animals as well as to the painting of dramatic effects of light.

The disparate elements of Sutherland's post-war interests and stylistic development first came together in a great composition, *Origins of the Land*,[6] commissioned in 1950 as a decoration for one of the pavilions at the Festival of Britain in 1951. The conception of the painting as a whole is,

[1] *Tree Form in Estuary* (1945), Colour Plate VI, was one of the last; in *Path through Plantation* or *Men Walking* (Plates 108, 109), both of 1950, he was more concerned with the relationship between man and nature than with nature itself, while *Landscape with Dry Waterway* (1952) (Plate 116b) was a study of stones. It is perhaps relevant that, from 1950 onwards, Sutherland was preoccupied with sculptural themes, portraits and the Coventry tapestry, which left him little time for painting other subjects. Plate 155 represents one of his rare recent landscapes.
[2] Letter to the author.
[3] e.g. Plates 95–9, 107, 110, 143–6, 148, 154.
[4] e.g. Plates 122a, 128, 132–6, Colour Plates X, XI.
[5] e.g. Plates 102–6, 118–21, 124b, 126, 129.
[6] Plates 112–16.

44

of course, symbolical, although the objects of which it is composed and the colours are not. This is an upward-moving composition divided into three parts, like the *Triple-tiered Landscape* of 1944.[1] But here, as one would expect in a primarily decorative work, no spatial experience is involved. The conception is that of a geological segment cut sheer through the earth's crust to the lowermost regions where there is fire. This segment is then used as a background for some animal and vegetable specimens – represented in half-relief – between which a complex organic relationship has developed under the ground during the process of decay and fossilization. In the uppermost section of the composition the eye is led above the surface of the earth, where it is met by a formidable array of eroded rocks. Thus, in the lower half of this picture, Sutherland confronts us with the consuming and fructifying process which goes on below ground, the hidden forces at work fashioning from the past the shape of things to come; while in the upper part he evokes the ageing process, the depraving forces of wind and water which eat into solid matter, giving character to things as they do so, and thus enrich the land. Time and history are therefore invoked obliquely, but so too, as I shall show, is man.

All the forms in this painting had their origin in real objects. Bird-life and the distant past are evoked by a pterodactyl, the model for which was found in a natural history museum.[2] The driftwood *Root Forms,* resembling blind-worms, had been picked up on a Mediterranean beach and painted many times during the previous three years. The rock formations are derived from some stones which Sutherland had found in a dry river-bed at Tourettes-sur-Loup[3] and which simultaneously suggested to him the image of a human *Head*.[4] Now here we have a typical example of the ambivalence of Sutherland's view of nature. For, looking in one way, he saw, as so often before, that the erosions in these stones were 'precisely reproducing, in miniature' the structure of a whole landscape,[5] while looking at them in another way, and 'paraphrasing' what he saw, he arrived at a formation resembling a skull. So through these stones nature appears directly related to man, and this seems to illustrate the meaning of one of Sutherland's enigmatic utterances: 'For myself I believe that a new vision must be grafted on reality – that the mysteriously intangible must be made immediate and tangible and vice versa'.[6] But this practice is even more vividly illustrated by the big *Standing Form* which occupies

Fig.7
**Stone Head** 1952 Watercolour and chalk
10×7½ in. Collection: the Artist

[1] Plate 55.
[2] Plates 112, 116.
[3] Plates 101a (1948), 116a, b, c.
[4] Plate 117. *vide* E. Sackville-West, *op. cit.* (1955 edn.) p.12: '. . . we recognize, with minimum delay, the form of abstraction which relates the head of an old military man to a lump of tufa'.
[5] *vide Horizon, op. cit.* p.235; also 'Thoughts on Painting', *op. cit.*
[6] 'On Painting', *op. cit.*

the left foreground of the composition, for this is simultaneously both a formalization of a piece of organic matter and a substitute for Man.

This form, a variation on the *Turning Form* and *Articulated Form* of 1948, had made its first appearance in paintings of 1949[1] and belongs to a group of similar forms with which Sutherland was preoccupied until 1954. What are these Forms? Where do they derive from, and what do they mean? 'They do not, of course, *mean* anything', replies the artist.[2] They are what he calls 'monuments and presences', but they have origins, nevertheless, in bits of trees or plants which the artist has 'emotionally modified from their natural prototype'[3] in accordance with some private visionary impulse. We have already encountered a similar imaginative transformation in the case of the *Thorns,* although in that case no figural image evolved. Yet another example of this mutative process, though of a different order, is to be found in the *Staring Tree Form* of 1945 which, vastly enlarged, becomes in 1946 the terrifying *Chimère*.[4] Here Sutherland starts with a fallen tree-trunk – from which a knot in the bark seems to glare at him like the eye of a Cyclops – and reinterprets the object until he has arrived at a dramatic but slightly grotesque apparition. Posed as it is on a sort of throne, this creature has the aloofness of a monument, yet as it fixes us with its eyes so it disquiets us with its presence. We find examples of similar 'presences' in the work of Picasso and Max Ernst.[5] However, unlike the frightening imaginative creations of these two artists, Sutherland's *Forms* are neither pictorial metaphors nor dream-world monsters but dummies like de Chirico's *Muses*.[6] As he himself has said, they are substitutes for human figures, fetish-like abstractions which proclaim their organic origins and so enable him by inference 'to catch the taste – the quality – the essence of the presence of the human figure'.[7] Sutherland looks at them from different sides and varies their setting according to whether he is trying to pin down his sudden awareness of 'the mysterious immediacy of a figure standing in a room or against a hedge, in its shadow'.[8] He had tried to capture this sort of 'awareness' with real figures in *Path through Plantation* (Plate 109) but was dissatisfied with the unreality of the

[1] Plates 102, 103.
[2] 'Thoughts on Painting', *op. cit.*
[3] *ibid.*
[4] Plates 69–71.
[5] e.g. a *Standing Bather* (1929) by Picasso, repr. in A. Barr, *Picasso, Fifty Years of His Art* (New York, 1946), p.162; or *The Elephant Celebes* (1921) by Max Ernst, repr. in P. Waldberg, *Max Ernst* (Paris, 1958), p.165.
[6] *vide* J. T. Soby, *Giorgio de Chirico* (New York, 1955), colour plate facing p.134. Compare *Armoured Form* (1950), Plate 119a, one of Sutherland's least convincing images, with Chirico's *Grand Metaphysician* or *Troubadour* (both 1917) repr. Soby pp.144, 234.
[7] 'Thoughts on Painting', *op. cit.*, on which much of this passage is based. It is only fair to state that Sutherland intended and still feels these *Forms* to be organic.
[8] Colour Plate VIII, Plates 102c, 121 show them in a garden. Plate 123a and c shows them in a landscape setting, i.e. 'thrown back, as it were, into the original cradle of impact' (*vide* 'Thoughts on Painting'); Plate 102d shows a 'monument' in a room.

Fig.8
**Standing Figure** 1952
Bronze cast from plaster model 21⅝ in. high
Edition of 6 produced by Marlborough
Fine Art

result. His fetish-like *Forms* are, in themselves, essentially unreal, but because they are painted in pseudo-sculptural terms and have human connotations they achieve a potent degree of pictorial reality.

It seems strange that during those very years when Sutherland was continuously at work on portraits of vital human beings he should have felt that the only expressive means by which he could bridge the gap between man, the visible world which we all inhabit, and the artist's world of the imagination, was through substitution and the creation of fetishes. But he maintains that he had to have recourse to these weird, magical forms because they gave him 'a sense of the shock of surprise which direct evocation could not do' and because they enabled him to make 'more real' to himself the sensation of being in the presence of other human beings.[1] We must therefore be content to interpret these puzzling and somewhat artificial paintings as expressions of a private visual and emotional obsession and as yet another example of the oblique ways in which Sutherland approaches reality. At the same time, we may remind ourselves of the encounter between Don Giovanni and the statue of the Commendatore. For Sutherland's *Forms* or 'presences' are in effect, like the Commendatore, sculptures[2] endowed with life. They are envisaged as three-dimensional objects, but represented, as were Picasso's bone structures of the late 1920's, in the two-dimensional terms of paint on canvas. And if we seek an explanation of why a modern painter works in this way we shall find ourselves approaching one of the basic dilemmas raised by the modern idiom. Why is it, for example, that two of the greatest painters of our time – Matisse and Picasso – have felt the need to treat the same *motif* in three as well as in two dimensions and have proved themselves in the doing to be great sculptors? Is not part of the answer to be found in the fact that since a true experience in the round is visually denied to painters by present-day pictorial practice they are driven at times to maintain their grasp on reality by modelling? At all events, sculpture has been closely integrated with their painting and, like Sutherland, when they have translated sculpture into pictorial terms they have used every means to give it roundness and to emphasize its figurative connotations.

In Sutherland's case this sculptural phase lasted, with variations, until about 1957. But it seems that as he became more at home in portraiture so his approach to nature became less indirect until he has now given up

[1] *vide* 'Thoughts on Painting', *op. cit.*: 'I feel that now we can perhaps enlarge the field of painting by setting our emotional paraphrases of reality ... within the ambience of optical reality'. In other words, Sutherland was attempting in these pictures to confront two pictorial realities, the natural scene and the imaginative concretion. He was thus trying to reconcile his own nature-bound vision with the conceptual or super-real imagery of a Picasso or an Ernst.
[2] Sutherland made about six sculptures in 1950–4; all were eventually destroyed except a *Standing Form* (Fig. 8) which has recently been cast in bronze. These sculptures related to the 'forms' in his paintings.

the process of substitution. At moments still, the engineer and the artificer within demands satisfaction, and some of his principal themes during the 1950's have been of a mechanistic nature. *Variation on a Theme* (1953), *Machine Form* (1953), *Hydrant* (1954) and *Chevaux de Frise* (1959),[1] for example, are images inspired by memories of things he had seen in factories and foundries during the war. We have only to look back at pictures such as *Moulds* or *Hydraulic Press*[2] of 1942 to discover the origins of the *motifs* which are now being imaginatively reinterpreted. Another theme which has occupied Sutherland greatly during the last few years involves equilibrium and a rotating or pendulum movement. This is sometimes represented by a pair of scales, as in *Still Life with Apples and Scales* (1957)[3] where the free movement of the hanging branch is contrasted with the up and down motion of the weighing pans. In *The Scales*[4] of 1959 this same movement is offset against the shifting balance created by light and shadow. While in paintings such as *Swinging Form and Monkey* (1953), *Swinging Form* (1954), *Hanging Form over Water* (1957), and *Hanging Form* (1959),[5] the movement of the mechanistic element is surrounded by mystery because the motivating force is never visible.

Fig.9
**Machine** 1956 Watercolour and chalk
$11\frac{1}{2} \times 8\frac{1}{2}$ in.   Collection: the Artist

Thorns have been a recurrent theme in Sutherland's work throughout the 1950's, but those executed since 1954,[6] which are based on drawings from nature made near Monte Carlo, have an altogether more violent, spiky, yet formalized appearance. They are dense and compact tangles of barbed twigs through which can be perceived an underlying cruciform structure. Indeed, the cross has become an element frequently met with in Sutherland's most recent works. Here private symbolism seems to be involved. For I believe that these images reflect the mental and moral anguish which Sutherland suffered in 1954 when single-handed he valiantly opposed what he held to be wrong practices in the administration of the Tate Gallery, was unsupported by colleagues, out-manoeuvred and eventually had no honourable alternative but to resign his Trusteeship. This was one of the bitterest moments of his life and for a while it coloured his outlook. But his painting at least seems to have gained indirectly by the experience, because this spurred Sutherland on to shun public life and concentrate on being a painter first and foremost. And this in turn has led to his style becoming less English and more European.

During the last few years, Sutherland has also hinted at some of his own preoccupations and dilemmas in a series of paintings taken from the

[1] Plates 128, 134c, 136, 157a.
[2] Plates 43, 44.
[3] Plate 148.
[4] Plate 154.
[5] Plates 133, 137, 149, 156.
[6] Plates 138, 140, 142, 150.

world of animals. Whereas in the past his animals were somewhat stylized and presented in the form of exhibits,[1] today he depicts them more naturalistically in romantically suggestive settings. The monkey imprisoned under his net appeals to be freed. One toad seeks to escape from imprisonment in a glass jar, while another, emerging from some dank corner, turns the beam of his orange eye on the world and stretches out his fierce claw-like paw as though to strike down some prey. The heron hangs around a sinister looking water-gate.[2] Sutherland has also painted eagles, bats and snakes, fierce, sinister and mysterious creatures all. In each case he has brought out the animal's hidden character and makes us see it in an unexpected way. Sutherland enjoys titillating us with mysterious and unexpected effects. Even the half-raised curtain in the open doorway of the Church of the Salute suggests something mysterious in its dark interior and enhances the emptiness and silence around the building.[3]

All of these are new subjects which Sutherland has treated in new ways since 1956. At the same time his compositions have become more complex and daring than in the past, he devises more ornate forms, and he has begun to introduce movement. Tendrils creep and curl around static constructions; foliage falls rhythmically in swags; there is a subtle play of light with dramatically contrasted shadows.[4] These are effects which he would not have attempted ten years ago but which he can manage today because, in the interval, he has acquired confidence, because his brushwork has become finer and because he has learnt to create a complex effect with economy in his use of means.[5] Gone are the errant lines and emphatic passages of the earlier works. Today, largely I think as a result of the discipline of painting portraits, Sutherland's work has the force and deceptive simplicity of one who is fully master of his medium.

### (iii) Portraits: 1949–60

Though the trend of Sutherland's art since the early 1940's had been continually moving towards figure painting, it was an unexpected departure when he started to paint portraits.[6] As we have seen, Sutherland had made a few studies of miners during the war years, followed in 1945 by the *Crucifixion* and the *Smiling Woman*,[7] and then in 1946 by the expressive

Fig.10
**Study of a Tin Miner**   1942  Pencil drawing
9 × 5 in.   Collection: the Artist

[1] Plate 98.
[2] Plates 139, 153, Colour Plate XIV.
[3] In 1957 Sutherland painted *St Mark's, Night* and *The Salute*.
[4] e.g. Plates 143, 145a, 147, 149, 150.
[5] Contrast two similar subjects: *Path in Wood II* of 1959 (Plate 155); and *Entrance to Lane* of 1939 (Plate 17).
[6] In childhood Sutherland had occasionally made self-portraits, but all were destroyed. He experimented with portraits in his student days in a style which he calls 'highly finished but not academic'; these too have been destroyed.
[7] Plate 61a.

49

if somewhat sketchy head entitled *Laughing Woman*.[1] But after these first tentative efforts at figure painting Sutherland had reverted to the painting of nature and still life, familiar genres in which he could more easily pursue the elaboration and evolution of his style. From this he was roused by chance rather than by design. During his stay at St Jean Cap Ferrat in the spring of 1948, Sutherland had occasionally encountered Mr Somerset Maugham, and after one of their meetings remarked casually to a mutual friend that were he to take up portraiture Mr Maugham's face and personality were of a type that would especially appeal to him. Sutherland gave no further thought to the matter, however, until a few months later he received to his surprise a letter from Mr Maugham asking him to paint his portrait. Here was an opportunity to launch out in a new direction which Sutherland could not refuse, for he is always keen to broaden his experience and the invitation to paint 'a real human animal' (to quote his own words[2]) was both a challenge to his capacities and a test of his interpretative powers. During the past few years Sutherland's technical proficiency had increased greatly and he had grown more confident. Yet for all that he was tempted by portraiture, Sutherland knew that it was a branch of painting about which he had much to learn and that he would have to create his own idiom. This first venture was, then, something of an experiment. The result, however, justified the hopes of both the sitter and the artist and the *Portrait of Somerset Maugham*,[3] an exceptional and striking work, therefore marks an important turning point in Sutherland's *œuvre*. The painting of it enabled Sutherland to gain experience which has affected the conception and execution of all his subsequent works, and it showed him how to reconcile his way of looking at nature with his observation of man.

A new vein of inspiration opened up for Sutherland when he began to see in the lines, forms and convolutions of a human face the same sort of expression of the process of growth and struggle as he found in the rugged surfaces and irregular contours of a boulder or a range of hills.[4] The significance of this discovery was its corollary, namely that, through portraiture, he could now extend the scope of his work and maintain its continuity. That is the sense of Sutherland's reference to his portraits as 'nature studies', and we may look for the link between the two – man and nature – in his sense of the picturesque.

[1] Plate 163.
[2] Unless otherwise indicated, the quotations in this section are taken from 'Thoughts on Painting', *op. cit.*; or from letters to and conversations with the author; or from notes of conversations with Graham Sutherland which Mr John Richardson has been kind enough to place at my disposal.
[3] Plate 165.
[4] Compare for example *Study of Boulders* (1942), Plate 35, and *Cairn* (1944), Plate 60b, with the study for the head of Mr Maugham, Plate 164.

Sutherland sees his own role in relation to a sitter as being somewhat that of a bird-watcher, that is to say an observer who remains detached and unobtrusive yet is constantly on the alert to detect and note down typical gestures, attitudes or facial expressions which give a clue to the type of behaviour or underlying character associated with the 'animal'. He does not approach a sitter with preconceived ideas of what he is like, nor of what he is going to see in him. Similarly, he does not make up his mind in advance on how he is going to paint his victim, nor does he try to impose on him some convenient pictorial formula. On the contrary, since Sutherland's principal tenet is that 'a portrait must be like', he remains passive in the sitter's presence for as long as possible and does not try to give a definitive form to his portrait until he has had a chance to observe and sense many different aspects of the individual.

Berenson has written[1] that: 'If British art has not been too strong on the side of decoration,[2] it has made up for it . . . by its success in that interesting and valuable realm of illustration, the effigy. It is that which turns the Royal Academy show into a spring fair.' The writer then goes on to define an effigy as concentrating on 'the social aspects of the subject, emphasizing the soldierliness of the soldier, the judiciousness of the judge, the clericality of the clergy, the self-importance of the business or professional man, the fashionableness of the woman of fashion, the club-ableness of the clubman'. And Berenson concludes sarcastically that the more the effigy-producing artist 'sees what his public thinks it wants to see, the more it admires, honours and rewards him'. The portrait, however, says Berenson, is a far more difficult, profound and rare form of art, since it consists in 'the rendering of an individual in terms of decoration, and of the individuality of the inner man as well as of his social standing'.

Judged by these standards, Sutherland is unquestionably a painter of portraits not of effigies. Not for him the type of impressive or inspiring 'illustration' which enables 'every frequenter of the Royal Academy to feel a tingle of "life-enhancement" ' as he looks at the portrait of a famous or successful person. Sutherland's portraits are meticulous, analytical, sincere and intimate records, but the sitters are never presented as inspiring examples and the spectator has no inclination to bask in reflected glory.

---

[1] B. Berenson, *Aesthetics and History* (London, 1950), p.188.

[2] Berenson used this word in a very personal sense, defining it as follows: 'Decoration comprises all the elements in a work of art that distinguish it from a mere reproduction of the shape of things: tactile values and movement of course, proportion, arrangement, space composition, in short everything in the field of visual representation that is made life-enhancing by means of ideated sensations.' Movement he defines as 'the manifest in-dwelling energy that vitalizes the delimiting outlines of an artifact'. And by 'ideated sensations' he means 'those that exist only in imagination, and are produced by the capacity of the object to make us realize its entity and live its life'. 'Decoration' as defined by Berenson corresponds well with the effect made on the beholder by Sutherland's portraits, *vide ibid.* pp.64, 67, 80.

Sutherland does not elaborate the setting, and the sort of 'likeness' that he aims at involves above all 'the individuality of the inner man', some indication of 'his social standing', and what he calls 'the atmosphere of a person', that is to say the impact made by accessory characteristics 'such as the sound of his voice, his smell and his distinctive colouring'.[1] What Sutherland is not interested in is that 'so-called "speaking likeness" of attempted imitation'. His concern is with a more meaningful 'likeness, which is the result of an attempt to fuse all the characteristic directions, movements and tensions of the head and body into terms of paint'. But to be able to distil this sort of likeness the artist must first amass an elaborate documentation, for the compiling of which he needs patience and much time for observation.

It is scarcely an exaggeration to say that Sutherland's practice amounts to waiting while the sitter reveals himself and composes his own portrait. 'As a person sits so I tend to accept him', Sutherland has written, and he has also confessed that he allows his subject's 'idiosyncrasies of pose and expression' to determine 'the actual layout' of his picture. For he maintains that if the artist alters the sitter's naturally assumed positions 'at the dictate of composition, he runs the certain risk that in falsifying physical truth he falsifies psychological truth'. In adopting this approach to portraiture Sutherland is maintaining a perfectly consistent attitude, for he wrote once in a letter that 'to seek deliberately qualities in form considered as likely to give art permanence is to be deceived'.[2] Thus we find in Sutherland's portraits that the individual sitter is, so to speak, the style of each painting, and this factor accounts for the changeability and lack of a repeated pattern which distinguishes them as a group from the work of most other portraitists. Or should I say producers of effigies?

Thus far I have discussed certain principles by which Sutherland tries to abide in his portraits. But naturalism is a very disruptive and exacting principle for an artist to follow, and Sutherland is the first to recognize the difficulties which it is apt to cause him. Among these is the risk that he may 'see too much or see the wrong things'. For instance, he may find himself confronted with a sitter who, because of vanity or for other motives, puts up a resistance to being properly identified and tries to camouflage his personality, that is to say tries to appear tougher and uglier or blander and more charming than in fact he is. Equally, Sutherland may find a sitter's body so awkwardly proportioned that it is difficult to arrive at a formally satisfactory composition. Or again a sitter may be unco-operative,

[1] Sutherland has spoken of the 'grey' colouring of Mr Maugham and the 'baby' colour of Sir Winston Churchill.
[2] Letter to Mr Hans Juda of 10 August 1950, repr. in facsimile in R. Melville, *op. cit.*, between Plates 13 and 14.

and he will then be obliged to drop his role of detached observer and turn hunter in order to be able to pin down his quarry. Faced with such problems, Sutherland has repeatedly proved his conscientiousness as an artist and has triumphed by virtue of his innate humanity. He does not cheat with the truth by concealment, evasion, distortion or exaggeration. He is not vindictive, does not underline weaknesses in a character, disdains the pitiable or pathetic strain, and checks his private sentiments. Instead, he clings to the visual evidence and tries to show the person as he really is. For this reason Sutherland's portraits are undoubtedly frank, but to call them 'brutal', 'cruel', 'callous' or even 'expressionistic',[1] as has been done, is nothing less than absurd, since these adjectives imply emotionalism and aggressive intentions on the part of the artist. Admittedly, Sutherland likes to get very close to his human sitters – closer even than to natural objects – in order to study physical details. As a result he gives as much importance to the furrows, flaws and fleshy folds on a face as to its finer features, its strength, expressiveness or bone structure. But since the two elements are, in fact, closely inter-related and together make up the reality of the human being, why should we reproach a portrait painter for revealing the truth? After all, his profession is not that of beautician. It might not be unjust to criticize Sutherland for allowing his view of a personality to be somewhat simplified and incomplete in so far as he often shows less than the totality of what he has seen. We should not forget, however, that it is virtually impossible to put into a single portrait the whole truth about so complex a creature as a human being without blurring the image and confusing the eye. Simplification enables Sutherland, as it does every other portraitist, to see sharply some truly significant aspects of a personality and to evoke with economy its concomitant ambience. Anything that he records he has actually seen, and that without prejudice. But the lasting value of his portraits lies in the exactness of his observation[2] and in the real life quality which his sitters conserve. Sutherland's portraits are for this reason no less records of our period than they are studies of human types.

Portrait painting has meant for Sutherland a tough artistic struggle, and there is evidence of this in the paintings themselves, where one can sometimes detect a certain hesitancy as well as a recurrent weakness in dealing with legs and feet. At the same time, this struggle has benefited Sutherland as an artist. For just as his pursuit of the human character has

[1] *vide* M. Wardell, 'The Beaverbrook Art Gallery', in *The Atlantic Advocate* (Fredericton, N.B.), September 1959, p.52.
[2] *vide* E. Sackville-West, *op. cit.*, (1955 edn.) p.13: . . . in each case the result has been an amazing likeness . . . As character studies . . . these portraits must count among the most perspicacious of our time.'

necessitated the sharpening of his vision,[1] so appreciation of the fact that 'portraits depend on hair-breadth accuracy' has urged him on to draw more firmly and to evolve a painting technique which is both finer and more *nuancé*. Not surprisingly, therefore, Sutherland's later portraits show a considerable advance over the first examples in that they are less picturesque, better organized and more subtle.

A basic difficulty for Sutherland is to reconcile the way an individual human being presents himself with the requirements of certain pictorial principles. Sutherland is denied – by the exigencies of his naturalistic idiom – the freedom of a Picasso,[2] whose conceptual method of representation enables him, after he has rearranged forms and features, to reconstitute a figure as an effective entity, to produce a likeness and to solve the problem of pictorial design. Instead, Sutherland is bound to respect the structural logic of the human body and face, as well as certain accepted proportional relationships. It is this factor which sets up many a conflict, because the natural, life-like pose seldom provides the formally satisfying composition. In consequence, Sutherland is sometimes obliged for compositional reasons to accept a pose which is awkward, as in the *Portrait of Lord Beaverbrook*,[3] and sometimes has to find a solution by cutting off part of the figure, as in the *Portrait of Maja Sacher*.[4] He is not disturbed by awkwardness because it carries with it a flavour of reality, and in any case there are good recent precedents in the work of Cézanne, Degas and Matisse. But cutting a figure is a device which Sutherland dislikes and tries to avoid, because it encourages the eye to imagine the body extending or the movement continuing beyond the containing frame. The effect is that of a snapshot, and is apt to suggest casualness and informality, qualities which unlike nineteenth-century painters he shuns.

Sutherland likes whatever he has painted to be complete in itself: he tries to make it self-contained and independent like a piece of sculpture. His portraiture thus ranges itself alongside the rest of his work. When painting a landscape subject, Sutherland has always avoided the scenic or panoramic because he likes to define the shape and character of a particular place. He must therefore resist the suggestion that what he is painting is part of a larger whole extending in all directions beyond the limits of the canvas. Similarly, in his recent Venetian paintings of St Mark's and the Salute[5] Sutherland has, so to speak, detached the buildings from their city

[1] *ibid*. 'Sutherland's profound sense of Original Sin, combined with a gimlet perception of some single but fundamental characteristic in his sitter, produces the portrait of a face in which the soul has been brought to the surface, displacing the usual mask . . .'
[2] Sutherland, however, regards the 'paraphrase' portraits of Picasso as being the highest form of the art.
[3] Plate 167.
[4] Plate 173.
[5] Both coll. Mr Arthur Jeffress, London.

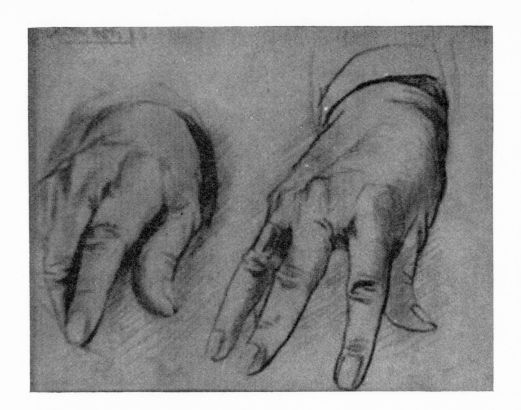

contexts and presented them like models. 'It is their *construction* that fascinates me primarily', he states, 'and they are like a human figure or a tree in that each part is clearly constructed and related to the next smaller part and so on down to the smallest detail.' Thus figures, buildings and natural objects all have this in common so far as Sutherland is concerned, that they are what he calls 'working machines', that is to say self-contained functioning organisms. And this provides us with a clue to the origins of such imaginative structures as *Golden Form, Hydrant* or *Hanging Form*,[1] which are part organic, part mechanical and sometimes near human. These three worlds impinge on each other constantly in Sutherland's imagination.

As a portraitist Sutherland has been no less selective than in his other works. 'If, for instance, I was not interested in the head and character of a portrait subject', he once said, 'I would not accept the commission because I would know that I could not make anything of it.' And he has been true to his word. We must, therefore, be prepared to find that Sutherland's range as a portraitist is limited, but equally we must recognize that once he undertakes a portrait he puts himself wholeheartedly into its realization. None of his portraits is, in consequence, superficial or banal. Indeed, banality, like insipidity, is one of the characteristics in a sitter which deters Sutherland.

Sutherland's interest is most keenly aroused by strong, passionate or

[1] Plates 136, 156, Colour Plate X.

life-weathered personalities, for within him lurks a romantic spirit which delights in signs of adventurousness, violence, fearlessness, idealism and power. The subjects of his portraits, male as well as female, therefore tend to fall into one or more of the following categories: the autocrat, the aristocrat, the tycoon, the buccaneer, the self-made man, the schemer, the materialist or the intellectually and artistically creative. Such people fascinate Sutherland in so far as they are extraordinary, that is to say they depart from the norm. He sees them, one might say, as fabulous creatures who – for good or for ill so far as the world is concerned – have been able to reach a dominating position by virtue of some innate super-sense, perhaps even by guile. Were Sutherland exclusively a portrait painter, he might have difficulty in finding enough sitters of the right type to keep him fully occupied. But since portrait painting is only one of the ways in which he expresses himself this problem does not arise and he is more likely to discourage than to welcome those who see themselves as being the Sutherland 'type'. For the initial impulse must come from Sutherland himself, *his* eye must be caught and *his* interest aroused by a combination of expressiveness and vitality, and he is as likely to experience this with the face of a gardener as with that of a general. In fact, Sutherland's sitters have come from many walks of life – they include a Prime Minister, politicians, noblemen, a cleric, newspaper proprietors, writers, musicians, business men and women, a publisher, a beauty specialist, representatives of the art world – as well as being of several nationalities.[1] They conform to no one facial type, belong to different age groups and come from different social strata. But, pictorially, there is a common bond between them in the artist's concentrated feeling for each as an extraordinary individual, whose face reveals in one way or another success or failure and the toll which life has taken of him or her.

Sutherland's first three portraits – those of Mr Somerset Maugham (1949)[2], Lord Beaverbrook (1951)[3] and Mr Edward Sackville-West (1953–54)[4] – were similar in conception, in that each shows a full-length

[1] A project for him to paint Pope Pius XII came to nothing, as did a projected portrait of Sir Anthony Eden commissioned by Christ Church, Oxford. At the moment negotiations are in progress for Sutherland to paint the Queen Mother of England, and Dr Adenauer.
[2] Begun 17 February 1949, finished in June. Plates 164, 165. Sutherland executed a second portrait of Mr Maugham in 1953. This was a lithographed drawing for an 80th birthday edition of *Cakes and Ale*, commissioned by Messrs Heinemann. He made new drawings of Mr Maugham from life on this occasion.
[3] Plates 166, 167. Presented to the sitter by the staff of his newspapers on his 75th birthday. Lord Beaverbrook asked Sutherland to undertake this commission after seeing his portrait of Mr Maugham. Begun May 1951, finished in November.
[4] Plate 169. Privately commissioned. Begun November 1953, finished December 1954. Misdated 1954–5 in R.A. Catalogue of *British Portraits*, No.794, London, 1956–57. This painting has been damaged as a result of varnishing by the present owner: certain passages on the trousers, the foot and the stool originally executed in charcoal have been obliterated. The *Head* (Plate 169b) was sketched in 1954 in connexion with a second projected portrait of Mr Sackville-West in bed, and was completed from memory later.

seated figure facing three-quarters right or left. They are not, however, uniform in handling, the degree of intensity decreases from one to the next, and they are not equally successful as paintings. In each the characterization of the sitter depends essentially on the set of the head, the facial expression and the hands, there being thus two centres of interest related by the attitude of the body. But the very different personalities of the subjects have provided Sutherland each time with a variation in the design and a differently expressive relationship between physical features. In Mr Maugham, the novelist, Sutherland has seen a self-satisfied and successful personality, a man who is sensitive, cynical and aloof, who appraises others but whose own inscrutability gives him something of the mysteriousness of an oriental.[1] Lord Beaverbrook, a politician and newspaper proprietor, is presented, on the contrary, as a robust high-powered executive, as a man of remarkable intelligence with a dynamic extrovert personality. At the same time, we are allowed a glimpse of a half-concealed jovial gnome with a taste for mischief. Mr Sackville-West, a belletrist and musicologist, makes a complete contrast with the other two because he is passive and sad. In him Sutherland has seen a hypersensitive, refined and vulnerable human being who has become sick through coping with the battle of life. Precariously perched on a high stool, his hands neurotically clasped, he seems literally to shrink into his clothes. This is perhaps the subtlest of the three portraits, yet I think this is only partly due to Sutherland having had the advantage, which he did not have with his two previous sitters, of knowing Mr Sackville-West well for a long time before he began to paint him. But what I would specially emphasize about this group of paintings is the evidence they provide of how Sutherland's control over a new genre developed. The essential change is that from the emphatic handling of the portrait of Mr Maugham, with its angularities, unhappy foreshortenings, simplifications and over-descriptive folds and creases, to the muted portrait of Mr Sackville-West, which is economical, tense and finely painted. In ridding his style of the coarseness which is visible in the Maugham portrait, Sutherland undoubtedly sacrificed something of his power of vigorous characterization. But this progression was decisive for his development as a portrait painter, for it reflects his realization that if his portraits were to come up to his own expectations he had to free himself from the descriptive, draughtsmanly approach of the

[1] The bamboo stool and the palm fronds at the top of the canvas heighten this impression.

Maugham portrait and cultivate a more painterly style.[1] This involved transforming his working methods, because at the start Sutherland relied on drawings, not painted sketches, to remind him of details of form and structure while he was working out his final portrait away from the model. This procedure contained, however, a seed of danger, because it allowed him to perpetuate his picturesque concern with facial crags, crannies and excrescences. Precision being his aim in portraiture, he needed to concentrate more on tonal nuances, modelling and the fullness of forms, for the other way could easily have led towards a form of expressionistic portraiture. In this connexion, painting the portrait of Mr Sackville-West was for Sutherland a decisive experience, because it was the first in which he substituted preliminary oil sketches for drawings and put a new technique to the test.

This experience was turned more fully to account in the portrait of Sir Winston Churchill, which was begun later[2] but finished before that of Mr Sackville-West. Sutherland received the commission to paint Sir Winston in the summer of 1954 from the Inter-Parliamentary Committee, acting on behalf of both Houses of Parliament, who were to present it to England's wartime Prime Minister on the occasion of his 80th birthday. The finished portrait, however, gave offence to Sir Winston who has not allowed it to be seen subsequently and has ordained that no reproduction may be published.[3] It is, however, remarkable as a likeness and telling as a study of character. There is no straining after effect and the execution is not laboured, while the expressiveness and structure of the head and hands are achieved solely through fine and subtle manipulation of paint.[4] Sir Winston is seen frontally and in full length, being seated in a chair the arms of which he is gripping with his two hands. He wears a black coat and striped trousers – the parliamentarian's dress – and his attitude suggests that he is about to rise. His expression is wistful and a trifle melancholy, but even in old age he is alert, and this portrait evokes a combative

[1] The following details illuminate the progressive changes in Sutherland's method. For the Maugham portrait he began by filling a whole sketch-book with small drawings from life; from these he made two or three large preparatory drawings (Plate 164) in the studio; then he began to paint the definitive portrait away from the model, but while he was working requested a few more sittings to make detailed drawings of the ears, mouth, etc. For the Beaverbrook portrait, Sutherland first made a series of drawings from life, then painted two free sketches in oils (one from memory, one from life), and then made a painting of the sitter's head before starting on the definitive canvas, during which time he again saw the sitter. For the Sackville-West portrait, however, Sutherland first made three or four slight drawings from life; then an oil sketch from life; then more drawings from life; then a head and shoulders study in oils; and lastly the definitive portrait. Sutherland destroys most of his preparatory drawings, and some of his oil sketches, because he regards them as notes and therefore too indefinite. Several that have survived are now in the Beaverbrook Art Gallery, Fredericton, N.B.

[2] Begun August 1954, finished 20 November. Official presentation 30 November 1954.

[3] Hence the inclusion of a preparatory sketch, Plate 168. For a reproduction of the original, readers are referred to the daily and weekly illustrated press of the days following the presentation.

[4] In preparation for this rapidly executed portrait Sutherland made from life, at Chequers and Chartwell, about twelve pencil or charcoal studies, six oil sketches, and several detail drawings of the sitter's hands, eyes, nose, mouth, shoes, etc., e.g. Fig.11.

politician used to fighting for his ideals, as well as the passionate temperament and forcefulness of one of the greatest personalities of our time. It is not a swagger official portrait such as Sir Winston is said to have wished for,[1] nor has Sutherland falsified the truth by painting his sitter as more youthful and handsome than he was. He has recorded accurately on canvas just what he saw, and for this reason his portrait is lively, convincing and impressive. Lord Beaverbrook, when he came to analyse Sir Winston's character,[2] described him as 'big-minded though self-willed', 'avid of power and office', self-confident, honest, dependable, ambitious although disinterestedly so, and lastly as 'a man almost devoid of rancour'. Sutherland has seen, and in some degree incorporated into his portrait, all these traits. But shortly before he began work on it Sir Winston had suffered a stroke, and while he was painting the reins of government were being snatched from Sir Winston's hands. It would be curious if these two potent factors had not in some way affected his expression and appearance, and Sutherland would have been dishonest if he had tried to ignore this. Therefore Sutherland's definition of Sir Winston may not be altogether personally convenient or flattering. On the other hand, it is not final but only one of many images – though probably the best – of the statesman which will be handed down to posterity, and in its favour are the facts that its view of the sitter is entirely original and that it is vigorous, positive, and life-like. Yet for personal reasons Sir Winston gave vent to fury and disgust when first shown this portrait and has never allowed it to be seen again since the day of its presentation. That he should object to it on grounds of insufficiency might be comprehensible, for it is not a full-dress portrait of a national hero but a personal impression of a great man. However, concealment cannot destroy its permanent value as a great artist's vision of a great English warrior when he finally laid down the burden of high office. And one of the chief virtues of portraiture is that it keeps man's past history alive by preserving in palpable form images of those by whom our destinies have been shaped.

Following the Churchill portrait, Sutherland painted a head and shoulders of his friend Mr Hans Juda,[3] and a full-length, seated portrait of another old friend, the dealer Mr Arthur Jeffress,[4] in which sadness vies with pertness, and exoticism with mundanity. Contemporaneously with these, Sutherland began work on two portraits of the German-Swiss

[1] Sir Winston would have liked to be painted 'as a *nobleman*', particularly in his robes as a Knight of the Garter (a sketch in this guise is now in the Beaverbrook Art Gallery). He presented himself for sittings on a dais.
[2] *vide Politicians and The War* (new ed., London, 1960), pp.125–7. On p.284 of the same work Lord Beaverbrook adds: 'Churchill on the top of the wave has in him the stuff of which tyrants are made'.
[3] Begun January 1955, finished in October, Plate 171.
[4] Begun July 1955, finished July 1956; Plate 170. Two heads of Mr Jeffress, in oils, were painted from life while the full-length portrait was being executed.

musician Herr Paul Sacher,[1] in which sensibility, intelligence, virility and elegance are subtly balanced against signs of the power of regimentation, administrative control and efficiency which a good conductor needs. A year later these two paintings were followed by a portrait of his wife, Frau Maja Sacher,[2] a great Swiss patroness and one of the surest judges of modern art and music. As a result of these two commissions, Sutherland's work has been incorporated into one of the outstanding private collections of paintings and sculpture by European artists such as Picasso, Braque, Chirico, Klee, Ernst, Arp, Ensor and Laurens. Other sitters portrayed by Sutherland since 1956 have included Mrs John Eaton, the wife of a Canadian multiple store proprietor,[3] Dean Hussey,[4] Mrs Ramsay Hunt, a New York socialite,[5] Dr Herschel Carey Walker, an American veterinary surgeon and well-known modern collector,[6] and Mr Alexander Frere, president of the publishing firm of Heinemann.[7] But Sutherland's two outstanding portraits of the last four years have been those of the cosmetics manufacturer Madame Helena Rubinstein (Princess Gourielli),[8] of which two versions (one seated, one standing) exist, and of the late Prince Fürstenberg, scion of a great south German dynasty, who was unique among latter-day aristocrats in his fearless patronage of modernism, which included a festival of the most advanced music at his residence Schloss Donaueschingen.[9] Here again the contrast between the sitters and the conception of their respective portraits is most striking. For where Madame Rubinstein in her richly embroidered velvet dress has the imperious air of a potentate and the ferocity of a bird of prey, Prince Fürstenberg, simply clad, gives no impression of an enterprising, daring man but seems a distinguished, friendly, cultured gentleman absorbed in his own affairs and dreaming of ideals unattained. Or is he looking into the Hereafter? The fact is that within a few hours of seeing this portrait, which gave him great pleasure, the Prince was dead.

Such, then, is the group of Sutherland's portraits. They are fascinating as character studies, remarkable as paintings, and yet surprising as works of art. There is nothing quite like them in contemporary art, and it is difficult

[1] Begun November 1955, finished October 1956. Plate 174. The two versions were worked on simultaneously. The version not reproduced shows the sitter facing left in strict profile; he wears a tie; instead of being in the foreground, the railing is behind him at shoulder height; the background is black with flashes of cerulean blue, instead of fawn and olive green as in the version reproduced. Sutherland attended rehearsals to watch Herr Sacher at work.
[2] Begun July 1957, finished February 1958.
[3] Begun June 1956, finished July 1957; now in the Beaverbrook Art Gallery, Fredericton, N.B.
[4] Begun May 1957; unfinished.
[5] Begun August 1957; unfinished.
[6] Begun summer 1958; finished April 1961.
[7] Begun May 1959, finished February 1960. (At that time Mr Frere was chairman of the firm.) Owned by the Windmill Press, London.
[8] Plate 172. Begun April 1956; a first version was burnt in the artist's studio in December 1956; the two existing versions, worked on concurrently, were finished in April 1957. The seated version belongs to the sitter.
[9] Colour Plate XV. Begun July 1958, finished April 1959.

to relate them to an old masterish tradition because they contain no obvious echoes. That Sutherland has a good knowledge of portraiture through the ages is sure, and he admires artists of several types. Thus, he is fascinated by the penetrating vision of Dürer, Grünewald and Holbein, as well as by the detachment of Raphael and Ingres. He is also greatly moved by the humanity and marvellous paint qualities of Titian and Rembrandt; by Velazquez, in whose portraits, he says, 'everything works'; and lastly by the perspicacity and mordant wit of Goya. All of these by assimilation have no doubt contributed their share to the formation of Sutherland's style, yet in his handling and compositional arrangements there is no manifest evidence of their several influences.

Sutherland's vision is incisive, individual and imaginative; he does not need to see people or things through the eyes of other artists, and his manner of painting is equally his own. Admittedly, it is exceptional for a leading twentieth-century artist to interest himself in portraiture, but portraiture is a great part of the English tradition and Sutherland's respect for the naturalistic convention is an essentially English trait. One of his outstanding achievements, however, is to have established an original portrait style which is modern, free of trappings and not reliant on false glamour or misplaced bravura. He has thus reasserted the importance of the human element in art and redeemed English portraiture from the progressive debasement imposed on it over the last hundred years by generations of academic effigy-makers. But we must beware of trying to detach Sutherland's portraiture from the rest of his work, or of following Mr Sackville-West[1] in regarding it as an unimportant, if brilliant, sideline. All his life as a painter Sutherland has been concerned with portraiture of a sort, for how else can one properly describe his pursuit of the *genius loci* and his insistence on defining the individual character of a place or an object? From nature to man has been a short step long delayed, but nevertheless we must learn to see Sutherland's portraits of human beings as integrally related to the rest of his *œuvre*. For this *œuvre* is coherent as a whole, one facet serving to illuminate another, and all are equally significant as expressions of the artist himself.

[1] *op. cit.*, (1955 edn.) p.13: 'I should be surprised if portraiture were ever to become more than a sideline, albeit a brilliant one, in Sutherland's career, for the centre of his interest continues to lie elsewhere.'

## V. Conclusion

In the foregoing text I have tried to explain what Sutherland wants to express in his painting and to describe his methods of working. I have also attempted to situate him in relation to various other contemporary artists, to show what he started with and how he has become one of the major artistic personalities of our time. But I have not said much about Sutherland as a man. Yet certain characteristics of the artist's personality cannot be ignored, because in many ways they correspond with and are reflected, unconsciously perhaps, in his work. He himself is by nature moody, introspective, apprehensive and falsely optimistic. The mood of his pictures, as I have tried to show, fluctuates constantly, the luscious fruit being followed by the harrowing thorn, the 'death colour' of the Crucifixion by the stimulating radiance of the colours of the south. But melancholy and anguish, solitude and suspense, fear and frustration provide dominating notes and there is little evidence of gaiety. Moreover, Sutherland's work is largely self-centred and replete with private symbolism. Again, Sutherland is distinguished by intellectual curiosity, by a will to know and see more for himself. This, too, comes out in his work and accounts not only for the constantly widening range of his interests, but also for what I have called his cyclical development, his continual return to earlier themes or *motifs* to try and pin down more exactly 'the essence of the likeness'. Then his insistence on making us feel the tingle of excitement and the thrill or disagreeableness of other sensations is typical of the man. For Sutherland is by nature something of a seeker after sensations: he likes driving fast cars, is addicted to gambling, relishes good food and drink. And lastly, the hesitancy and ambiguity apparent in much of his work corresponds with an element of self-doubt which haunts him, as does its elegance and mannered perfectionism with a certain uneasy dandyism which he cultivates in his private life.

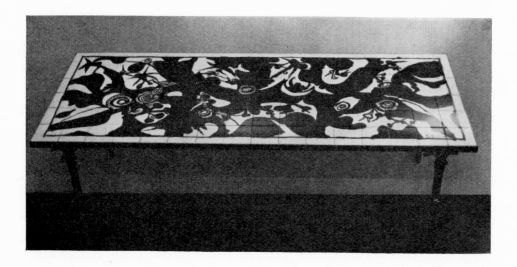

Fig.12
**Ceramic Table Top** 1959
Design in black and white on tiles
99 × 37 in.
In the possession of the Artist

Like all romantics, Sutherland defies classification, and the more one studies and tries to understand his work the more one comes to recognize and respect his uniqueness and independence. He belongs to no school of contemporary painters and excels by virtue of his own pictorial talents and imagination. His basic Englishness cannot be doubted, yet his outlook and manner of painting have come increasingly close to those of some European artists. At the same time, he is something of an anomaly among contemporary European artists by virtue of his vital interest in portraiture and in the painting of nature, both of them typically English preoccupations. Within the context of English painting, however, he is anomalous by virtue of his sophisticated international style, which he owes to contact with the European scene and with European artists. He began, in his etchings, as a delineator on a small scale of the good life of the countryman. He became a romantic landscape painter, and then broadened out as a factual painter of the wartime scene. During the last fifteen years he has painted religious subjects, still lifes of natural objects, portraits of human beings and latterly studies of animals. In these, naturalism has vied with romantic sentiments, fear with fascination, and admiration with horror. At each stage, then, Sutherland has been able to add to his stature and has disclosed concealed layers of emotion and understanding. But, in addition, his paintings of the last ten years show how greatly he has enlarged his technical vocabulary. Nowadays he ventures on more subtle painterly effects than before and is currently concerned with problems of chiaroscuro in a shallow pictorial space.

Sutherland's romantic temperament is undeniable, and his belief that man, like nature, is subject to the same inimical forces has led him to cultivate an element of the picturesque. Yet, fundamentally, Sutherland's art is an art of feeling and mystery, and he seems particularly susceptible to manifestations of violence – understandable, surely, in a twentieth-century artist, though this may also correspond to some private obsession. At the same time, Sutherland starts from the evidence of his eyes and is not an intellectual painter living in a world of poetic conceits or ideas. His great contribution, it seems to me, has been his discovery of pictorial images which should assist us to bridge the gap imaginatively between the separate realms of the human, the organic and the mechanical. His evolution has proceeded by cycles so that, as with Picasso, certain characteristic *motifs* and themes recur at intervals and are treated each time in a subtler, more audacious or more elaborate manner. Sutherland has a remarkable colour sense and, like Matisse, delights in playing variations by transposing a subject into a different key for the sake of emotional effect. His work does not, therefore, tend to become monotonous or repetitive, and he is able to go on developing and improving as a painter year by year.

Today, Sutherland stands at the top of his profession in England and is recognized in European artistic circles as the only significant English painter since Constable and Turner. That he has reached this eminence is due to his seriousness of purpose, to his imaginative inspiration, and, above all, to innate artistic gifts such as have been granted to few English-born painters.

D.C.  *Argilliers, July 1961*

# Biographical Summary

| | |
|---|---|
| 1903 | 24 August: Graham Sutherland born in London. |
| 1903–12 | Lives with his parents at Merton Park, Surrey; then at Rustington in Sussex. |
| 1912 | The family moves to Sutton in Surrey. |
| 1913 | Spends his first holiday in Dorset and visits Swanage. |
| 1914–18 | Attends Epsom College. |
| 1919–20 | Serves an apprenticeship at the Midland Railway works in Derby. |
| 1921–26 | Studies at The Goldsmiths' College School of Art in London. |
| | Draws from nature in Kent and Sussex. |
| | Studies engraving techniques under Stanley Anderson and Malcolm Osborne. |
| | Friendship with F. L. Griggs. |
| 1923 | First etchings issued in small editions. *Barn Interior* exhibited at the Royal Academy, where he exhibits annually until 1929. |
| | Helps Clive Gardiner to execute decorations for a pavilion at the Wembley International Exhibition (1924). |
| 1925 | Finalist in engraving section for Prix de Rome (unsuccessful). |
| | Elected an Associate of the Royal Society of Painter-Etchers and Engravers. |
| | First one-man exhibition at XXI Gallery, London (drawings and engravings). |
| 1926 | Lives at Blackheath. Converted to Roman Catholic Church. |
| 1927 | Teaches at an art school in Kingston. |
| | 29 December: Marries Kathleen Frances Barry; they move to Farningham in Kent. |
| 1928 | Second one-man exhibition at the XXI Gallery (September). |
| | Visits Dorset (summer). |
| | Appointed to teach engraving at the Chelsea School of Art (till 1932). |
| 1929 | Visits Dorset (June–July). |
| 1930 | Visits Dorset (spring) and Devonshire (summer). |
| | Abandons engraving following the collapse of the market. |
| 1931 | Takes up painting. Visits Dorset (summer). |
| | Moves to Eynsford in Kent. |
| 1932–39 | Concentrates on painting, but earns a living by teaching and by designing posters for Shell-Mex, the London Passenger Transport Board, the Post Office, etc. Also designs for china and fabrics. |
| 1932 | Visits Dorset (spring). |
| | Appointed to teach Composition and Book Illustration at the Chelsea School of Art (till 1939). |
| 1933 | Visits Cornwall and Dorset (summer). |
| | Expelled from the Royal Society of Painter-Etchers and Engravers. |
| | Moves to Sutton-at-Hone in Kent. |

| 1934 | First visit to Wales (Pembrokeshire) in summer leads to first creative paintings. |
|---|---|
| 1935–39 | Annual painting trips to Wales in vacations from teaching; these provide the subject-matter of all Sutherland's work. He visits St David's, Solva, Dale, Haverfordwest, Sandy Haven, Crickhowell. The English Landscape period begins (1935–45). |
| 1936 | Rents a house at Trottiscliffe in Kent (spring). |
| | Publishes 'A Trend in English Draughtsmanship' in *Signature* (July). |
| 1937 | Publishes 'An English Stone Landmark' (Brimham Rocks) in *The Painter's Object*. |
| 1938 | First one-man exhibition of paintings at Rosenberg and Helft Gallery, London (September). |
| 1939 | Loses his teaching job at the Chelsea School of Art on the outbreak of war. Invited by Sir Kenneth Clark to move to Upton House, Tetbury, Gloucestershire, where he continues to paint. Does illustrations for *Henry VI, Part I* by Shakespeare (Limited Editions Club, New York, 1940). Visits Wales at Christmastime. |
| 1940 | Second exhibition of paintings at The Leicester Galleries, London (May). |
| | Appointed an Official War Artist (August). First commissions take him to airfields in Wiltshire, then to bomb-damaged Swansea. |
| | Returns to Trottiscliffe (autumn). |
| | Designs décor and costumes for *The Wanderer*, a ballet by Frederick Ashton, presented by The Sadler's Wells Company at the New Theatre, London, in January 1941. |
| 1940–45 | Employed as a War Artist and has little time for painting on his own. Sent to armaments factories and bomb-damaged areas in London and the Midlands; to Wales (1941, 1942, 1943, 1944); to Cornwall (1942); to Derbyshire (1943); and to France (1944). Sutherland adopts a more factual idiom. |
| 1942 | 'A Welsh Sketchbook' published in *Horizon* (April). |
| 1944 | Canon Walter Hussey commissions a *Crucifixion* for St Matthew's Church, Northampton (September). |
| | Stylistic changes become apparent in Sutherland's painting: a transitional phase begins. |
| | First visit to Paris, on return journey from Trappes and St Leu (autumn). |
| 1945 | Ceases to be a War Artist. |
| | Buys The White House at Trottiscliffe. |
| | At work on the *Crucifixion*. Series of *Thorn Trees* and *Thorn Heads* (1945–46). |
| | Visits Wales (summer). |
| 1946 | First one-man exhibition in New York at the Buchholz Gallery run by Curt Valentin (February). |
| | Short visit to Paris (summer). |
| | The *Crucifixion* finished (November). |
| 1947 | First visit to the South of France. Works at Villefranche (April–May, October–December). |
| | Sees Picasso Museum at Antibes. |
| | Takes up meridional subjects: *Vine Pergolas, Palm Palisades, Cactus, Banana, Cigale*. |
| | Meets Picasso and Matisse (November). |
| 1948 | Works at Villefranche (August–September, October–December). |
| | One-man exhibitions at the Hanover Gallery, London (June); also Buchholz Gallery, New York (November). |
| | The transitional phase in Sutherland's painting ends. A second period begins in which he is to be concerned with Man, Nature and Machinery. |

| | |
|---|---|
| 1949 | Works at St Jean Cap Ferrat (February–June, November–January 1950); paints the portrait of Mr Somerset Maugham. |
| | Designs *Birds and Foliage* tapestry for the Edinburgh Tapestry Company. |
| | Appointed a Trustee of the Tate Gallery. |
| | Phase of sculptural 'monuments and presences' begins (till 1957). |
| 1950 | *The Origins of the Land* commissioned for the Festival of Britain (1951). |
| | Works at Villefranche (August). First visit to Venice (September). |
| 1951 | Works at St Jean Cap Ferrat (January), then returns to England to paint *The Origins of the Land* (February–March). |
| | One-man exhibition at the Hanover Gallery, London (June). |
| | Starts portrait of Lord Beaverbrook (May). |
| | *Thoughts on Painting* broadcast by the B.B.C. (August). |
| | Returns to Villefranche (November). |
| 1952 | Works at Villefranche (January–March). Makes some sculpture. |
| | Visits to Jersey (March) and Paris (June). |
| | Visits Venice on the occasion of an exhibition of his works in the British Pavilion at the Biennale (June). Awarded a prize by the Museum of Modern Art, São Paulo. |
| | An enlarged version of this retrospective exhibition is subsequently shown at the Musée d'Art Moderne, Paris (November). |
| | Works at St Jean Cap Ferrat (June–July). |
| | Visits Paris (November). |
| | Commissioned to design a vast tapestry – *Christ in Glory in the Tetramorph* – for the new Coventry Cathedral. |
| | Works at Pont St Jean, A.M. (November–December). |
| | B.B.C. Television starts to make a film of Sutherland at work. |
| 1953 | Works at Pont St Jean (January–March). |
| | Retrospective exhibitions at the Stedelijk Museum, Amsterdam (January); then at Kunsthaus, Zürich (March). |
| | One-man exhibition at the Curt Valentin Gallery, New York (March). |
| | Retrospective exhibition at the Tate Gallery, London (May). |
| | Begins portrait of Hon. E. Sackville-West (November). |
| | His brushwork becomes finer. |
| | Works on lithographs with Mourlot in Paris (October–November). |
| 1954 | Works at Roquebrune (January–April) and St Jean Cap Ferrat (April–May). |
| | The Tate Row. Obliged to resign as a Trustee of the Tate Gallery (January). |
| | Visits Venice (July–August). |
| | Paints portrait of Sir Winston Churchill (August–November). |
| | Retrospective exhibition at Akademie der bildenden Künste, Vienna, which goes on to Innsbruck, Berlin, Cologne, Stuttgart, Mannheim and Hamburg (1954–55). |
| 1955 | Works at Cap d'Ail (February–March) and St Jean Cap Ferrat (June). |
| | Buys a house at Menton (May; moves in in November). |
| | Works in Venice (August). |

Allotted a room at the 3rd Biennial Exhibition at the Museum of Modern Art, São Paulo (November).

Works in Basle on portrait of Herr Paul Sacher (November).

1955–61    Predominantly occupied painting portraits and supervising the design and execution of the Coventry tapestry.

1956    Works in Menton (January–April).

In Venice (June).

B.B.C. Television shows a documentary film of Sutherland at work.

Visits Venice (September); in Menton (September–October).

1957    Commissioned by H.M. The Queen and Prince Philip to paint a composition symbolizing *The Common Interests of Portugal and England* for presentation to the President of Portugal on the occasion of their State visit.

Works in Venice (May–July): first Venetian subjects *The Church of the Salute* and *St Mark's, Night*.

In Menton (July).

Completes design for the Coventry tapestry (September). Exhibits at the Fourth International Art Exhibition in Japan (Tokyo, Osaka, Nagoya, Fukvoka) and is awarded the Foreign Minister's Prize.

1958    Works in Menton (March–May).

In Venice (May–June).

Weaving of tapestry begins at Felletin.

Goes to Donaueschingen to start portrait of Prince Fürstenberg (July).

1959    One-man exhibition in Frankfurt a. Main (January).

Designs ceramic table-tops.

Works in Menton (April–May, July–August, October–December).

In Venice (June).

One-man exhibition at the Paul Rosenberg Gallery, New York (November).

1960    Awarded the Order of Merit (April).

Works in Menton (April–May, July–August).

In Venice (June).

Commissioned to paint a *Noli Me Tangere* for the Chapel of St Mary Magdalen in Chichester Cathedral; also a *Crucifixion* for St Aidan's Church, Acton.

1961    Works in Menton (February–March, April–May).

In Venice (June–July).

# List of Plates

*Entries which do not mention a collection refer to works in the possession of the artist*

2a **Barn Interior**
1922
Drypoint 6″ × 8″
Exhibited Royal Academy 1923 Catalogue No.1072
Edition not known

2b **Mill Interior**
1923
Pen and wash drawing in sepia 5⅛″ × 6½″

3a **Pecken Wood**
1925
Etching 5½″ × 7½″
Edition: 77 proofs. Three published states
Plate destroyed
Published by The Twenty One Gallery, London

3b **Cray Fields**
1925
Etching 4¾″ × 5″
Edition: 77 proofs. Two published states
Plate destroyed
Published by The Twenty One Gallery, London

3c **St Mary Hatch**
1926
Etching 4¾″ × 7¼″
Edition: 77 proofs. Three published states; 11 in 1st state; 5 in second state; 61 in 3rd state
Plate destroyed
Published by The Twenty One Gallery, London

3d **Lammas**
1926
Etching 4¼″ × 6¼″
Edition: 77 proofs. One state only
Plate destroyed
Published by The Twenty One Gallery, London

4a **Welsh Landscape**
1936
Etching and aquatint 7½″ × 5½″
Published in 'Signature', 1936

4b **Pastoral**
1930
Etching 5″ × 7½″
Small edition. Number of proofs not known

5a **Sand Hills, Dorset**
1932–3
Watercolour 7⅞″ × 12¼″

5b **Men-an-Tol**
1931
Pen and watercolour 18¼″ × 26¾″
Collection: Mrs Nicolette Gray, London

5c **Landscape, Sketch of Hills**
1932
Watercolour 4″ × 7″

5d **Tree Form, Dorset**
1933–4
Pen and sepia, touched with white 7⅜″ × 12¾″

5e **Lobster Claw**
1935
Gouache 8″ × 12¾″

5f **Ideas for a Fallen Tree, Purbeck**
probably 1935–6
incorrectly dated 1937
Pen and wash 5½″ × 9″
Inscribed in margin: Ideas for picture 1937
Collection: Mrs Graham Sutherland

6a **Solva and Valley above Porthclais**
1935
Pen and wash 5½″ × 8¼″
Sketch book page
'Valley above Porthclais' is first sketch for plates 8f, 9a
Collection: Mrs Graham Sutherland

6b **Camomile Flowers in Landscape**
1935
Gouache 12¾″ × 8¾″

7a **Hills at Solva**
1935
Pen and wash 5⅜″ × 9″

7b **Pembrokeshire Landscape**
1936
Gouache 14″ × 21½″
Collection: National Museum of Wales, Cardiff

7c **Pembrokeshire Landscape**
1937
Pencil and watercolour 5⅛″ × 8½″

8a **Welsh Landscape**
1936
Gouache and watercolour approx. 13″ × 22″,
Present owner not known

8b **Road with Rocks**
1936
Pen and wash 13½″ × 22″
Collection: Sir Kenneth Clark, Saltwood, Kent

8c **Landscape with Turning Roads**
1936
Gouache and watercolour 17¼″ × 25½″
Collection: National Gallery of Canada, Ottawa

8d **Rock in Estuary**
1936
Pen and wash 5″ × 8¼″
Inscribed: Rock in S. Haven Pill

8e **Rocky Landscape with Gateway**
1936
Gouache and watercolour $12\frac{7}{8}'' \times 19\frac{3}{4}''$
Collection: National Gallery of Canada, Ottawa

8f **Welsh Landscape with Roads**
1936
Oil on canvas $22'' \times 15''$
Study for plate 9a
Collection: Mrs Ruth Simon, London

9a **Welsh Landscape with Roads**
1936
Oil on canvas $26'' \times 36''$
First exhibited Rosenberg & Helft, London
1938 Catalogue No. 3
Collection: Tate Gallery, London

9b **Red Tree**
1936
Oil on canvas $22'' \times 36''$
First exhibited Rosenberg & Helft, London
1938 Catalogue No. 2
Collection: Sir Kenneth Clark, Saltwood, Kent

10a **Landscape, Green, Pink and Brown**
1937
Gouache and pastel $13'' \times 20''$
First exhibited Rosenberg & Helft, London
1938 Catalogue No. 24
Collection: Mrs Ruth Simon, London

10b **Welsh Mountains**
1937
Oil on canvas $22'' \times 36''$
First exhibited Rosenberg & Helft, London
1938 Catalogue No.14
Previous collection: R. D. S. May
Collection: Government of New South Wales, Australia

10c **Black Landscape**
1937
Watercolour $18\frac{1}{4}'' \times 31\frac{1}{2}''$
First exhibited Rosenberg & Helft, London
1938 Catalogue No.18
Previous collection: Sir Kenneth Clark
Collection: Glasgow Art Gallery

11a **Study of Rocks**
1937
Ink and watercolour $4\frac{1}{2}'' \times 3\frac{1}{4}''$

11b **Study for 'Blasted Tree'**
1937
Pen and watercolour $4\frac{1}{2}'' \times 3\frac{3}{8}''$

11c **Study for 'Blasted Tree'**
1937
Pen and watercolour $7\frac{1}{2}'' \times 5''$

11d **Blasted Tree**
1938
Watercolour $22\frac{3}{8}'' \times 15\frac{3}{4}''$
First exhibited Rosenberg & Helft, London
1938 Catalogue No.17
Previous collection: R. D. Morss
Present owner not known

12a **Study for 'Tree Trunk Sprawling'**
1937
Pen and watercolour $8'' \times 6''$
Study for the painting 'Tree Trunk Sprawling', 1938
Present owner not known

12b **Studies for 'Red Monolith'**
1937
Pen and watercolour $8'' \times 6''$
Present owner not known

12c **Damp Tree Roots**
1938
Watercolour $18\frac{1}{4}'' \times 31\frac{1}{2}''$
First Exhibited Rosenberg & Helft, London
1938 Catalogue No.23
Previous collection: Peter Watson
Collection: James Bomford, Aldbourne, Wiltshire

13 **Red Monolith**
1938
Oil on canvas $39\frac{1}{4}'' \times 24\frac{1}{4}''$
First exhibited Rosenberg & Helft, London
1938 Catalogue No.8
Collection: Joseph H. Hirshhorn, New York City

14a **Sun Setting Between Hills**
1938
Watercolour $9\frac{7}{8}'' \times 14''$
Collection: Sir Kenneth Clark, Saltwood, Kent

14b **Rocky Landscape with Cairn**
1940
Gouache $20'' \times 33''$
First exhibited Leicester Galleries, London
1940 Catalogue No.28
Collection: Viscountess Hinchingbrooke, London

14c **Dark Hill with Hedges and Fields**
1940
Pen and wash $19'' \times 27\frac{1}{2}''$
First exhibited Leicester Galleries, London
1940 Catalogue No.21
Collection: Hiram Winterbotham, Woodchester, Gloucestershire

15a **Steep Road**
1938
Gouache $11\frac{1}{2}'' \times 9''$
Collection: John Craxton, London

15b **Landscape with Rocks (Wolf's Castle)**
1939
Watercolour $19\frac{1}{2}'' \times 26\frac{3}{8}''$
Collection: Mrs Barbara Bagenal, Lewes, Sussex

16a **Study for 'Entrance to Lane'**
10 July 1939
Pen and watercolour $5\frac{5}{16}'' \times 4\frac{5}{8}''$
Collection: Dean Hussey, Chichester

16b **Study for 'Entrance to Lane'**
10 July 1939
Pen and watercolour $5\frac{5}{16}'' \times 4\frac{5}{8}''$
Collection: Dean Hussey, Chichester

16c **Study for 'Entrance to Lane'**
11 July 1939
Pen and watercolour $5\frac{5}{16}'' \times 4\frac{5}{8}''$
Collection: Dean Hussey, Chichester

16d **Study for 'Entrance to Lane'**
July 1939
Pen and gouache $7\frac{1}{8}'' \times 5\frac{3}{8}''$

17 **Entrance to Lane**
1939
Oil on canvas $19\frac{1}{2}'' \times 23\frac{1}{2}''$
First exhibited Leicester Galleries, London, 1940
under the title 'Approach to Woods' Catalogue No.30
Previous collection: Peter Watson
Collection: Tate Gallery, London

18 **Four studies for 'Gorse on Sea Wall'**
1938–9
Pen and watercolour
top left $2\frac{3}{4}''$ × $2\frac{1}{8}''$; top right $3\frac{1}{8}''$ × $2\frac{1}{4}''$; bottom left $2\frac{5}{8}''$ × $2\frac{1}{8}''$; bottom right $3\frac{1}{8}''$ × $2\frac{1}{4}''$
From a sheet originally containing five studies.
See reproduction *Horizon* April 1942. Bibl.
Collection: Mr and Mrs Philip James, Beaconsfield, Buckinghamshire

19a **Road Mounting Between Hedges: Sunrise**
1940
Watercolour 27″ × 19″
First exhibited Leicester Galleries, London
1940 Catalogue No.14
Collection: City Art Gallery, Birmingham

19b **Hollow Tree Trunk**
1938
Watercolour $22\frac{3}{8}''$ × $15\frac{3}{8}''$
First exhibited Rosenberg & Helft, London
1938 Catalogue No.21
Previous collection: Sir Edward Marsh
Collection: Laing Art Gallery, Newcastle

20 **Four Studies of Rocks**
1939–40
Pen and wash, touched with pink $8\frac{1}{4}''$ × $5\frac{1}{8}''$

21 **Sheet of Three Studies**
Two studies of interlocking stones in landscape 1939
landscape study 1937
Pen and watercolour $7\frac{3}{8}''$ × $3\frac{7}{8}''$
Collection: Dr Henry M. Roland, London

22 **Green Tree Form: Interior of Woods**
1939
Pen and watercolour 27″ × 19″
First exhibited Leicester Galleries, London
1940 Catalogue No.11
Collection: Sir Colin Anderson, London

23a **Study for 'Green Tree Form'**
1939
Pen and watercolour $4\frac{3}{8}''$ × $3\frac{3}{8}''$

23b **Study for 'Green Tree Form'**
1939
Pen and watercolour $4\frac{3}{8}''$ × $3\frac{3}{8}''$

23c **Green Tree Form: Interior of Woods**
1940
Oil on canvas 30″ × $41\frac{1}{8}''$
First exhibited Leicester Galleries, London
1940 Catalogue No.23
Collection: Tate Gallery, London

24 **Sheet of Four Studies**
1939
Pen and watercolour 8″ × 6″
Includes study for 'Tree Forms in an Estuary' pl.31
and study for 'Association of Oaks' pl.25
First exhibited without study middle right under the title
'Three Studies of Trees', Temple Newsam, Leeds
1941 Catalogue No.146
Collection: Sir Kenneth Clark, Saltwood, Kent

25 **Association of Oaks**
1940
Gouache 27″ × 19″
First exhibited Leicester Galleries, London
1940 Catalogue No.22
Collection: Mrs Edward W. Root, New York City

26 **Studies for 'Midsummer Landscape'**
1940
Pen and watercolour 8″ × 6″

27 **Midsummer Landscape**
1940
Gouache $26\frac{3}{4}''$ × $18\frac{1}{2}''$
First exhibited Temple Newsam, Leeds
1941 Catalogue No.150
Collection: City Art Gallery, Birmingham

28a **Welsh Mountain Top**
1939
Pen and watercolour 3″ × $5\frac{3}{8}''$

28b **Study for 'Red Landscape'**
1941–2
Watercolour $3\frac{3}{4}''$ × 5″
Study for painting 'Red Landscape' 1942 reproduced
Penguin Modern Painters, 1st Edition, pl.9
Collection: Dr Andrew Revai, London

28c **Fallen Tree**
1940
Watercolour $5\frac{3}{8}''$ × 8″

29 **Cliff Road**
1941
Oil on canvas $46\frac{1}{2}''$ × 34″
First exhibited British Institute of Adult Education, London 1942
Collection: Felton Bequest, Melbourne Art Gallery, Australia

30a **Design for 'The Wanderer' Act I**
1940
Gouache 8″ × 10″
First exhibited Temple Newsam, Leeds
July/Sept. 1941 Catalogue No.56
Collection: Sir Kenneth Clark, Saltwood, Kent

30b **Design for 'The Wanderer' Act II**
1940
Gouache 8″ × 9″
First exhibited Temple Newsam, Leeds
July/Sept. 1941 Catalogue No.57
Collection: Sir Kenneth Clark, Saltwood, Kent
Designs for two backcloths for 'The Wanderer', a ballet performed by the Vic Wells Company at the New Theatre, London, January 1941

31 **Tree Forms in an Estuary**
1940
Pen and watercolour 19″ × 27″
First exhibited Leicester Galleries, London
1940 Catalogue No.10
Collection: Ian Phillips, Charlton Mackrell, Somerset

32a **Tree Form**
1941
Oil on canvas $15\frac{1}{2}''$ × 12″
First exhibited Temple Newsam, Leeds 1941 Catalogue No.138
Collection: Temple Newsam, Leeds

32b **Study for 'Tree Form'**
1940
Pen and wash 9″ × 7″

33 **Blasted Oak**
1941
Pen and wash 15″ × 12″
Previous collection: The Hon. Edward Sackville-West
Collection: Sir Colin Anderson, London

34a **Study of Boulders**
1942
Pen and wash $4\frac{3}{4}''$ × $7\frac{3}{4}''$

34b **Gower Landscape**
1941
Indian ink, coloured chalk and watercolour $14\frac{1}{2}'' \times 18''$
Private collection, London

35 **Study of Boulders**
1942
Pen, chalk and wash $7\frac{3}{4}'' \times 6\frac{1}{4}''$

36a **Devastation – City – Burnt-out Interior**
1941
Pen, chalk and wash $21\frac{1}{2}'' \times 31\frac{1}{2}''$
Collection: Imperial War Museum, London

36b **Devastation – House in Wales**
6 September 1940
Pen and watercolour $6\frac{3}{4}'' \times 5\frac{1}{2}''$
Study for painting reproduced Penguin Modern Painters, 1st Edition, pl.17

37 **Devastation – City – Twisted Girders**
1941
Pen, pencil, chalk and wash $7'' \times 5\frac{1}{4}''$

38a **Devastation – City – Ruined Machinery**
1941
Pen, chalk and wash $8\frac{3}{4}'' \times 6\frac{1}{2}''$
Inscribed: Machinery fallen through floor of city factory

38b **Devastation – City – Ruined Machinery**
1941
Pen, chalk and wash $8\frac{1}{4}'' \times 5\frac{3}{4}''$

39a **Devastation – City – Fallen Lift Shaft**
1941
Pen and gouache $5\frac{1}{2}'' \times 4\frac{3}{4}''$

39b **Devastation – City – Fallen Lift Shaft**
1941
Pen, chalk and gouache $9'' \times 6\frac{1}{4}''$

39c **Devastation – City – Fallen Lift Shaft**
1941
Chalk and gouache $12\frac{7}{8}'' \times 18\frac{1}{4}''$
Collection: Imperial War Museum, London
On loan to Wakefield City Art Gallery

40a **Devastation – East End – Burnt-out Paper Rolls**
1941
Pen, chalk and wash $12\frac{7}{8}'' \times 18\frac{1}{4}''$
Collection: Imperial War Museum, London

40b **Devastation – East End – Burnt-out Paper Rolls**
1941
Pen, chalk and wash approx. $6'' \times 9''$
Present owner not known

41a **Devastation – East End Houses**
1941
Pen, chalk and gouache $25\frac{1}{4}'' \times 44\frac{3}{4}''$
Exhibited by the War Artists Committee 1941
Destroyed by enemy action

41b **Study – An East End Street**
1941
Pen, chalk and wash $5'' \times 10''$
Collection: Mrs Jennie Bevan, Asheridge, Bucks.

41c **Study for 'Devastation – East End Street'**
1941
Pen, chalk and wash $4'' \times 7\frac{1}{2}''$
Study for painting reproduced
Penguin Modern Painters, 1st Edition, pl.21
Collection: Felix H. Man, Frankfurt, Germany

41d **Study – An East End Street**
1941
Pen, chalk and wash $4'' \times 7\frac{1}{2}''$

41e **Collapsed Roofs – London Suburbs**
1941
Pen, chalk and wash $4\frac{1}{2}'' \times 7''$

41f **East End Public House**
1941
Pen, chalk and wash $5\frac{1}{4}'' \times 9\frac{5}{8}''$

42a **Devastation – Chancery Chambers, Swansea**
1941
Gouache $4'' \times 3\frac{1}{8}''$
Collection: National Museum of Wales, Cardiff

42b **Devastation – Chancery Chambers, Swansea**
1941
Gouache $6\frac{3}{4}'' \times 4''$
Collection: National Museum of Wales, Cardiff

43a **Moulds: Iron Foundry**
1942
Pen, chalk and wash $3\frac{3}{4}'' \times 3\frac{1}{4}''$

43b **Moulds: Iron Foundry**
1942
Pen, chalk and wash $5\frac{1}{4}'' \times 4\frac{3}{4}''$

43c **Moulds: Iron Foundry**
1942
Pen, chalk and wash $6\frac{3}{8}'' \times 8\frac{1}{8}''$

43d **Moulds: Iron Foundry**
1942
Pen, chalk and wash $7\frac{1}{8}'' \times 8''$

43e **Moulds: Iron Foundry**
1942
Pen, chalk and wash $6\frac{5}{8}'' \times 7\frac{7}{8}''$

43f **Manufacturing Bombs**
1942
Oil on hardboard $36'' \times 43''$
Collection: Imperial War Museum, London
On loan to The Tate Gallery

44a **Man Looking into Furnace**
1942
Pen, chalk and wash $10'' \times 11\frac{1}{4}''$
Private collection, London

44b **Steel Workers**
1942
Pen, chalk and gouache $4\frac{3}{4}'' \times 4\frac{1}{2}''$
Collection: Dr Andrew Revai, London

44c **Small Furnaces, Woolwich**
1942
Pen, chalk and wash $19\frac{1}{2}'' \times 15\frac{1}{2}''$
Collection: Imperial War Museum, London
On loan to Sheffield Art Gallery

44d **Hydraulic Press, Woolwich**
1944
Pen, chalk and wash $29\frac{3}{8}'' \times 17\frac{1}{2}''$
Collection: Imperial War Museum, London
On loan to Manchester Art Gallery

45 **Tapping a Steel Furnace**
1942
incorrectly dated 1943
Pen, chalk and watercolour $11'' \times 8''$
Collection: Dr Andrew Revai, London

46a **Tin Mine – A Declivity**
1942
Pen, gouache and watercolour 37½″ × 19½″
Collection: Imperial War Museum, London

46b **Sheet of Tin Mine Studies**
1942
Pen, chalk and wash 7¾″ × 5⅞″
Includes study of miner emerging, for painting
'Tin Mine, Miner Emerging', in collection of Temple Newsam,
Leeds

46c **Tin Mine – Miner Approaching**
1942
Ink, chalk and wash 46¼″ × 29⅜″
Collection: British Council, London

47a **Limestone Quarry – Loosening Stone**
1943
Pen, chalk and watercolour 25½″ × 22½″
Collection: British Council, London

47b **Outcast Coal Production – Dragline Depositing Excavated Earth**
1943
Pen, chalk and watercolour 27¼″ × 26″
Collection: Imperial War Museum, London
On loan to Leeds City Art Gallery

47c **Outcast Coal Production – Excavators Uncovering Coal Seam**
1943
Pen, chalk and watercolour 17½″ × 34″
Collection: Imperial War Museum, London
On loan to Leeds City Art Gallery

48a **Flying Bomb Site, St. Leu d'Esserent**
1944
Chalk and wash 9½″ × 7¾″
Collection: Imperial War Museum, London
On loan to South London Art Gallery

48b **Trappes – Study for 'Wrecked Locomotive'**
1944
Pen, chalk and wash 10″ × 7″
Collection: E. Millington-Drake, Este

48c **Trappes – Study for 'Wrecked Locomotive'**
1944
Chalk and wash 16⅜″ × 13⅝″
Collection: Temple Newsam, Leeds

48d **Trappes – Wrecked Locomotive**
1944
Oil on hardboard 50½″ × 41¼″
Collection: Temple Newsam, Leeds

49 **Trappes – Wrecked Locomotive**
1944
Pen, chalk and wash approx. 12″ × 8″
Present owner not known

50a **Pembrokeshire Landscape**
1944
Gouache 9″ × 11″
Collection: Dr Henry M. Roland, London

50b **Carn Llydi, Wales**
1944
Gouache 6¼″ × 9¼″

50c **Mountain in Wales**
1944
Pen, pencil, chalk and watercolour 3⅞″ × 6″

51 **Landscape with Mounds**
1943
Pen and wash 9″ × 7″

52a **Folded Hills**
1943
Oil on canvas 20″ × 27″
Previous collection: Eardley Knollys
Collection: Guy Dixon, London

52b **Landscape with Pointed Rocks**
1944
Chalk and gouache 16″ × 22″
Collection: British Council, London

52c **Landscape with Pointed Rocks**
1944
Chalk and gouache 16″ × 22″
Collection: Dr Youngman, Cambridge

52d **Landscape with Pointed Rocks**
1944
Gouache 16¼″ × 21¼″
Collection: James Bomford, Aldbourne, Wiltshire

52e **Landscape with Pointed Rocks**
1944
Chalk and watercolour 10″ × 14″
Present owner not known

52f **Landscape with Pointed Rocks**
1944
Chalk and gouache 4¼″ × 5⅜″
Collection: Felix H. Man, Frankfurt, Germany

53a **Landscape with Pointed Hills**
1944
Oil on hardboard 17″ × 14⅛″
First exhibited Buchholz Gallery, New York
1946 Catalogue No.7
Collection: West Riding Education Committee, Yorkshire

53b **Root Form**
1944
Pen, chalk and watercolour 18¾″ × 15½″
First exhibited Buchholz Gallery, New York
1946 Catalogue No.34
Collection: George Dix, New York City

53c **Landscape with Pointed Rocks**
1945
Oil on canvas approx. 32″ × 22″
Present owner unknown

53d **Horned Tree Form**
1944
Pen, chalk and gouache approx. 24″ × 20″
Collection: Mrs Lois Orswell, Pomfret Center, Connecticut

54a **Study of Lane Opening**
1945
Pen, chalk and gouache 6″ × 4¼″
Collection: Sir Michael Balcon, London

54b **Study of Burning Coal**
1945
Watercolour 7¼″ × 6″

54c **Triple-tiered Landscape**
1944
Gouache and chalk 29″ × 21½″
Collection: Santa Barbara Museum of Art, California

54d **Man and Fields**
1944
Chalk and watercolour 8⅞″ × 6¾″

55 **Triple-tiered Landscape**
1944
Pen, chalk and watercolour 22″ × 16″
First exhibited Redfern Gallery 1944
Collection: Raymond Mortimer, London

56a **Thistles and Sun**
1945
Chalk and gouache 17¾″ × 15⅞″
First exhibited Buchholz Gallery, New York
1946 Catalogue No.18
Collection: Mr and Mrs John Macdonell, Sarasota, Florida

56b **Red Thistles**
1945
Chalk and gouache 24¾″ × 21″
First exhibited Buchholz Gallery, New York
1946 Catalogue No.17
Present owner not known

56c **Fire Basket**
1944
Pen, chalk and gouache 18½″ × 16″
First exhibited Buchholz Gallery, New York
1946 Catalogue No.26
Collection: Mrs Malcolm McBride, Cleveland, Ohio

56d **Association of Thistles**
1945
Oil on hardboard 22″ × 21″
First exhibited Buchholz Gallery, New York
1946 Catalogue No.10
Collection: Dr Robert Strauss-Hupé, Philadelphia, U.S.A.

57 **Thistles**
1945
Oil on canvas 24½″ × 28½″
First exhibited Buchholz Gallery, New York
1946 Catalogue No.5
Collection: Mrs Lois Orswell, Pomfret Center, Connecticut

58a **Study for 'Horned Forms'**
1944
Pen, chalk and gouache 3⅝″ × 4⅝″

58b **Study for 'Horned Forms'**
1944
Pen, chalk and gouache 4¼″ × 4½″

58c **Study for 'Horned Forms'**
1944
Chalk and gouache 5¼″ × 5¼″

58d **Study for 'Horned Forms'**
1944
Chalk and gouache 5″ × 5″

59 **Horned Forms**
1944
Oil on canvas 26″ × 20″
Collection: Wilfred Evill, London
Another version is in the collection of the Museum of Modern Art, New York

60a **Study of Road between Hills**
1944
Watercolour 8¼″ × 7¾″
Collection: Frankland Dark, London

60b **Cairn**
1944
Pen, chalk and gouache 15¾″ × 16″
First exhibited Buchholz Gallery, New York
1946 Catalogue No.23
Collection: Society of the Four Arts, Palm Beach, Florida

60c **Study of Leaf**
1943
Pencil, ink and gouache 10¾″ × 8″

60d **Study of Foliage**
1944
Chalk and gouache 27″ × 22″
Collection: Jocelyn Baines, London

61a **Smiling Woman**
1945
Oil on canvas 33″ × 28½″
First exhibited Lefevre Gallery, 1945
Catalogue No.38
Collection: Gibson Smith, London

61b **Woman Picking Vegetables**
1945
Oil on hardboard 24″ × 20″
First exhibited Buchholz Gallery, New York
1946 Catalogue No.3
Collection: Wilfred Evill, London

61c **The Lamp**
1944
Oil on hardboard 30″ × 25″
First Exhibited Lefevre Gallery, London, 1945 Catalogue No.36
Collection: Roderick Cameron, Paris

61d **The Lamp**
1945
Oil on canvas 24″ × 25″
First exhibited Buchholz Gallery, New York
1946 Catalogue No.6
Collection: Andrew C. Ritchie, New Haven, Connecticut

62a **Corn and Stone**
1945
Chalk and gouache 21″ × 20½″
Collection: James Grady, Atlanta, Georgia

62b **Study of Corn**
1945
Ink, chalk and gouache 10″ × 9¼″

62c **Interlocking Tree Forms**
1945
Pen, chalk and gouache 21″ × 21″
First exhibited Buchholz Gallery
1946 Catalogue No.29
Collection: The Redfern Gallery, London

62d **Tree Form**
1945
Pen, chalk and gouache 22″ × 21″
Collection: Wilfred Evill, London

63a **Woman in a Garden**
1945
Pen, chalk and gouache 24″ × 17″
First exhibited Buchholz Gallery, New York
1946 Catalogue No.30
Collection: Wilfred Evill, London

63b **Still Life with Apples**
1944
Gouache and chalk 6¼″ × 8″
Collection: Mr and Mrs Philip James, Beaconsfield, Bucks.

64a **Sun over Cornfield**
1946
Pen, chalk and gouache 16½″ × 10⅞″
Collection: W. A. Brandt, Saffron Walden, Essex

64b **Sun over Cornfield**
1945
Pen, chalk and gouache 27″ × 16″
On reverse: 'Landscape with Estuary' plate 67a
Collection: British Council, London

64c **Landscape**
1947
Oil on canvas 12″ × 19⅝″
Inscribed on reverse: 'G. Sutherland 1947 Antibes Homage to Picasso –
Free copy after seeing a painting by Picasso and noticing
similarity of certain forms to some I have used in Wales'
Present owner not known

65 **Landscape with Fields**
1945
Pen, chalk and gouache 27⅝″ × 10¾″
First exhibited Buchholz Gallery, New York
1946 Catalogue No.35
Collection: Mr and Mrs John Macdonell, Sarasota, Florida

66a **Woods and Estuary**
1945
Pen, chalk and gouache 16⅞″ × 16¾″
Collection: Wilfred Evill, London

66b **Estuary with Rocks**
1946
Gouache 8½″ × 11″
Collection: British Council, London

67a **Landscape with Estuary**
1945
Pen, chalk and gouache 16¼″ × 26¾″
On reverse: 'Sun over Cornfield' plate 64b
Collection: British Council, London

67b **Landscape with Estuary**
1945
Pen, chalk and watercolour 15½″ × 29″
Collection: C. J. Hayshaw, Manchester

67c **Estuary Foreshore**
1946
Pen, chalk and gouache 14¾″ × 29¼″
Collection: H. P. Juda, London

68a **Green Lane**
1945
Oil on canvas 24½″ × 19¾″
Collection: Southampton Art Gallery

68b **Entrance to Lane**
1945
Oil on canvas 21½″ × 15½″
Collection: H. P. Juda, London

68c **Entrance to Lane with Interlacing Foliage**
1945
Pen, chalk and gouache 21½″ × 21¼″
First exhibited Buchholz Gallery, New York
1946 Catalogue No.15
Collection: Mrs Joseph Phillips, U.S.A.

68d **Entrance to Lane**
1945
Pen, chalk and gouache 21½″ × 21¼″
First exhibited Buchholz Gallery, New York
1946 Catalogue No.11
Collection: Andrew C. Ritchie, New Haven, Connecticut

69a **Staring Tree Form**
1945
Chalk and gouache 18⅝″ × 16″
First exhibited Buchholz Gallery, New York
1946 Catalogue No.21
Collection: Wilfred Evill, London

69b **Study for 'Staring Tree Form'**
Pen and watercolour approx. 4″ × 5″

69c **Study for 'Staring Tree Form'**
Chalk and watercolour on tracing paper approx. 4″ × 7″

70 **Chimère I**
1946
Oil on canvas 78½″ × 47½″
First exhibited Exposition Internationale d'Art
Moderne, Paris 1946
Collection: Mrs Somerville, London

71 **Chimère II**
1946–7
Oil on canvas 70″ × 36″
First exhibited Hanover Gallery, London
1948 Catalogue No.25
Collection: Frank McEwen, Salisbury, Rhodesia

72a **Study for the Northampton Crucifixion**
1946
Oil on hardboard 35¾″ × 48″
First exhibited Lefevre Gallery, London 1947
Collection: Tate Gallery, London

72b **Study for the Northampton Crucifixion**
1946
Oil on hardboard 40″ × 48″
First exhibited Lefevre Gallery, London 1947
Collection: British Council, London

73 **Deposition**
1946
Oil on hardboard 47″ × 36⅞″
First exhibited Lefevre Gallery, London 1947
Collection: Wilfred Evill, London

74a **Stone Head**
1946
Black chalk 4½″ × 5¾″
First exhibited Innsbruck and Vienna 1953/4

74b **Detail of Crucifixion,** plate 75, in course of execution

75 **Crucifixion**
1946
Oil on hardboard 96″ × 90″
St Matthew's Church, Northampton

76 **Two Studies for a Crucifixion**
1946
Black chalk 26″ × 16″
Collection: Mrs Graham Sutherland

77 **Study for a Crucifixion**
1946
Oil on hardboard 13″ × 9¾″
Collection: Lady Clark, Saltwood, Kent

78a **Thorns**
1945
Pen and watercolour 16¼″ × 12½″
Collection: British Council, London

78b **Thorn Trees**
1945
Pen and gouache on tracing paper 8¾″ × 7″
Previous collection: Peter Watson
Collection: Norman Fowler, U.S.A.

79 **Thorn Trees**
1945
Oil on hardboard 42¾″ × 40″
First exhibited Buchholz Gallery, New York
1946 Catalogue No.1
Collection: Albright Art Gallery, Buffalo, New York

80 **Thorn Tree**
1945
Oil on canvas 26″ × 20″
Collection: Sir Kenneth Clark, Saltwood, Kent

81 **Thorn Trees**
1946
Oil on canvas 50″ × 40″
First exhibited Lefevre Gallery, London, 1946
Catalogue No.12
Collection: British Council, London

82 **Thorns**
1945
Pen, chalk and gouache 29½″ × 16½″
First exhibited Buchholz Gallery, New York
1946 Catalogue No.28
Collection: Mr and Mrs John Macdonell, Sarasota, Florida

83a **Thorn Head**
1945
Oil on canvas 24″ × 24¼″
Collection: Frankland Dark, London

83b **Thorn Head**
1946
Pen, chalk and gouache 22″ × 21″
First exhibited Buchholz Gallery, New York
1946 Catalogue No.14
Collection: James Thrall Soby, New Canaan, Connecticut

83c **Thorn Head**
1946
Oil on canvas 43¾″ × 30½″
Collection: Dr Henry M. Roland, London

83d **Thorn Head**
1946
Ink and gouache 16″ × 10″
Collection: William Roerich, New York City

84a **Thorn Heads**
1946
Oil on canvas 47″ × 36″
Previous collection: Ian Greenlees
Collection: Museum of Modern Art, New York City

84b **Thorn Heads**
1946
Pastel and gouache 27″ × 20″
First exhibited Lefevre Gallery, London
1946 Catalogue No.13
Collection: Sir Colin Anderson, London

85a **Thorn and Wall**
1946
Oil on canvas 16″ × 20″
First exhibited Hanover Gallery, London
1948 Catalogue No.17
Collection: Vancouver Art Gallery, Canada

85b **Thorn Trees**
1947
Oil on canvas 34½″ × 35¾″
Collection: Toledo Museum of Art, Ohio

86a **The Intruding Bull**
1944
Oil on hardboard 30″ × 25½″
First exhibited Lefevre Gallery, London, 1945
Catalogue No. 37
Collection: Sir Colin Anderson, London

86b **Tethered Cow**
1944
Gouache 20½″ × 16″
Collection: Alan Roger, London

87 **Tree Form**
1946
Oil on canvas 22¾″ × 21¼″
Collection: Gimpel Fils, London

88a **Study of Vine Pergola**
1947
Pencil, ink and watercolour 4¾″ × 9⅞″
Collection: Frankland Dark, London

88b **Study of Vine Pergola**
1947
Pencil, ink and watercolour 4½″ × 9″
Collection: Mrs Graham Sutherland

88c **Study of Vine Pergola**
1947
Pen, chalk and watercolour 4½″ × 9″
Collection: Mrs Graham Sutherland

88d **Vine Pergola with Figure**
1947
Oil on paper 4½″ × 9″
Collection: Mrs Graham Sutherland

88e **Large Vine Pergola**
1948
Oil on canvas 37⅞″ × 68¼″
First exhibited Hanover Gallery, London
1948 Catalogue No.23
Collection: British Council, London

88f **Figure and Vine Structure**
1948
Oil on canvas 11″ × 20″
First exhibited Hanover Gallery, London
1948 Catalogue No.18
Collection: W. A. Brandt, Saffron Walden, Essex

89a **Blue Vine**
1948
Oil on hardboard 22½″ × 33″
First exhibited Hanover Gallery, London
1948 Catalogue No.4
Collection: Godfrey Winn, London

89b **Figure and Vine**
1947
Oil on canvas 21¼″ × 25½″
First exhibited Hanover Gallery, London
1948 Catalogue No.6
Previous collection: Dr A. Hunter
Collection: F. J. Lyons, London

90a **Green Vine Pergola**
1948
Oil on canvas 22″ × 18½″
First exhibited Hanover Gallery, London
1948 Catalogue No.14
Collection: Musée Royal des Beaux Arts, Brussels

90b **Vine Pergola**
1947
Oil on canvas 13″ × 16″
First exhibited Buchholz Gallery, New York
1948 Catalogue No.2
(Incorrectly titled 'Palms')
Collection: Phillips Memorial Gallery, Washington, D.C.

91 **Large Vine Pergola**
1948
Oil on canvas 52½″ × 33″
First exhibited Buchholz Gallery, New York
1948 Catalogue No.11
Previous collection: Dr Andrew Revai
Collection: National Gallery of Canada, Ottawa

92a **Palm Palisade**
1947
Chalk and gouache 12½″ × 9¾″
Study for plate 93b
Collection: British Council, London

92b **Landscape with Palm**
1947
Watercolour 9″ × 11¼″
First exhibited Hanover Gallery, London
1948 Catalogue No.5 (watercolours)
Collection: G. F. Williams, London

92c **Palm and Landscape**
1948
Chalk and gouache 15¼″ × 19½″
First exhibited Buchholz Gallery, New York
1948 Catalogue No.37
Collection: M. Bech, U.S.A.

93a **Palm and House**
1947
Oil on canvas 43¾″ × 36½″
First exhibited Hanover Gallery, London
1948 Catalogue No.2
Collection: University of Nebraska, Lincoln, Nebraska

93b **Palm Palisade**
1948
Oil on canvas 43½″ × 36½″
First exhibited Hanover Gallery, London
1948 Catalogue No.3
Collection: Wright Ludington, Santa Barbara, California

93c **Palm Palisade**
1947
Oil on canvas 43½″ × 36½″
First exhibited Buchholz Gallery, New York
1948 Catalogue No.7
Collection: Burton Tremaine, Meriden, Connecticut

93d **Palm Palisade**
1947
Oil on canvas 19½″ × 15½″
Collection: H. P. Juda, London

94a **Study for 'Palm and Wall'**
1948
Black chalk 14″ × 21¾″

94b **Palm and Wall**
1948
Oil on hardboard 22⅛″ × 39½″
First exhibited Hanover Gallery, London
1948 Catalogue No.10
Collection: Phillips Memorial Gallery, Washington, D.C.

94c **The Garden**
1947
Oil on canvas 15″ × 23⅝″
Collection: Mr and Mrs Manuel Seff, New York City

95a **Maize**
1948
Ink and watercolour 8¾″ × 11″
First exhibited Buchholz Gallery, New York
1948 Catalogue No.22
Collection: Albert Valentin, Arvada, Colorado

95b **Maize**
1948
Pen and gouache 15″ × 19½″
Collection: Peter Godden, Canterbury

95c **Hanging Maize**
1948
Ink and gouache 8¾″ × 11″
First exhibited Buchholz Gallery, New York
1948 Catalogue No.26b
Collection: Mr and Mrs Sam Jaffe, Beverly Hills, California

95d **Study for 'Hanging Maize'**
1948
Black chalk 9¼″ × 10¼″

95e **Maize and Gourd**
1948
Pencil and gouache 15½″ × 19½″
First exhibited Buchholz Gallery, New York
1948 Catalogue No.34
Collection: Dr. J. Rosenberg, Buffalo, New York

95f **Maize and Landscape**
1948
Gouache 8¾″ × 11″
First exhibited Buchholz Gallery, New York
1948 Catalogue No.23
Reproduced in colour in *Graham Sutherland*
Ambassador Editions, London 1950 (Plate 36)
Collection: Myron Ybarra O'Higgins, New York City

96a **The Gourd**
1948
Oil on hardboard 20″ × 20¼″
First exhibited Hanover Gallery, London
1948 Catalogue No.9
Collection: Museum of Modern Art, New York City

96b **Still Life with Gourds**
1948
Oil on canvas 18½″ × 21¾″
First exhibited Hanover Gallery, London
1948 Catalogue No.8
Collection: Mrs Dorothy Morland, London

96c **Study for 'Still Life with Gourds'**
1947
Watercolour 9″ × 11¼″
First exhibited Hanover Gallery, London
1948 Catalogue No.6 (watercolours)
Collection: Arthur Jeffress, London
Damaged by fire 1951, not yet restored

96d **Hanging Gourds**
1948
Gouache 10″ × 12½″
Collection: The Arts Council of Great Britain, London

97a **Cactus**
1947
Pen and watercolour 9″ × 11¼″
First exhibited Hanover Gallery, London
1948 Catalogue No.9 (watercolours)
Collection: James Bomford, Aldbourne, Wiltshire

97b **Cactus**
1947
Conté crayon and watercolour 8½″ × 12″
Collection: British Council, London

98a **Cigale**
1948
Oil on canvas 27″ × 20″
First exhibited Hanover Gallery, London
1948 Catalogue No.27
Collection:Mr and Mrs Peter Adam, London

98b **Cigale**
1948
Oil on canvas 27″ × 20″
First exhibited Hanover Gallery, London
1948 Catalogue No.16
Collection: Arthur Tooth and Sons, London

98c **Mantis**
1953
Oil on canvas 35½ × 27½″
Collection: F. J. Lyons, London

98d **Mantis**
1949
Oil on canvas 14⅞″ × 11″
Collection: Frankland Dark, London

98e **Cigale**
1947
Pen and watercolour 9″ × 11¼″
First exhibited Hanover Gallery, London
1948 Catalogue No.10 (watercolours)
Collection: Mrs H. P. Juda, London

98f **Insects**
1948
Pen and gouache 8¾″ × 11″
First exhibited Buchholz Gallery, New York
1948 Catalogue No.25
Collection: Mrs Benjamin P. Watson, New York City

99a **Still Life with Banana Leaf**
1947
Oil on hardboard 10¾″ × 21″
First exhibited Hanover Gallery, London
1948 Catalogue No.15
Collection: Frankland Dark, London

99b **Study of Banana Leaves**
1948
Chalk and watercolour on blue paper 9½″ × 17½″
Collection: Dr Andrew Revai, London

100a **Turning Form**
1948
Chalk and gouache 8¾″ × 11″
First exhibited Buchholz Gallery, New York
1948 Catalogue No.30
Collection: Mr and Mrs John Macdonell, Sarasota, Florida

100b **Study of a Palm Tree**
1948
Black crayon on coloured paper touched with white 10¼″ × 12½″
Collection: The Albertina, Vienna

100c **Reclining Stone Form**
1948
Pen, chalk and gouache 8¾″ × 11″
First exhibited Buchholz Gallery, New York
1948 Catalogue No.31
Collection: Dr W. R. Valentiner, Los Angeles

101a **Tourettes**
1948
Gouache 8¾″ × 11″
First exhibited Buchholz Gallery, New York
1948 Catalogue No.24
Collection: Mrs Benjamin P. Watson, New York City

101b **Banana Leaf and Landscape**
1947
Chalk and gouache 9″ × 11¼″
First exhibited Hanover Gallery, London
1948 Catalogue No.3 (watercolours)
Collection: Mr and Mrs Cecil H. Wills, London

101c **Articulated Forms**
1948
Pen, chalk and gouache 8¾″ × 11″
First exhibited Buchholz Gallery, New York
1948 Catalogue No.26a
Collection: Mrs Benjamin P. Watson, New York City

101d **Maize and Gourd**
1947
Oil on board 10″ × 13″
Collection: Mrs William A. Bernoudy, St Louis, Missouri

101e **Banana Leaves and Wall**
1948
Gouache 8¾″ × 11″
First exhibited Buchholz Gallery, New York
1948 Catalogue No.28
Collection: George Rickey, Indiana

101f **Figure in Enclosure**
1948
Ink, crayon and gouache 15½″ × 19½″
First exhibited Buchholz Gallery, New York
1948 Catalogue No.33
Collection: Wright Ludington, Santa Barbara, California

102a **Three Standing Forms, Yellow Background**
1949
Chalk and watercolour 21″ × 19″
Collection: Assis Chateaubriand, São Paulo, Brazil

102b **Two Stone Forms**
1950
Gouache 13¾″ × 14″
Collection: W. J. Strachan, Bishops Stortford, Hertfordshire

102c **Three Forms**
1950
Oil on canvas 18¼″ × 15¼″
First exhibited Hanover Gallery, London
1951 Catalogue No.5
Previous collection: Peter Watson
Collection: Marlborough Fine Art Ltd and The Arthur Jeffress Gallery, London

102d **Standing Form – Hot Summer Room**
1951
Oil on canvas 18″ × 15″
First exhibited Hanover Gallery, London
1951 Not in Catalogue
Collection: G. F. Williams, London

103a **Two Standing Forms against a Palisade**
1949
Oil on canvas 30⅛″ × 26⅛″
First exhibited Hanover Gallery, London
1951 Catalogue No.3
Collection: Vancouver Art Gallery, Canada

103b **Root Form, Green Background**
1948
Crayon and watercolour 8¾″ × 10¼″
Collection: British Council, London

104a **Horizontal Form, Mauve Background**
1950
Oil on hardboard 14½″ × 30½″
First exhibited Hanover Gallery, London
1951 Catalogue No.11
Collection: R. Morris, Paris

104b **Articulated Form, Yellow Background**
1949
Oil on canvas 10⅛″ × 22⅛″
First exhibited Hanover Gallery, London
1951 Catalogue No.2
Collection: H. P. Juda, London

104c **Articulated Form in Landscape**
1949
Chalk and watercolour 8½″ × 19½″
Collection: F. R. S. Yorke, London

105a **Study for Two Forms**
1949
Conté crayon and coloured chalk 3½″ × 9¼″

105b **Two Forms in a Terraced Landscape**
1951
Oil on canvas 20¼″ × 36¼″
First exhibited Hanover Gallery, London
1951 Catalogue No.16
Collection: Mr and Mrs R. T. S. Grigg, Uckfield, Sussex

105c **Horizontal Form in Grasses**
1951
Oil on canvas 20⅛″ × 36⅛″
First exhibited Hanover Gallery, London
1951 Catalogue No.13
Collection: Peter Meyer, London

106a **Articulated Form**
1951
Chalk and gouache 15″ × 18″
Collection: E. Rosenberg, London

106b **Organic Forms**
1950
Oil on hardboard approx. 18″ × 16″
Collection: Charles Brasch, Dunedin, New Zealand

106c **Organic Forms**
1948
Conté crayon and gouache 8¾″ × 11″
First exhibited Buchholz Gallery, New York
1948 Catalogue No.32
Collection: Robert J. Schoelkopf, Jr., New York City

106d **Study of a Cactus**
1948
Ink and watercolour 9″ × 7″

107a **Still Life with Grapes**
1950
Oil on canvas 19¾″ × 15¾″
Collection: Frankland Dark, London

107b **Roses**
1951
Oil on canvas 26½″ × 14½″
First exhibited Hanover Gallery, London
1951 Not in Catalogue
Collection: Mr and Mrs Alan Sainsbury, London

107c **Roses**
1951
Oil on canvas 26½″ × 20⅛″
First exhibited Hanover Gallery, London
1951 Catalogue No.14
Collection: Eric Newton, London

107d **Roses**
1950
Oil on canvas 25″ × 20″
Collection: Roger Senhouse, London

108a **Path through Plantation**
1950
Oil on canvas 36⅛″ × 20⅛″
First exhibited Hanover Gallery, London
1951 Catalogue No.8
Collection: Maurice Stuart, Chicago, Illinois

108b **Men Walking**
1950
Oil on canvas 57¼″ × 38½″
Previous collection: Robert Melville, London
Collection: Beaverbrook Foundation, Fredericton, New Brunswick,
Canada

109 **Path through Plantation**
1951
Oil on canvas 30″ × 25″
Collection: Beaverbrook Foundation, Fredericton, New Brunswick,
Canada

110a **Aubergines**
1951
Gouache 8⅜″ × 21½″
Collection: W. A. Brandt, Saffron Walden, Essex

110b **Artichokes** (detail)
1951
Watercolour 9½″ × 13⅝″
Collection: Mrs M. Balint, London

110c **Pomegranates**
1951
Oil on canvas 16″ × 35″
First exhibited Arts Council 'Three Young Collectors'
1952 Catalogue No.22
Previous collection: R. D. S. May
Collection: Mrs Peter Adam, London

111a **Thorn Head**
1949
Oil on canvas 17⅞″ × 23¾″
Present owner not known

111b **Study for 'Thorn Head'**
1949
Black chalk 14½″ × 11″
Collection: Mrs Graham Sutherland

111c **Thorn Head**
1950–1
Oil on canvas 26½″ × 19¾″
First exhibited Venice Biennale, 1952
(British Council Catalogue No.51)
Collection: Peter Meyer, London

111d **Thorn Head**
1950
Gouache 26″ × 22″
Collection: Contemporary Art Society, London

112a **Head of Bird: Study for 'Origins of the Land'**
1950–51
Black chalk 12″ × 24″

112b **Pterodactyl: Study for 'Origins of the Land'**
1950–51
Conté crayon and gouache 12½″ × 29¼″
First exhibited Redfern Gallery, October 1953
Collection: Peter Cox, Totnes, Devon

113a **Study for 'Origins of the Land'**
1950
Gouache 7″ × 5⅝″

113b **Study for 'Origins of the Land'**
1950
Pencil and watercolour 3½″ × 3½″
One of two studies on a single sheet

113c **Origins of the Land** (Plate 115) in course of execution

113d **Origins of the Land** (Plate 115) in course of execution

114a **Working Drawing for 'Origins of the Land'**
1951
Chalk and gouache 24¾″ × 19½″
Collection: Sir Kenneth and Lady Clark, Saltwood, Kent

114b **Study for 'Origins of the Land'**
1951
Conté crayon and watercolour 3⅝″ × 2¾″

115 **Origins of the Land**
1951
Oil on canvas 167½″ × 131¼″
Commissioned for the Pavilion 'The Origins of the Land' at the
Festival of Britain, South Bank, London 1951. Later acquired by the
Arts Council of Great Britain and presented to the Tate Gallery
Collection: The Tate Gallery, London

116a **Barren Landscape with Rocks**
1951
Gouache 13⅛″ × 9⅝″
First exhibited Curt Valentin Gallery, New York
1953 Catalogue No.17
Collection: Mr & Mrs S. Day, London

116b **Landscape with Dry Waterway**
1952
Pen, chalk and gouache 22½″ × 14¾″
First exhibited Curt Valentin Gallery, New York
1953 under title 'Landscape with Rocks'
Catalogue No.25
Collection: Redfern Gallery, London

116c **Rocks in a Landscape**
1952
Pencil, chalk and gouache 7¼″ × 7¾″
First exhibited Curt Valentin Gallery, New York
1953 Catalogue No.28

116d **Birds**
1952
Pen, chalk and gouache 22½″ × 21½″
First exhibited Curt Valentin Gallery, New York
1953 Catalogue No.22
Collection: Reginald Denham, New York City

117a **Head**
1951
Chalk and gouache 15¼″ × 12″

117b **Head**
1951
Chalk and gouache 13″ × 9½″
First exhibited Venice Biennale 1952
(British Council Catalogue No.61)
Collection: Rex Nan Kivell, London

117c **Head**
1951
Oil on canvas 24″ × 20″
First exhibited Hanover Gallery, London
1951 Catalogue No.15
Previous collection: Curt Valentin
Collection: National Gallery of Canada, Ottawa

117d **Head**
1951
Oil on canvas 24″ × 20″
First exhibited Venice Biennale 1952
(British Council Catalogue No.58)
Collection: Mrs Graham Sutherland

118a **Standing Form, Orange Background**
1949
Chalk and gouache 16″ × 6½″
First exhibited Hanover Gallery, London
1951 Catalogue No.26
Collection: Wilfred Evill, London

118b **Form in Reeds**
1952
Gouache 17¼″ × 7″
Collection: The Redfern Gallery, London

118c **Standing Form, Red Background**
1950
Pen and gouache 14⅞″ × 5½″
Collection: Angus W. Robertson, Montreal

118d **Standing Form, Red Background**
1949
Chalk and gouache 16″ × 7″
Collection: Ronald Alley, London

119a **Armoured Form**
1950
Oil on canvas 65″ × 32½″

119b **Standing Form**
1952
Oil on canvas 86½″ × 40¼″
Collection: Musée National d'Art Moderne, Paris

120 **Standing Forms**
1952
Oil on canvas 71¼″ × 55¾″
First exhibited Curt Valentin Gallery, New York
1953 Catalogue No.7
Collection: Myron Ybarra O'Higgins, New York City

121 **Three Standing Forms in a Garden**
1952
Oil on canvas 52¾″ × 45⅝″
First exhibited Musée National d'Art Moderne, Paris
1952 Catalogue No.56a
Collection: Mrs Graham Sutherland

122a **Form against Foliage**
1952
Oil on canvas 66½″ × 33½″
First exhibited Venice Biennale 1952
(British Council Catalogue No.65)
Collection: Robert J. Schoelkopf, Jr., New York City

122b **Forms against Reeds**
1952
Oil on canvas 24″ × 20″
First exhibited Curt Valentin Gallery, New York
1953 Catalogue No.12
Collection: Max Weinstein, Seattle, Washington

123a **Landscape with Stones and Grasses**
1952
Oil on canvas 18¾″ × 36¼″
First exhibited Curt Valentin Gallery, New York
1953 Catalogue No.11
Collection: Myron Ybarra O'Higgins, New York City

123b **Vine Pergola**
1952
Oil on canvas 18″ × 36″
First exhibited Curt Valentin Gallery, New York
1953 Catalogue No.9
Collection: Miss Carmen Mathews, New York City

123c **Monuments against a Landscape**
1952
Ink, chalk and gouache 8″ × 21¼″
First exhibited Curt Valentin Gallery, New York
1953 Catalogue No.27
Collection: Joseph H. Hirshhorn, New York City

124a **Cynocéphale**
1952
Oil on canvas 52″ × 23¾″
First exhibited Venice Biennale 1952
(British Council Catalogue No.63)
Collection: Joseph H. Hirshhorn, New York City

124b **Predatory Form**
1952
Chalk and gouache 22¼″ × 7″
First exhibited Curt Valentin Gallery, New York
1953 Catalogue No.24
Collection: Mrs Leslie Gill, New York City

125 **Standing Forms**
1953
Oil on canvas 71½″ × 56″ (destroyed by artist)

126a **Head**
1952
Oil on canvas 36″ × 28″
First exhibited Curt Valentin Gallery, New York
1953 Catalogue No.10
Present owner not known

126b **Head**
1952
Oil on canvas 28¾″ × 26″
First exhibited Venice Biennale 1952
(British Council Catalogue No.65b)
Previous collection: Dr Jesi, Milan
Collection: Alfred Hecht, London

126c **Form on a Pedestal**
1952
Chalk and gouache 29½″ × 14¼″
Collection: Dr Andrew Revai, London

127 **Head III**
1953
Oil on canvas 45″ × 34¾″
First exhibited Tate Gallery
1953 Catalogue No.77 (size given incorrectly)
Collection: The Tate Gallery, London

128 **Variation on a Theme I**
1953
Oil on canvas 36″ × 27¾″
First exhibited Tate Gallery
1953 (Not in Catalogue)
Collection: Frankland Dark, London

129 **Poised Form**
1953
Oil on paper 41″ × 20¼″
First exhibited Curt Valentin Gallery, New York City
1953 Catalogue No.14
Collection: Andrew C. Ritchie, New Haven, Connecticut

130 **Study of a Cut Tree I**
1953
Ink and charcoal 78½″ × 30″
First exhibited Tate Gallery
1953 Catalogue No.74
Collection: Roloff Beny, New York City

131 **Study of a Cut Tree II**
1953
Ink and charcoal 78½″ × 30″
First exhibited Tate Gallery
1953 Catalogue No.75
Collection: Art Institute of Chicago, Chicago, Illinois

132 **La Petite Afrique**
1953
Oil on canvas 72″ × 36″
First exhibited Tate Gallery
1953 (Not in Catalogue)
Collection: James Bomford, Aldbourne, Wiltshire

133 **Swinging Form and Monkey**
1953
Ink, gouache and pastel 11⅝″ × 8⅜″
First exhibited The Arthur Jeffress Gallery, London
1959 Catalogue No.10
Collection: Richard Attenborough, London

134a **Study for 'Golden Form'**
1953
Pastel and gouache 11½″ × 8½″
Collection: Arthur Tooth and Sons, London

134b **Study for 'Golden Form'**
1953
Gouache 11¾″ × 8½″

134c **Machine Form**
1953
Gouache 11¾″ × 8½″

135 **Study**
1953
Lithographic chalk and ink 11½″ × 8½″
Collection: Le Roux S. Le Roux, London

136 **Hydrant**
1954
Oil on canvas 44″ × 36″
Collection: Mrs Paul Rankine, Bethesda, Maryland

137 **Swinging Form**
1954
Oil on canvas 30″ × 25″
Collection: Mrs Martha Jackson, New York City

138a **Thorn Cross and Sun**
1954
Ink and gouache 13″ × 20½″

138b **Thorn Cross**
1954
Oil on canvas 18½″ × 36½″
Collection: Victor Laufen, Düsseldorf

138c **Study for Thorn Cross**
1954
Oil, ink and chalk 13″ × 20½″

139 **Monkey**
1955
Oil on canvas 30″ × 25″
Collection: Mrs Doreen H. Thompson, Co. Durham

140 **Thorn Tree**
1954
Oil on canvas 53″ × 24″
Collection: Dr Andrew Revai, London

141 **La Petite Afrique III**
1955
Oil on canvas 56″ × 48″
Previous collection: Alfred Hecht, London
Collection: Wilfred Evill, London

142 **Thorn Form**
1955
Oil on canvas 44″ × 36¼″
First exhibited São Paulo Biennal 1955
(British Section Catalogue No.19)
Collection: São Paulo Museum, Brazil

143 **Study for Apple Tree**
1955
Oil on hardboard 13½″ × 9½″
Inscribed 'Study for Apple Tree/September 1955/GS'
Collection: Mr and Mrs John Montgomery, Esher, Surrey

144 **Apple Bough**
1955
Oil on canvas 21½″ × 18″
Collection: Arthur Jeffress, London

145a **Study for Apple Tree**
1955
Oil on canvas 11″ × 16¼″
Collection: David Gibbs, London

145b **Still Life with Apples**
1955
Oil on hardboard 6¾″ × 14½″
Collection: Alastair Roger, London

146 **Cypress Cones**
1956
Oil on canvas 40″ × 30″
Collection: Mr and Mrs I. Bloomfield, London

147 **Palm Tree**
1957
Oil on canvas 25¾″ × 21¼″
First exhibited 'Five English Painters', The Arthur Jeffress Gallery,
London, 1957 Catalogue No.21
Collection: D. L. Breeden, London

148 **Still Life with Apples and Scales**
1957
Oil on canvas 25¾″ × 21¼″
First exhibited 'Five English Painters', The Arthur Jeffress Gallery,
London, 1957 Catalogue No.22
Collection: G. W. Rickinson, London

149 **Hanging Form over Water**
1957
Oil on canvas 39½″ × 31½″
Collection: Mrs William H. Brown, Media, Pennsylvania

150 **Thorn Cross in Oval**
1959
Oil on canvas 25½″ × 21½″
First exhibited Paul Rosenberg & Co., New York
1959 Catalogue No.22
Collection: Paul Rosenberg & Co., New York

151a **The Lamp**
1958
Oil on canvas 29″ × 24″
First exhibited Paul Rosenberg & Co., New York,
1959 Catalogue No.10
Collection: Paul Rosenberg & Co., New York

151b **Attached Form, Root**
1959
Oil on canvas 25½″ × 21½″
First exhibited Paul Rosenberg & Co., New York
1959 Catalogue No.21
Collection: Paul Rosenberg & Co., New York

152a **The Tank**
1959
Oil on canvas 39″ × 31¾″
First exhibited Paul Rosenberg & Co., New York
1959 Catalogue No.17
Collection: Paul Rosenberg & Co., New York

152b **The Oracle**
1959
Oil on canvas 39″ × 31¾″
First exhibited Paul Rosenberg & Co., New York
1959 Catalogue No.18
Collection: Paul Rosenberg & Co., New York

153 **Dark Entrance**
1959
Oil on canvas 52″ × 38¼″
First exhibited Paul Rosenberg & Co., New York
1959 Catalogue No.14
Collection: Phillips Memorial Gallery, Washington, D.C.

154 **The Scales**
1959
Oil on canvas 50″ × 40″
First exhibited Paul Rosenberg & Co., New York
1959 Catalogue No.15
Collection: Sir Kenneth Clark, Saltwood, Kent

155 **Path in Wood II**
1958
Oil on canvas 24″ × 20″
First exhibited Paul Rosenberg & Co., New York
1959 Catalogue No.8
Collection: Paul Rosenberg & Co., New York

156 **Hanging Form**
1959
Oil on canvas 65¾″ × 56″
First exhibited 'Documenta II', Kassel, 1959, No.3
Collection: Kunstmuseum, Basel, Switzerland
(Emanuel Hoffmann Foundation)

157 **Chevaux de Frise**
1959
Oil on canvas 51″ × 38″
First exhibited Paul Rosenberg & Co., New York
1959 Catalogue No.13
Collection: Paul Rosenberg & Co., New York

158 **Cartoon for the Coventry Tapestry 'Christ in Glory'**
1957
Oil on hardboard 74″ × 40″
Collection: The Provost and Chapter of Coventry Cathedral
This design has been subsequently modified in several respects

# List of Illustrations appearing in the Text

# Colour Plates

I **Road and Hills in Setting Sun**
1938
Oil on canvas 24″ × 20″
First exhibited Rosenberg & Helft, London
1938 Catalogue No.6
Previous collection: James Bomford
Collection: Frankland Dark, Crawleydown Park, Sussex

II **Gorse on Sea Wall**
1939
Oil on canvas 24½″ × 19″
First exhibited Leicester Galleries, London
May 1940 Catalogue No.8
Previous collection: Peter Watson
Collection: Norman Fowler, U.S.A.

III **Mountain Road with Boulder**
1940
Oil on canvas 24½″ × 44″
Collection: Kerrison Preston, Merstham, Surrey

IV **Studies for Interlocking Hills**
1943
Chalk and gouache 8″ × 6″
Inscribed 'Idea for Interlocking Hills/1943'

V **Landscape with Estuary**
1945
Chalk and gouache 9¾″ × 15″
Collection: Captain D. de Pass, R.N., Den Mead, Hampshire

VI **Tree Form in Estuary**
1945
Oil and gouache on paper 9½″ × 10½″
Collection: Galleria Galatea, Turin

VII **Christ Carrying the Cross**
1953
Oil on canvas 71½″ × 55¾″
Inscribed bottom left: Preparatory sketch for composition "Christ carrying the Cross"
First exhibited International Exposition, São Paulo, Brazil, 1955
Collection: Myron Ybarra O'Higgins, New York City

VIII **Standing Form Against Hedge**
1950
Oil on canvas 52⅛″ × 45⅝″
First exhibited Hanover Gallery, London 1951 Catalogue No.6
Collection: The Arts Council of Great Britain, London

IX **Variation on a Theme II**
1953
Oil on canvas 35½″ × 27½″
First exhibited Tate Gallery 1953
(Not in catalogue)
Collection: Mrs Elliott Jaques, London

X **Golden Form against Black Background**
1954
Oil on canvas 52¼″ × 23¾″
Collection: Arthur Tooth & Sons, London

XI **Thorn Cross**
1954
Oil on canvas 44½″ × 37½″
Previous collection: Le Roux S. Le Roux, London
Collection: Galerie des 20 Jahrhunderts, Berlin

XII **Monkey**
1953
Chalk and gouache 11½″ × 8½″
Private collection, London

XIII **Hanging Form over Water**
1955
Oil on canvas 43″ × 34″
First exhibited 'Critic's Choice 1955' (Eric Newton)
Arthur Tooth & Sons, London, Catalogue No.4
Collection: Mrs Audrey Bevan, London

XIV **Toad II**
1958–59
Oil on canvas 50¾″ × 38¼″
First exhibited Paul Rosenberg & Co., New York, 1959, Catalogue No.3
Collection: Marlborough Fine Art Ltd and The Arthur Jeffress Gallery

XV **Portrait of Max Egon, Prince Fürstenberg**
1958–59
Oil on canvas 65″ × 55″
Collection: Fürstenbergsche Gemäldesammlung, Donaueschingen

# Plates

Up to Plate 160, the illustrations are arranged, with few exceptions, in chronological sequence. The group of 'Figures and Portraits' which follows has been deliberately separated from the rest but is also arranged chronologically.

2a **Barn Interior** 1922 Drypoint 6 × 8 in.

2b **Mill Interior** 1923 Pen and wash $5\frac{1}{8} \times 6\frac{1}{2}$ in.

3a **Pecken Wood** 1925 Etching 5½ × 7½ in.

3b **Cray Fields** 1925 Etching 4¾ × 5 in.

3c **St Mary Hatch** 1926 Etching 4¾ × 7¼ in.

3d **Lammas** 1926 Etching 4¼ × 6¼ in.

4a **Welsh Landscape** 1936 Etching and aquatint $7\frac{1}{2} \times 5\frac{3}{4}$ in.

4b **Pastoral** 1930 Etching $5 \times 7\frac{1}{2}$ in.

5a **Sand Hills, Dorset** 1932–3 Water-colour 7⅞ × 12¼ in.

5b **Men-an-Tol** 1931 Pen and water-colour 18¼ × 26¾ in.

5c **Landscape, Sketch of Hills** 1932 Water-colour 4 × 7 in.

5d **Tree Form, Dorset** 1933–4
Pen and sepia touched with white 7⅞ × 12¾ in.

5e **Lobster Claw** 1935 Gouache 8 × 12¾ in.

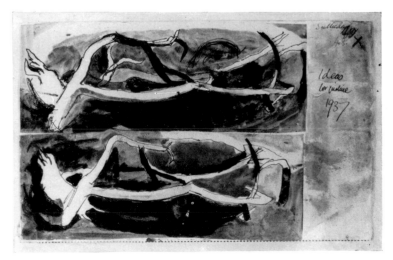

5f **Ideas for a Fallen Tree, Purbeck** probably 1935–6
Pen and wash 5½ × 9 in.

6a  **Solva and Valley above Porthclais**  1935  Pen and wash  $5\frac{1}{2} \times 8\frac{1}{4}$ in.

6b  **Camomile Flowers in Landscape**  1935  Gouache  $12\frac{3}{4} \times 8\frac{3}{4}$ in.

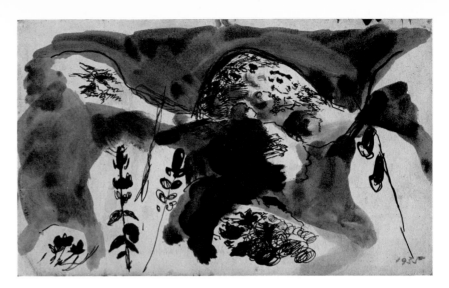

7a **Hills at Solva** 1935 Pen and wash $5\frac{3}{8} \times 9$ in.

7b **Pembrokeshire Landscape** 1936 Gouache $14 \times 21\frac{1}{2}$ in.

7c **Pembrokeshire Landscape** 1937 Pencil and water-colour $5\frac{1}{8} \times 8\frac{1}{2}$ in.

8a **Welsh Landscape** 1936
Gouache and water-colour approx. 13 × 22 in.

8b **Road with Rocks** 1936 Pen and wash 13½ × 22 in.

8c **Landscape with Turning Roads** 1936
Gouache and water-colour 17¼ × 25½ in.

8d **Rock in Estuary** 1936 Pen and wash 5 × 8¼ in.

8e **Rocky Landscape with Gateway** 1936
Gouache and water-colour 12⅞ × 19¾ in.

8f **Welsh Landscape with Roads** 1936 Oil on canvas 22 × 15 in.

I   **Road and Hills in Setting Sun**   1938 Oil on canvas 24 × 20 in.

9a **Welsh Landscape with Roads** 1936 Oil on canvas 26 × 36 in.

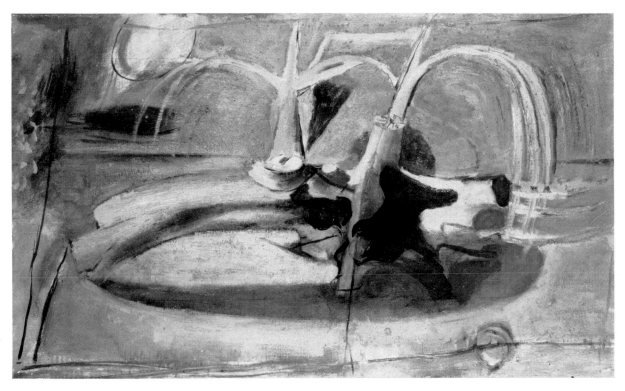

9b **Red Tree** 1936 Oil on canvas 22 × 36 in.

10a **Landscape, Green, Pink and Brown** 1937 Gouache and pastel 13 × 20 in.

10b **Welsh Mountains** 1937 Oil on canvas 22 × 36 in.

10c **Black Landscape** 1937 Water-colour 18¼ × 31½ in.

11a **Study of Rocks** 1937 Ink and water-colour $4\frac{1}{2} \times 3\frac{1}{4}$ in.

11b **Study for 'Blasted Tree'** 1937
Pen and water-colour $4\frac{1}{2} \times 3\frac{3}{8}$ in.

11c **Study for 'Blasted Tree'** 1937
Pen and water-colour $7\frac{1}{2} \times 5$ in.

11d **Blasted Tree** 1938 Water-colour $22\frac{3}{8} \times 15\frac{3}{4}$ in.

12a **Study for 'Tree Trunk Sprawling'** 1937
Pen and water-colour 8 × 6 in.

12b **Studies for 'Red Monolith'** 1937
Pen and water-colour 8 × 6 in.

12c **Damp Tree Roots** 1938 Water-colour 18¼ × 31½ in.

13    **Red Monolith**   1938  Oil on canvas  $39\frac{1}{4} \times 24\frac{1}{4}$ in.

14a **Sun Setting between Hills**  1938  Water-colour  $9\frac{7}{8} \times 14$ in.

14b **Rocky Landscape with Cairn**  1940  Gouache  $20 \times 33$ in.

14c **Dark Hill with Hedges and Fields**  1940  Pen and wash  $19 \times 27\frac{1}{2}$ in.

15a  **Steep Road**  1938  Gouache  11½ × 9 in.

15b  **Landscape with Rocks (Wolf's Castle)**  1939  Water-colour  19½ × 26⅜ in.

16a **Study for 'Entrance to Lane'** 10 July 1939
Pen and water-colour $5\frac{5}{16} \times 4\frac{5}{8}$ in.

16b **Study for 'Entrance to Lane'** 10 July 1939
Pen and water-colour $5\frac{5}{16} \times 4\frac{5}{8}$ in.

16c **Study for 'Entrance to Lane'** 11 July 1939
Pen and water-colour $5\frac{5}{16} \times 4\frac{5}{8}$ in.

16d **Study for 'Entrance to Lane'** July 1939
Pen and gouache $7\frac{1}{8} \times 5\frac{3}{8}$ in.

17    **Entrance to Lane**   1939  Oil on canvas   $19\frac{1}{2} \times 23\frac{1}{2}$ in.

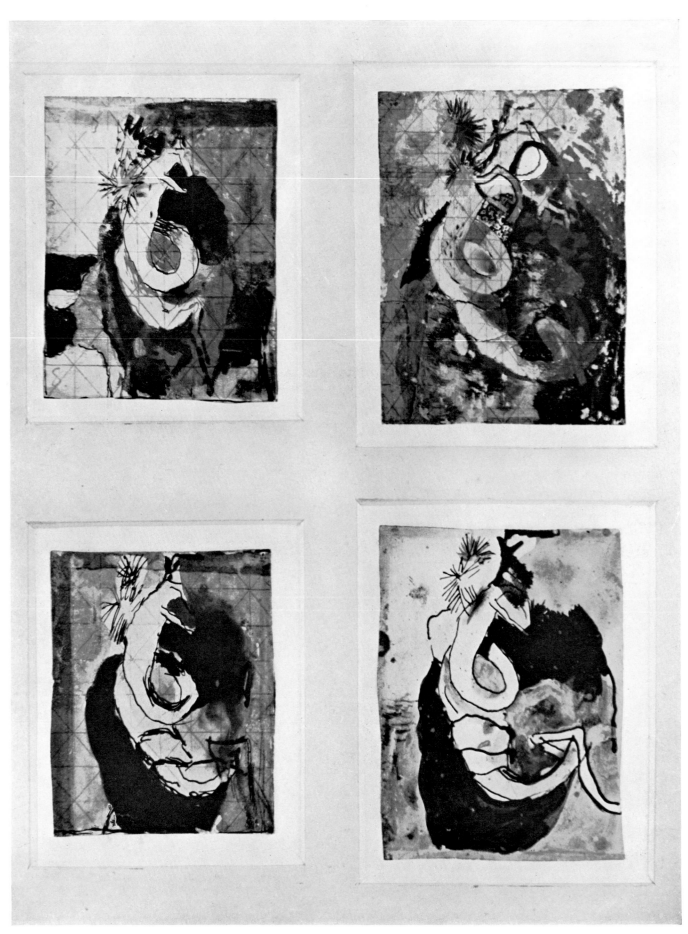

18   **Four Studies for 'Gorse on Sea Wall'**   1938–9
Pen and water-colour
top left, 2¾ × 2⅛ in.; top right, 3⅛ × 2¼ in.; bottom left, 2⅝ × 2⅛ in.; bottom right, 3⅛ × 2¼ in.

19a **Road Mounting between Hedges: Sunrise** 1940
Water-colour 27 × 19 in.

19b **Hollow Tree Trunk** 1938 Water-colour 22⅜ × 15⅜ in.

20   **Four Studies of Rocks**   1939–40
Pen and wash touched with pink   $8\frac{1}{4} \times 5\frac{1}{8}$ in.

II    **Gorse on Sea Wall**    1939 Oil on canvas $24\frac{1}{2} \times 19$ in.

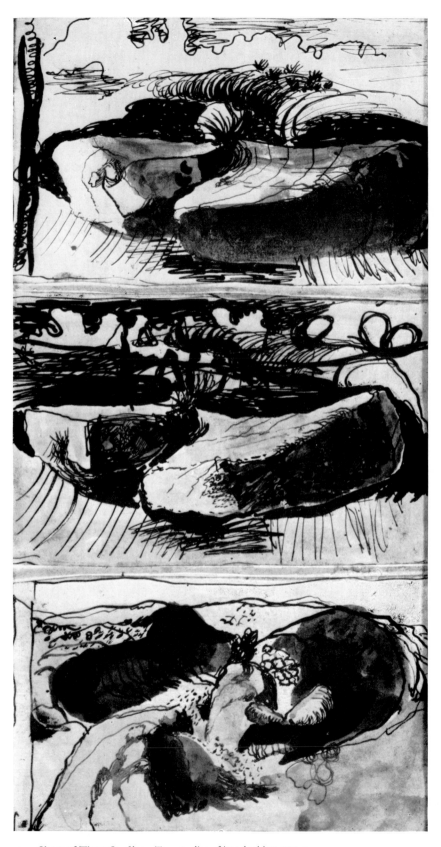

21  **Sheet of Three Studies**  Two studies of interlocking stones
in landscape, 1939; landscape study, 1937
Pen and water-colour  $7\frac{3}{8} \times 3\frac{7}{8}$ in.

22 **Green Tree Form: Interior of Woods** 1939
Pen and water-colour 27 × 19 in.

23a **Study for 'Green Tree Form'** 1939
Pen and water-colour 4⅜ × 3⅜ in.

23b **Study for 'Green Tree Form'** 1939
Pen and water-colour 4⅜ × 3⅜ in.

23c **Green Tree Form: Interior of Woods** 1940 Oil on canvas 30 × 41⅛ in.

24   **Sheet of Four Studies**   1939  Pen and water-colour  8 × 6 in.

25   **Association of Oaks**   1940 Gouache 27 × 19 in.

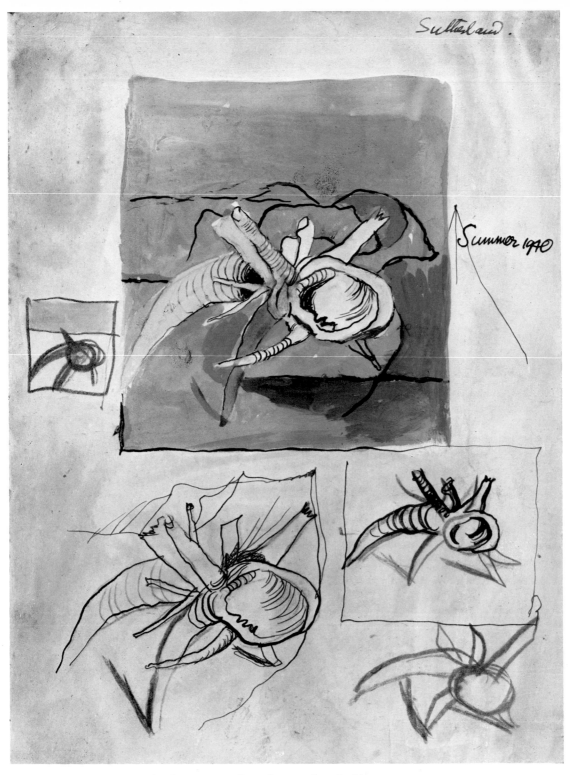

26   **Studies for Midsummer Landscape**   1940  Pen and water-colour  8 × 6 in.

27 **Midsummer Landscape** 1940 Gouache 26¾ × 18½ in.

28a **Welsh Mountain Top** 1939 Pen and water-colour 3 × 5⅜ in.

28b **Study for 'Red Landscape'** 1941–2
Water-colour 3¾ × 5 in.

28c **Fallen Tree** 1940 Water-colour 5⅜ × 8 in.

III    **Mountain Road with Boulder**    1940 Oil on canvas $24\frac{1}{2} \times 44$ in.

29  **Cliff Road**  1941  Oil on canvas  $46\frac{1}{2} \times 34$ in.

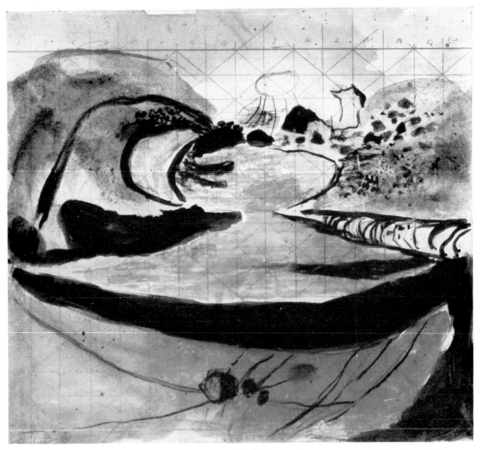

30a  **Design for 'The Wanderer' Act I**   1940  Gouache  8 × 10 in.

30b  **Design for 'The Wanderer' Act II**   1940  Gouache  8 × 9 in.

31   **Tree Form in an Estuary**   1940  Pen and water-colour  19 × 27 in.

32a   **Tree Form**   1941 Oil on canvas 15½ × 12 in.           32b   **Study for 'Tree Form'**   1940 Pen and wash 9 × 7 in.

33  **Blasted Oak**  1941  Pen and wash  15 × 12 in.

34a  **Study of Boulders**  1942  Pen and wash  $4\frac{3}{4} \times 7\frac{3}{4}$ in.

34b  **Gower Landscape**  1941  Indian ink, coloured chalk and water-colour  $14\frac{1}{2} \times 18$ in.

35  **Study of Boulders**  1942  Pen, chalk and wash  $7\frac{3}{4} \times 6\frac{1}{4}$ in.

36a  **Devastation – City – Burnt-out Interior**  1941
Pen, chalk and wash  $21\frac{1}{2} \times 31\frac{1}{2}$ in.

36b  **Devastation – House in Wales**  6 September 1940
Pen and water-colour  $6\frac{3}{4} \times 5\frac{1}{2}$ in.

37   **Devastation – City – Twisted Girders**   1941
Pen, pencil, chalk and wash   7 × 5¼ in.

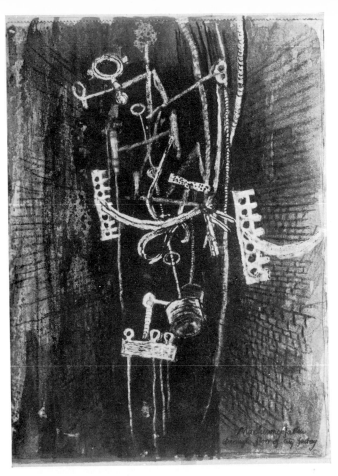

**38a** **Devastation – City – Ruined Machinery** 1941
Pen, chalk and wash 8¾ × 6½ in.

**38b** **Devastation – City – Ruined Machinery** 1941
Pen, chalk and wash 8¼ × 5¾ in.

39a **Devastation – City – Fallen Lift Shaft** 1941
Pen and gouache 5½ × 4¾ in.

39b **Devastation – City – Fallen Lift Shaft** 1941
Pen, chalk and gouache 9 × 6¼ in.

39c **Devastation – City – Fallen Lift Shaft** 1941 Chalk and gouache 12⅞ × 18¼ in.

40a **Devastation – East End – Burnt-out Paper Rolls** 1941
Pen, chalk and wash $12\frac{7}{8} \times 18\frac{1}{4}$ in.

40b **Devastation – East End – Burnt-out Paper Rolls** 1941
Pen, chalk and wash approx. $6 \times 9$ in.

41a **Devastation – East End Houses** 1941 Pen, chalk and gouache $25\frac{1}{4} \times 44\frac{3}{4}$ in.

41b **Study – An East End Street** 1941 Pen, chalk and wash $5 \times 10$ in.

41c **Study for 'Devastation – East End Street'** 1941
Pen, chalk and wash $4 \times 7\frac{1}{2}$ in.

41d **Study – An East End Street** 1941
Pen, chalk and wash $4 \times 7\frac{1}{2}$ in.

41e **Collapsed Roofs – London Suburbs** 1941
Pen, chalk and wash $4\frac{1}{2} \times 7$ in.

41f **East End Public House** 1941 Pen, chalk and wash $5\frac{1}{4} \times 9\frac{5}{8}$ in.

42a **Devastation – Chancery Chambers, Swansea**
1941 Gouache 4 × 3⅛ in.

42b **Devastation – Chancery Chambers, Swansea**
1941 Gouache 6¾ × 4 in.

43a **Moulds: Iron Foundry** 1942
Pen, chalk and wash 3¾ × 3¼ in.

43b **Moulds: Iron Foundry** 1942
Pen, chalk and wash 5¼ × 4¾ in.

43c **Moulds: Iron Foundry** 1942
Pen, chalk and wash 6⅝ × 8⅛ in.

43d **Moulds: Iron Foundry** 1942
Pen, chalk and wash 7⅛ × 8 in.

43e **Moulds: Iron Foundry** 1942
Pen, chalk and wash 6⅝ × 7⅞ in.

43f **Manufacturing Bombs** 1942
Oil on hardboard 36 × 43 in.

44a **Man Looking into Furnace** 1942
Pen, chalk and wash 10 × 11¼ in.

44b **Steel Workers** 1942 Pen, chalk and gouache 4¾ × 4½ in.

44c **Small Furnaces, Woolwich** 1942
Pen, chalk and wash 19½ × 15½ in.

44d **Hydraulic Press, Woolwich** 1944
Pen, chalk and wash 29⅜ × 17½ in.

45 **Tapping a Steel Furnace** 1942 Pen, chalk and water-colour 11 × 48 in.

46a **Tin Mine – A Declivity** 1942 Pen, gouache and water-colour $37\frac{1}{2} \times 19\frac{1}{2}$ in.

46b **Sheet of Tin Mine Studies** 1942
Pen, chalk and wash $7\frac{3}{4} \times 5\frac{7}{8}$ in.

46c **Tin Mine – Miner Approaching** 1942
Ink, chalk and wash $46\frac{1}{4} \times 29\frac{3}{8}$ in.

47a **Limestone Quarry – Loosening Stone** 1943
Pen, chalk and water-colour $25\frac{1}{2} \times 22\frac{1}{2}$ in.

47b **Outcast Coal Production – Dragline Depositing Excavated Earth** 1943 Pen, chalk and water-colour $27\frac{1}{4} \times 26$ in.

47c **Outcast Coal Production – Excavators Uncovering Coal Seam** 1943 Pen, chalk and water-colour $17\frac{1}{2} \times 34$ in.

**48a   Flying Bomb Site, St Leu d'Esserent**   1944
Chalk and wash  9½ × 7¾ in.

**48b   Trappes – Study for 'Wrecked Locomotive'**   1944
Pen, chalk and wash  approx. 10 × 7 in.

**48c   Trappes – Study for 'Wrecked Locomotive'**   1944
Chalk and wash  16⅜ × 13⅜ in.

**48d   Trappes – Wrecked Locomotive**   1944
Oil on hardboard  50½ × 41¼ in.

49   **Trappes – Wrecked Locomotive**   1944  Pen, chalk and wash approx. 12 × 8 in.

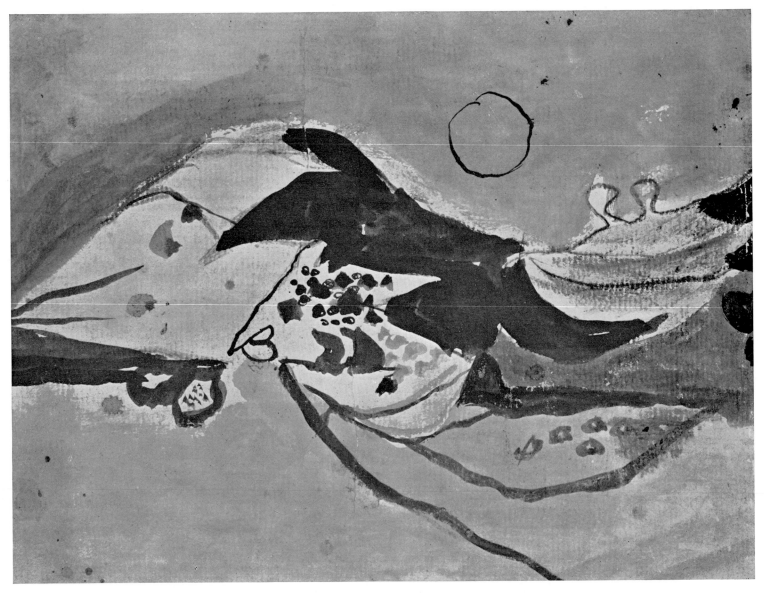

50a **Pembrokeshire Landscape** 1944 Gouache 9×11 in.

50b **Carn Llydi, Wales** 1944 Gouache 6¼×9¼ in.

50c **Mountain in Wales** 1944 Pen, pencil, chalk and water-colour 3⅞×6 in.

51 **Landscape with Mounds** 1943 Pen and wash 9×7 in.

52a **Folded Hills** 1943 Oil on canvas 20 × 27 in.

52b **Landscape with Pointed Rocks** 1944
Chalk and gouache 16 × 22 in.

52c **Landscape with Pointed Rocks** 1944
Chalk and gouache 16 × 22 in.

52d **Landscape with Pointed Rocks** 1944 Gouache 16¼ × 21¼ in.

52e **Landscape with Pointed Rocks** 1944
Chalk and water-colour 10 × 14 in.

52f **Landscape with Pointed Rocks** 1944
Chalk and gouache 4¼ × 5⅜ in.

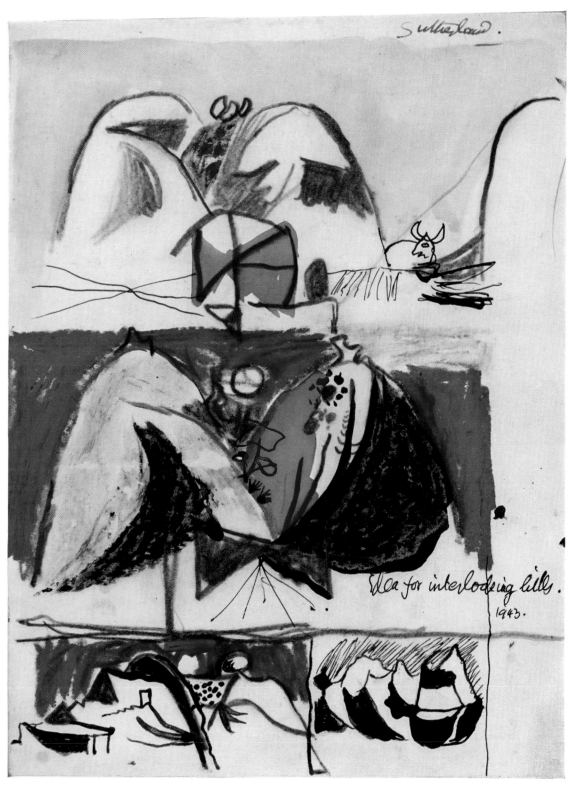

IV    **Studies for Interlocking Hills**    1943 Chalk and gouache 8 × 6 in.

53a **Landscape with Pointed Hills**  1944
Oil on hardboard  17 × 14⅛ in.

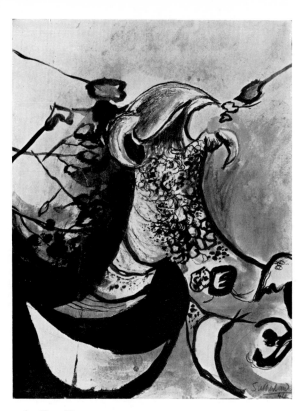

53b **Root Form**  1944
Pen, chalk and water-colour  18¾ × 15½ in.

53c **Landscape with Pointed Rocks**  1945
Oil on canvas approx. 32 × 22 in.

53d **Horned Tree Form**  1944
Pen, chalk and gouache  approx. 24 × 20 in.

54a **Study of Lane Opening**   1945
Pen, chalk and gouache $6 \times 4\frac{1}{4}$ in.

54b **Study of Burning Coal**   1954 Water-colour $7\frac{1}{4} \times 6$ in.

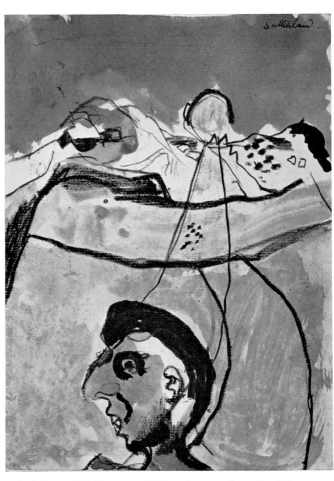

54c **Triple-tiered Landscape**   1944
Gouache and chalk   $29 \times 21\frac{1}{2}$ in.

54d **Man and Fields**   1944 Chalk and water-colour $8\frac{7}{8} \times 6\frac{3}{4}$ in.

55　**Triple-tiered Landscape**　1944 Pen, chalk and water-colour 22 × 16 in.

56a **Thistles and Sun** 1945 Chalk and gouache 17¾ × 15⅞ in.

56b **Red Thistles** 1945 Chalk and gouache 24¾ × 21 in.

56c **Fire Basket** 1944 Pen, chalk and gouache 18½ × 16 in.

56d **Association of Thistles** 1945 Oil on hardboard 22 × 21 in.

57   **Thistles**   1945   Oil on canvas   $24\frac{1}{2} \times 28\frac{1}{2}$ in.

58a **Study for 'Horned Forms'** 1944
Pen, chalk and gouache $3\frac{1}{8} \times 4\frac{5}{8}$ in.

58b **Study for 'Horned Forms'** 1944
Pen, chalk and gouache $4\frac{1}{4} \times 4\frac{1}{2}$ in.

58c **Study for 'Horned Forms'** 1944 Chalk and gouache $5\frac{1}{4} \times 5\frac{1}{4}$ in.

58d **Study for 'Horned Forms'** 1944 Chalk and gouache $5 \times 5$ in.

59   **Horned Forms**   1944 Oil on canvas 26 × 20 in.

60a **Study of Road between Hills** 1944 Water-colour $8\frac{1}{4} \times 7\frac{3}{4}$ in.

60b **Cairn** 1944 Pen, chalk and gouache $15\frac{3}{4} \times 16$ in.

60c **Study of Leaf** 1943 Pencil, ink and gouache $10\frac{3}{4} \times 8$ in.

60d **Study of Foliage** 1944 Chalk and gouache $27 \times 22$ in.

V   **Landscape with Estuary**   1945 Chalk and gouache $9\frac{3}{4} \times 15$ in.

61a **Smiling Woman** 1945 Oil on canvas 33 × 28½ in.

61b **Woman Picking Vegetables** 1945 Oil on hardboard 24 × 20 in.

61c **The Lamp** 1944 Oil on hardboard 30 × 25 in.

61d **The Lamp** 1945 Oil on canvas 24 × 25 in.

62a **Corn and Stone** 1945 Chalk and gouache 21 × 20½ in.

62b **Study of Corn** 1945 Ink, chalk and gouache 10 × 9¼ in.

62c **Interlocking Tree Forms** 1945
Pen, chalk and gouache 21 × 21 in.

62d **Tree Form** 1945 Pen, chalk and gouache 22 × 21 in.

63a **Woman in a Garden** 1945 Pen, chalk and gouache 24 × 17 in.

63b **Still Life with Apples** 1944 Gouache and chalk 6¼ × 8 in.

64a **Sun over Cornfield** 1946
Pen, chalk and gouache 16½ × 10⅞ in.

64b **Sun over Cornfield** 1945
Pen, chalk and gouache 27 × 16 in.

64c **Landscape** 1947 Oil on canvas 12 × 19⅝ in.

65   **Landscape with Fields**   1945  Pen, chalk and gouache  $27\frac{5}{8} \times 10\frac{3}{4}$ in.

66a **Woods and Estuary** 1945 Pen, chalk and gouache $16\frac{7}{8} \times 16\frac{3}{4}$ in.

66b **Estuary with Rocks** 1946 Gouache $8\frac{1}{2} \times 11$ in.

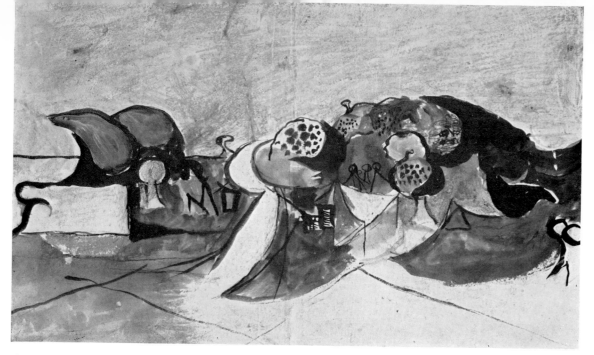

67a **Landscape with Estuary** 1945 Pen, chalk and gouache $16\frac{1}{4} \times 26\frac{3}{4}$ in.

67b **Landscape with Estuary** 1945 Pen, chalk and water-colour $15\frac{1}{2} \times 29$ in.

67c **Estuary Foreshore** 1946 Pen, chalk and gouache $14\frac{3}{4} \times 29\frac{1}{4}$ in.

68a  **Green Lane**  1945 Oil on canvas  $24\frac{1}{2} \times 19\frac{3}{4}$ in.

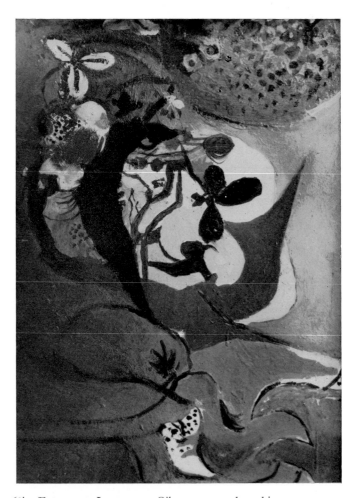

68b  **Entrance to Lane**  1945 Oil on canvas  $21\frac{1}{2} \times 15\frac{1}{2}$ in.

68c  **Entrance to Lane with Interlacing Foliage**  1945
Pen, chalk and gouache  $21\frac{1}{2} \times 21\frac{1}{4}$ in.

68d  **Entrance to Lane**  1945 Pen, chalk and gouache  $21\frac{1}{2} \times 21\frac{1}{4}$ in.

VI    **Tree Form in Estuary**    1945 Oil and gouache on paper $9\frac{1}{2} \times 10\frac{1}{2}$ in.

69a **Staring Tree Form** 1945 Chalk and gouache 18⅝ × 16 in.

69b **Study for 'Staring Tree Form'**
Pen and water-colour approx. 4 × 5 in.

69c **Study for 'Staring Tree Form'**
Chalk and water-colour on tracing paper approx. 4 × 7 in.

70    **Chimère I**   1946  Oil on canvas  $78\frac{1}{2} \times 47\frac{1}{2}$ in.

71    **Chimère II**   1946–7 Oil on canvas 70 × 36 in.

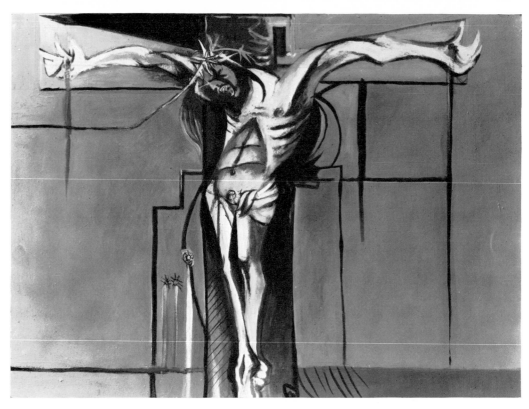

**72a  Study for the Northampton 'Crucifixion'**  1946
Oil on hardboard  $35\frac{3}{4} \times 48$ in.

**72a  Study for the Northampton 'Crucifixion'**  1946
Oil on hardboard  $40 \times 48$ in.

73  **Deposition**  1946 Oil on hardboard  47 × 36⅞ in.

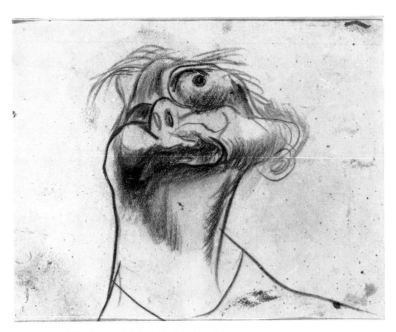

74a   **Stone Head**   1946 Black chalk   $4\frac{1}{2} \times 5\frac{3}{4}$ in.

74b   Detail of plate 75

75  **Crucifixion, St Matthew's Church, Northampton**  1946  Oil on hardboard  96 × 90 in.

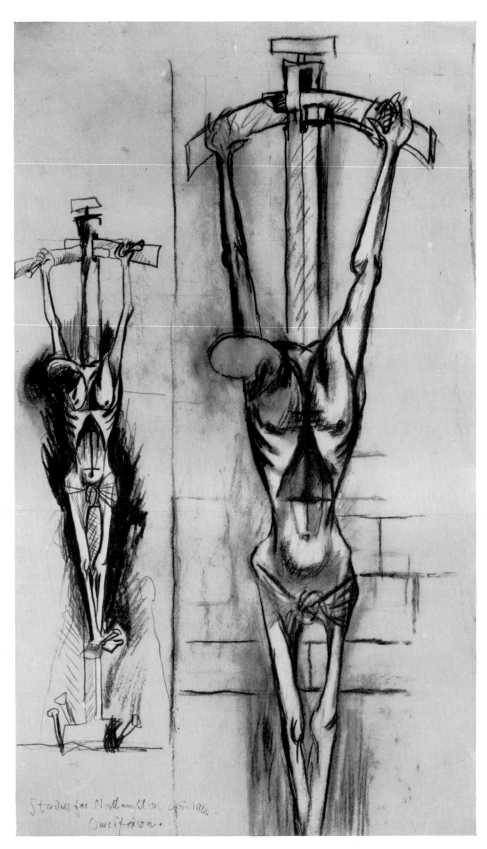

Studies for Northampton 45. 1946.
Crucifixion.

76   **Two Studies for a Crucifixion**  1946  Black chalk  26 × 16 in.

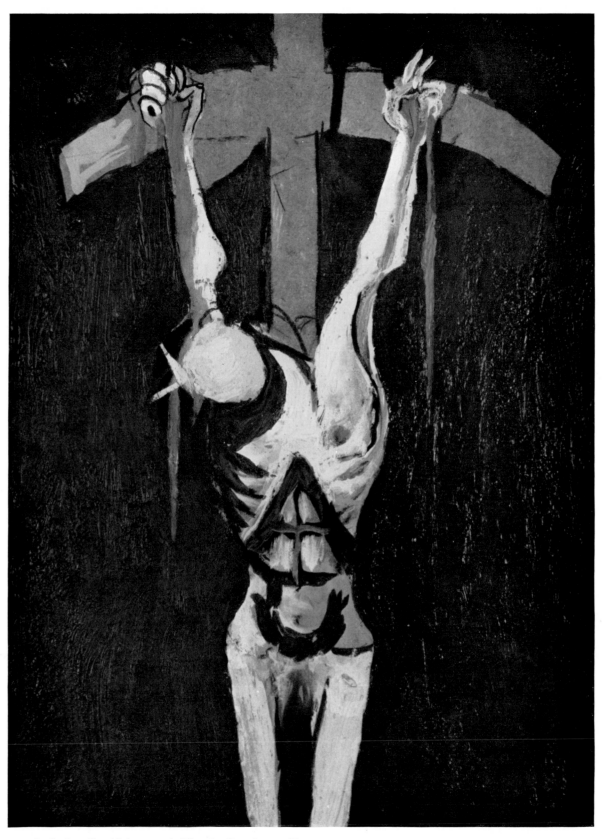

77  **Study for a Crucifixion**  1946  Oil on hardboard  13 × 9¾ in.

78a  **Thorns**  1945  Pen and water-colour  $16\frac{1}{4} \times 12\frac{1}{2}$ in.

78b  **Thorn Trees**  1945  Pen and gouache on tracing paper  $8\frac{3}{4} \times 7$ in.

79   **Thorn Trees**   1945  Oil on hardboard  $42\frac{3}{4} \times 40$ in.

80   **Thorn Tree**   1945 Oil on canvas 26 × 20 in.

81   **Thorn Trees**   1946 Oil on canvas  50×40 in,

82  **Thorns**  1945  Pen, chalk and gouache  $29\frac{1}{2} \times 16\frac{1}{2}$ in.

83a **Thorn Head** 1945 Oil on canvas 24 × 24¼ in.

83b **Thorn Head** 1946 Pen, chalk and gouache 22 × 21 in.

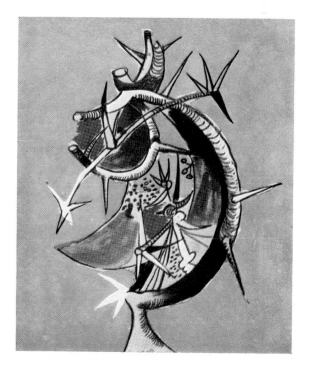

83c **Thorn Head** 1946 Oil on canvas 43¾ × 30½ in.

83d **Thorn Head** 1946 Ink and gouache 16 × 10 in.

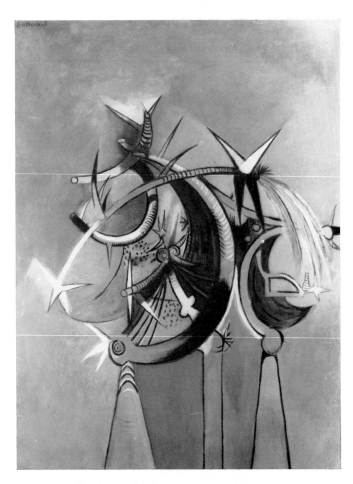

84a   **Thorn Heads**   1946  Oil on canvas  47 × 36 in.

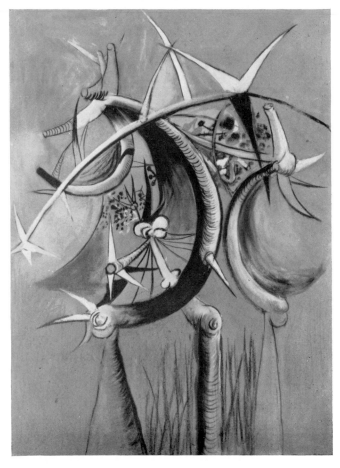

84b   **Thorn Heads**   1946  Pastel and gouache  27 × 20 in.

85a  **Thorn and Wall**  1946  Oil on canvas  16 × 20 in.

85b  **Thorn Trees**  1947  Oil on canvas  $34\frac{1}{2} \times 35\frac{3}{4}$ in.

86a **The Intruding Bull** 1944 Oil on hardboard 30 × 25½ in.

86b **Tethered Cow** 1944 Gouache 20½ × 16 in.

87    **Tree Form**    1946  Oil on canvas  $22\frac{3}{4} \times 21\frac{1}{4}$ in.

88a **Study of Vine Pergola** 1947
Pencil, ink and water-colour $4\frac{3}{4} \times 9\frac{7}{8}$ in.

88b **Study of Vine Pergola** 1947
Pencil, ink and water-colour $4\frac{1}{2} \times 9$ in.

88c **Study of Vine Pergola** 1947
Pen, chalk and water-colour $4\frac{1}{2} \times 9$ in.

88d **Vine Pergola with Figure** 1947 Oil on paper $4\frac{1}{2} \times 9$ in.

88e **Large Vine Pergola** 1948 Oil on canvas $37\frac{3}{8} \times 68\frac{1}{4}$ in.

88f **Figure and Vine Structure** 1948 Oil on canvas $11 \times 20$ in.

89a **Blue Vine** 1948 Oil on hardboard 22½ × 33 in.

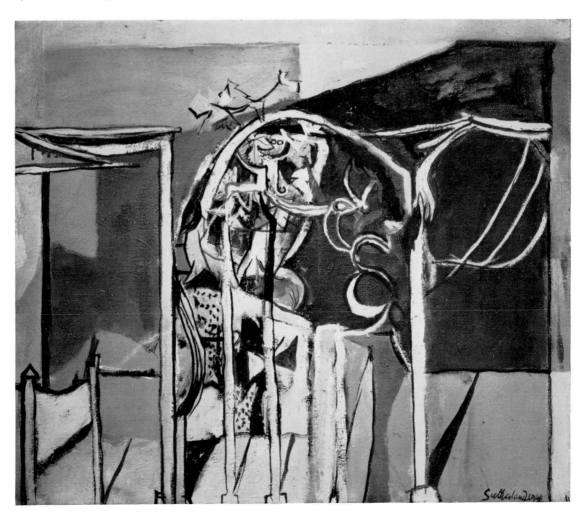

89b **Figure and Vine** 1947 Oil on canvas 21¼ × 25½ in.

90a   **Green Vine Pergola**   1948  Oil on canvas  22 × 18½ in.

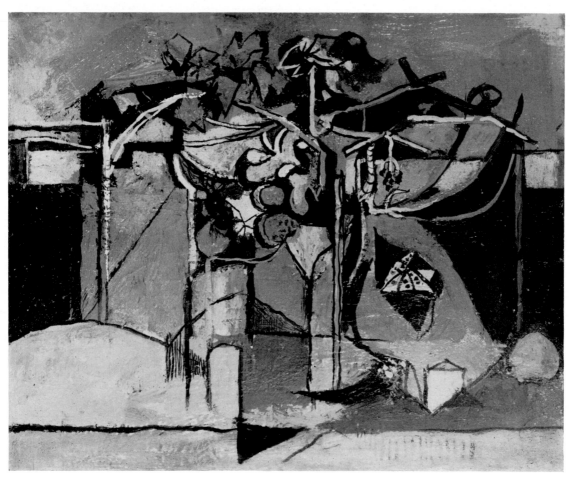

90b   **Vine Pergola**   1947  Oil on canvas  13 × 16 in.

91 **Large Vine Pergola** 1948 Oil on canvas 52½ × 33 in.

92a **Palm Palisade**  1947
Chalk and gouache  12½ × 9¾ in.

92b **Landscape with Palm**  1947  Water-colour  9 × 11¼ in.

92c **Palm and Landscape**  1948  Chalk and gouache  15¼ × 19½ in.

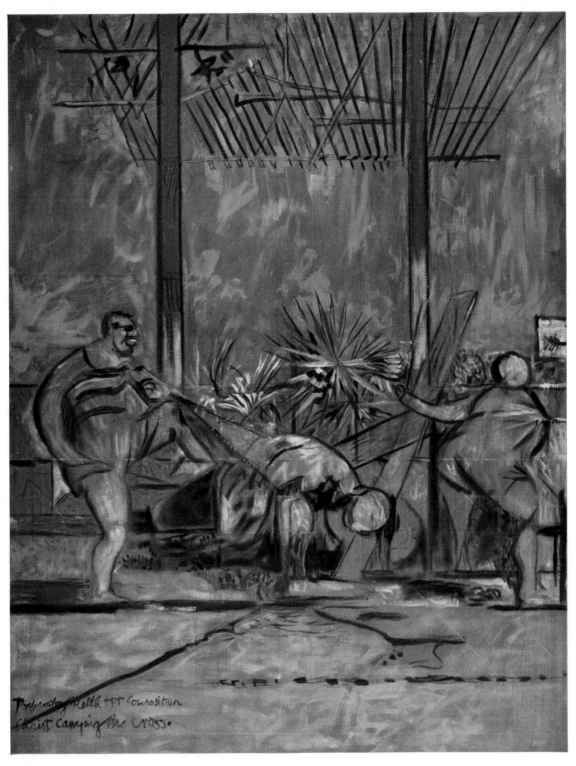

VII    **Christ Carrying the Cross**    1953 Oil on canvas $71\frac{1}{2} \times 55\frac{3}{4}$ in.

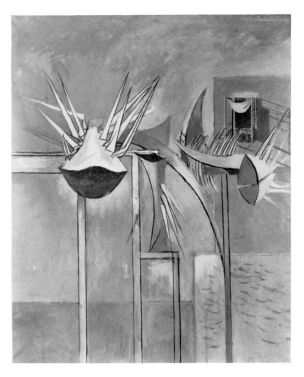

93a  **Palm and House**  1947  Oil on canvas  $43\frac{3}{4} \times 36\frac{1}{2}$ in.

93b  **Palm Palisade**  1948  Oil on canvas  $43\frac{1}{2} \times 36\frac{1}{2}$ in.

93c  **Palm Palisade**  1947  Oil on canvas  $43\frac{1}{2} \times 36\frac{1}{2}$ in.

93d  **Palm Palisade**  1947  Oil on canvas  $19\frac{1}{2} \times 15\frac{1}{2}$ in.

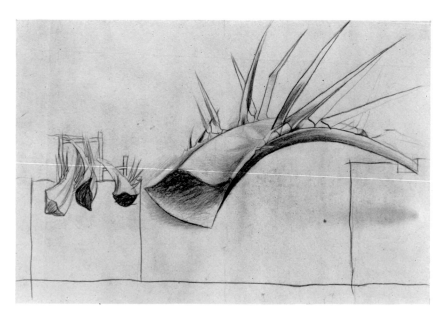

94a  **Study for 'Palm and Wall'**  1948  Black chalk  $14 \times 21\frac{3}{4}$ in.

94b  **Palm and Wall**  1948  Oil on hardboard  $22\frac{1}{8} \times 39\frac{1}{4}$ in.

94c  **The Garden**  1947  Oil on canvas  $15 \times 23\frac{5}{8}$ in.

95a  **Maize**  1948  Ink and water-colour  8¾ × 11 in.

95b  **Maize**  1948  Pen and gouache  15 × 19½ in.

95c  **Hanging Maize**  1948  Ink and gouache  8¾ × 11 in.

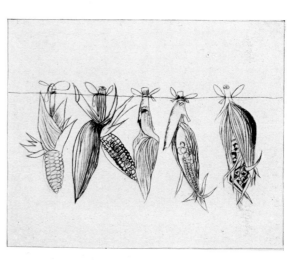

95d  **Study for 'Hanging Maize'**  1948
Black chalk  9¼ × 10¼ in.

95e  **Maize and Gourd**  1948
Pencil and gouache  15½ × 19½ in.

95f  **Maize and Landscape**  1948  Gouache  8¾ × 11 in.

96a  **The Gourd**  1948  Oil on hardboard  20 × 20¼ in.

96b  **Still Life with Gourds**  1948  Oil on canvas  18½ × 21¾ in.

96c  **Study for 'Still Life with Gourds'**  1947
Water-colour  9 × 11¼ in.

96d  **Hanging Gourds**  1948  Gouache  10 × 12½ in.

97a **Cactus** 1947 Pen and water-colour 9 × 11¼ in.

97b **Cactus** 1947 Conté crayon and water-colour 8½ × 12 in.

98a **Cigale** 1948 Oil on canvas 27 × 20 in.

98b **Cigale** 1948 Oil on canvas 27 × 20 in.

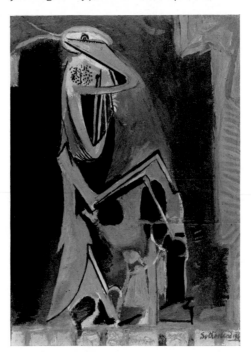

98c **Mantis** 1953 Oil on canvas $35\frac{1}{2} \times 27\frac{1}{2}$ in.

98d **Mantis** 1949 Oil on canvas $14\frac{7}{8} \times 11$ in.

98e **Cigale** 1947 Pen and water-colour $9 \times 11\frac{1}{4}$ in.

98f **Insects** 1948 Pen and gouache $8\frac{3}{4} \times 11$ in.

99a   **Still Life with Banana Leaf**   1947  Oil on hardboard  10¾ × 21 in.

99b   **Study of Banana Leaves**   1948  Chalk and water-colour on blue paper  9½ × 17½ in.

100a   **Turning Form**   1948 Chalk and gouache  $8\frac{3}{4} \times 11$ in.

100b   **Study of a Palm Tree**   1948
Black crayon on coloured paper touched with white  $10\frac{1}{4} \times 12\frac{1}{2}$ in.

100c   **Reclining Stone Form**   1948
Pen, chalk and gouache  $8\frac{3}{4} \times 11$ in.

VIII    **Standing Form Against Hedge**    1950 Oil on canvas $52\frac{1}{8} \times 45\frac{5}{8}$ in.

101a **Tourettes** 1948 Gouache $8\frac{3}{4} \times 11$ in.

101b **Banana Leaf and Landscape** 1947
Chalk and gouache $9 \times 11\frac{1}{4}$ in.

101c **Articulated Forms** 1948
Pen, chalk and gouache $8\frac{3}{4} \times 11$ in.

101d **Maize and Gourd** 1947 Oil on board $10 \times 13$ in.

101e **Banana Leaves and Wall** 1948 Gouache $8\frac{3}{4} \times 11$ in.

101f **Figure in Enclosure** 1948
Ink, crayon and gouache $15\frac{1}{2} \times 19\frac{1}{2}$ in.

102a **Three Standing Forms, Yellow Background** 1949
Chalk and water-colour 21 × 19 in.

102b **Two Stone Forms** 1950 Gouache 13¾ × 14 in.

102c **Three Forms** 1950 Oil on canvas 18¼ × 15¼ in.

102d **Standing Form – Hot Summer Room** 1951
Oil on canvas 18 × 15 in.

103a  **Two Standing Forms against a Palisade**  1949  Oil on canvas  $30\frac{1}{8} \times 26\frac{1}{8}$ in.

103b  **Root Form, Green Background**  1948  Crayon and water-colour  $8\frac{3}{4} \times 10\frac{1}{4}$ in.

104a   **Horizontal Form, Mauve Background**   1950   Oil on hardboard   14½ × 30½ in.

104b   **Articulated Form, Yellow Background**   1949   Oil on canvas   10⅛ × 22⅛ in.

104c   **Articulated Form in Landscape**   1949   Chalk and water-colour   8½ × 19½ in.

105a **Study for Two Forms** 1949 Conté crayon and coloured chalk $3\frac{1}{2} \times 9\frac{1}{4}$ in.

105b **Two Forms in a Terraced Landscape** 1951 Oil on canvas $20\frac{1}{4} \times 36\frac{1}{4}$ in.

105c **Horizontal Form in Grasses** 1951 Oil on canvas $20\frac{1}{8} \times 36\frac{1}{8}$ in.

106a **Articulated Form** 1951 Chalk and gouache 15 × 18 in.

106b **Organic Forms** 1950
Oil on hardboard approx. 18 × 16 in.

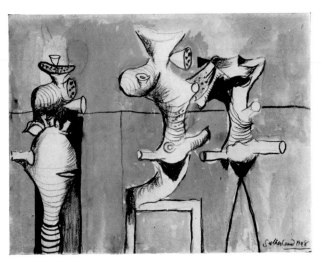

106c **Organic Forms** 1948 Conté crayon and gouache 8¾ × 11 in.

106d **Study of a Cactus** 1948
Ink and water-colour 9 × 7 in.

107a **Still Life with Grapes** 1950
Oil on canvas 19¾ × 15¾ in.

107b **Roses** 1951
Oil on canvas 26½ × 14½ in.

107c **Roses** 1951 Oil on canvas 26½ × 20⅛ in.

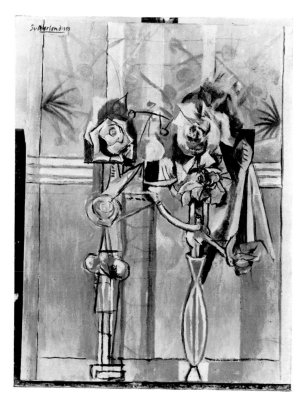

107d **Roses** 1950 Oil on canvas 25 × 20 in.

108a  **Path through Plantation**  1950
Oil on canvas  36⅛ × 20⅛

108b  **Men Walking**  1950  Oil on canvas  57¼ × 38½ in.

109    **Path through Plantation**    1951  Oil on canvas  30 × 25 in.

110a  **Aubergines**  1951  Gouache $8\frac{3}{8} \times 21\frac{1}{2}$ in.

110b  **Artichokes** (detail)  1951  Water-colour $9\frac{1}{2} \times 13\frac{5}{8}$ in.

110c  **Pomegranates**  1951  Oil on canvas  $16 \times 35$ in.

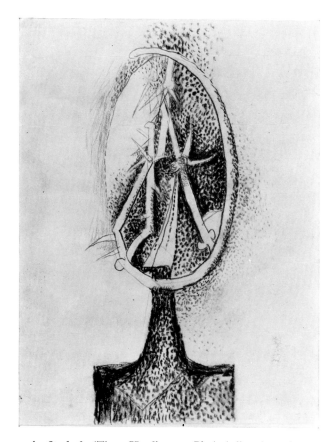

111a **Thorn Head** 1949 Oil on canvas 17⅞ × 23¾ in.

111b **Study for 'Thorn Head'** 1949 Black chalk 14½ × 11 in.

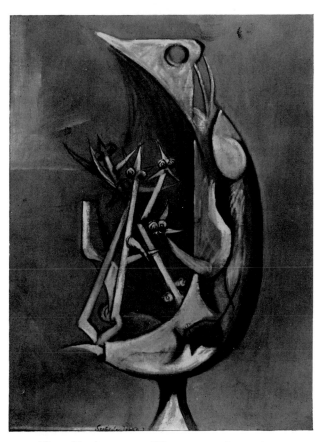

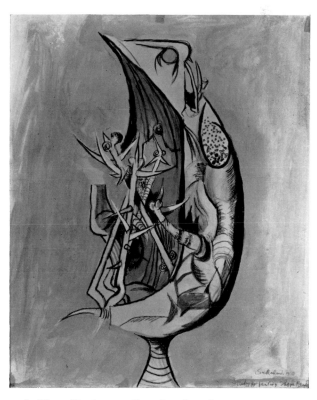

111c **Thorn Head** 1950–51 Oil on canvas 26½ × 19¾ in.

111d **Thorn Head** 1950 Gouache 26 × 22 in.

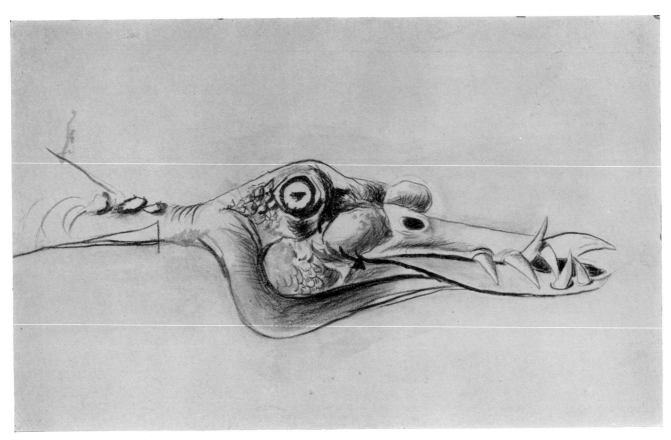

112a  **Head of Bird: Study for 'Origins of the Land'**  1950–51  Black chalk  12 × 24 in.

112b  **Pterodactyl: Study for 'Origins of the Land'**  1950–51  Conté crayon and gouache  12½ × 29¼ in.

113a **Study for 'Origins of the Land'** 1950
Gouache 7 × 5⅝ in.

113b **Study for 'Origins of the Land'** 1950
Pencil and water-colour 3½ × 3½ in.

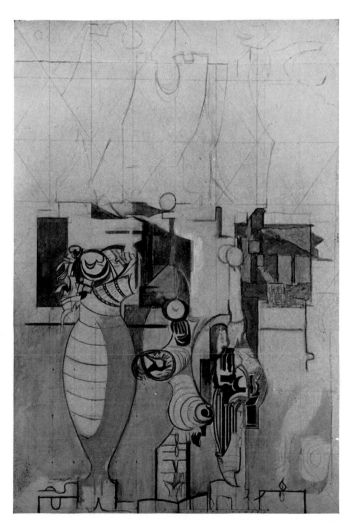

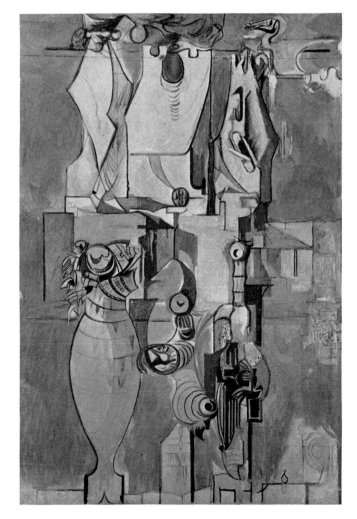

113c **Origins of the Land** – in course of execution

113d **Origins of the Land** – in course of execution

114a **Working Drawing for 'Origins of the Land'** 1951
Chalk and gouache  $24\frac{3}{4} \times 19\frac{1}{2}$ in.

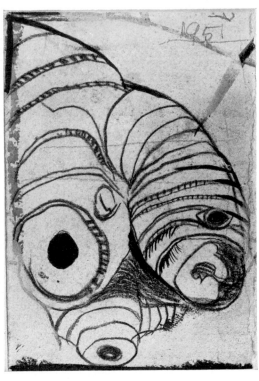

114b **Study for 'Origins of the Land'** 1951
Conté crayon and water-colour  $3\frac{5}{8} \times 2\frac{3}{4}$ in.

115   **Origins of the Land**   1951  Oil on canvas  $167\frac{1}{2} \times 131\frac{1}{4}$ in.

116a **Barren Landscape with Rocks** 1951
Gouache 13⅛ × 9⅝ in.

116b **Landscape with Dry Waterway** 1952
Pen, chalk and gouache 22½ × 14¾ in.

116c **Rocks in a Landscape** 1952
Pencil, chalk and gouache 7¼ × 7¾ in.

116d **Birds** 1952 Pen, chalk and gouache 22½ × 21½ in.

117a **Head** 1951 Chalk and gouache 15¼ × 12 in.

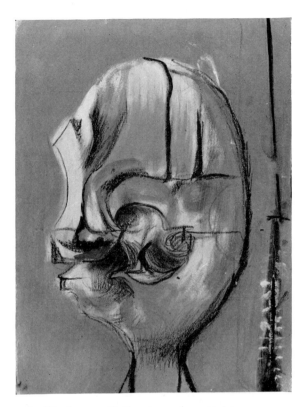

117b **Head** 1951 Chalk and gouache 13 × 9½ in.

117c **Head** 1951 Oil on canvas 24 × 20 in.

117d **Head** 1951 Oil on canvas 24 × 20 in.

118a **Standing Form, Orange Background**
1949 Chalk and gouache 16×6½ in.

118b **Form in Reeds** 1952
Gouache 17¼×7 in.

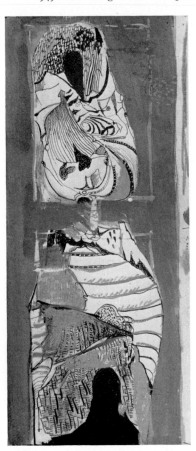

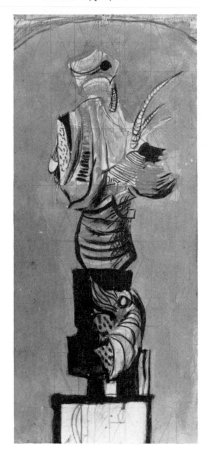

118c **Standing Form, Red Background**
1950 Pen and gouache 14⅞×5½ in.

118d **Standing Form, Red Background**
1949 Chalk and gouache 16×7 in.

119a **Armoured Form**  1950  Oil on canvas  65 × 32½ in.

119b **Standing Form**  1952  Oil on canvas  86½ × 40¼ in.

120  **Standing Forms**  1952 Oil on canvas  71¼ × 55¾ in.

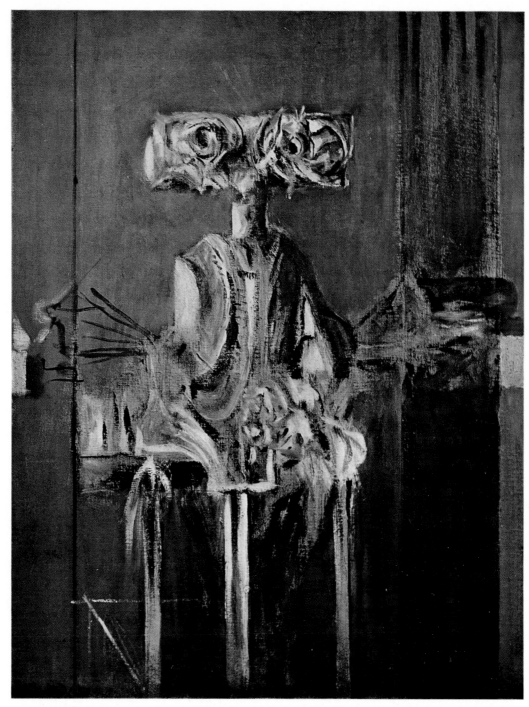

IX    **Variation on a Theme II**    1953 Oil on canvas $35\frac{1}{2} \times 27\frac{1}{2}$ in.

121   **Three Standing Forms in a Garden**   1952  Oil on canvas  $52\frac{3}{8} \times 45\frac{5}{8}$ in.

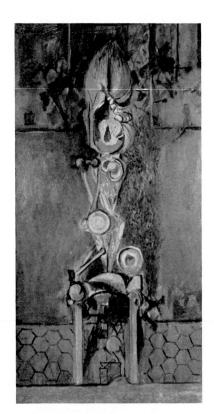

122a **Form against Foliage** 1952
Oil on canvas $66\frac{1}{2} \times 33\frac{1}{2}$ in.

122b **Forms against Reeds** 1952 Oil on canvas $24 \times 20$ in.

123a   **Landscape with Stones and Grasses**   1952  Oil on canvas  $18\frac{3}{4} \times 36\frac{1}{4}$ in.

123b   **Vine Pergola**   1952  Oil on canvas  $18 \times 36$ in.

123c   **Monuments against a Landscape**   1952  Ink, chalk and gouache  $8 \times 21\frac{1}{4}$ in.

124a **Cynocéphale** 1952 Oil on canvas 52 × 23¾ in.

124b **Predatory Form** 1952
Chalk and gouache 22¼ × 7 in.

125　**Standing Forms**　1953　Oil on canvas　$71\frac{1}{2} \times 56$ in. (destroyed by artist)

126a **Head** 1952 Oil on canvas 36 × 28 in.

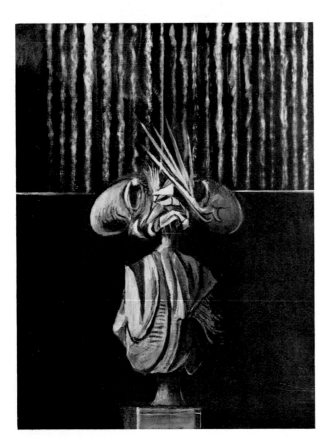

126b **Head** 1952 Oil on canvas 28¾ × 26 in.

126c **Form on a Pedestal** 1952 Chalk and gouache 29½ × 14¼ in.

127   **Head III**   1953  Oil on canvas  45 × 34¾ in.

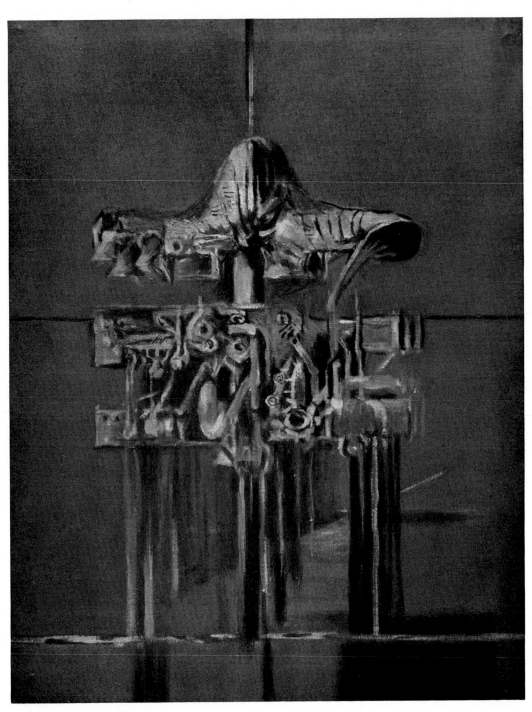

128  **Variation on a Theme I**  1953  Oil on canvas  $36 \times 27\frac{3}{4}$ in.

129    **Poised Form**   1953  Oil on paper  41 × 20¼ in.

130   **Study of a Cut Tree I**   1953  Ink and charcoal  78½ × 30 in.

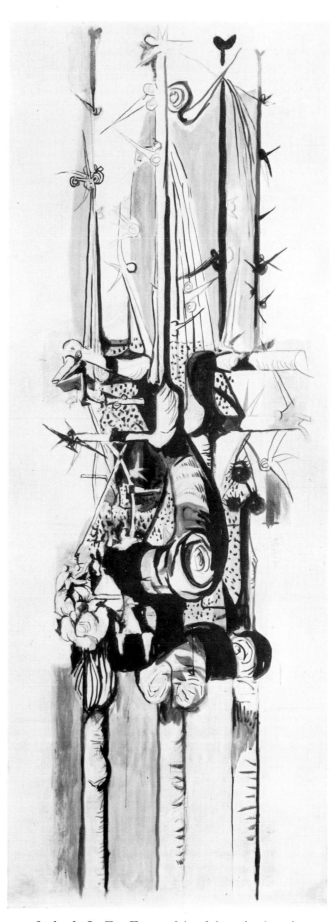

131    **Study of a Cut Tree II**    1953  Ink and charcoal  $78\frac{1}{2} \times 30$ in.

132   **La Petite Afrique**  1953  Oil on canvas  72 × 36 in.

X     **Golden Form against Black Background**   1954 Oil on canvas
$52\frac{1}{4} \times 23\frac{3}{4}$ in.

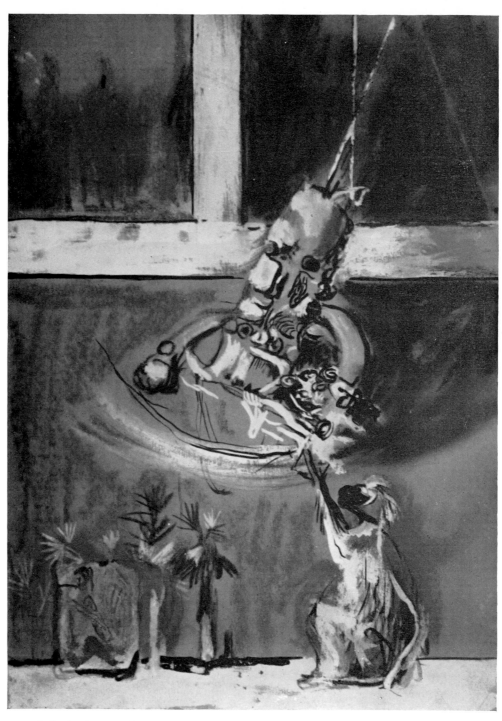

133   **Swinging Form and Monkey**   1953  Ink, gouache and pastel  $11\frac{5}{8} \times 8\frac{3}{8}$ in.

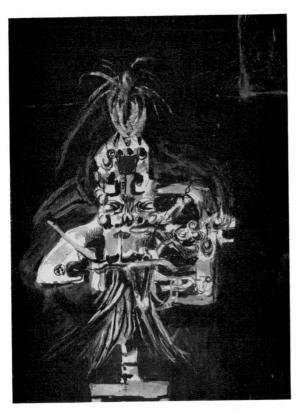

134a **Study for 'Golden Form'** 1953 Pastel and gouache
$11\frac{1}{2} \times 8\frac{1}{2}$ in.

134b **Study for 'Golden Form'** 1953 Gouache $11\frac{3}{4} \times 8\frac{1}{2}$ in.

134c **Machine Form** 1953 Gouache $11\frac{3}{4} \times 8\frac{1}{2}$ in.

135   **Study**   1953   Lithographic chalk and ink   $11\frac{1}{2} \times 8\frac{1}{2}$ in.

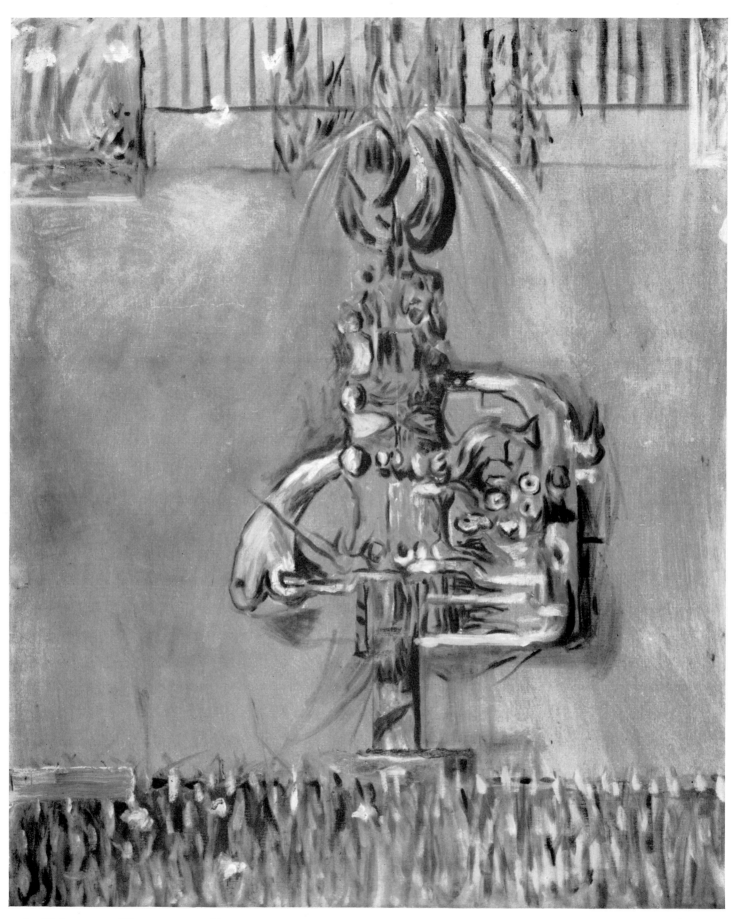

136 **Hydrant** 1954 Oil on canvas 44×36 in.

XI    **Thorn Cross**    1954 Oil on canvas $44\frac{1}{2} \times 37\frac{1}{2}$ in.

137  **Swinging Form**  1954 Oil on canvas 30×25 in.

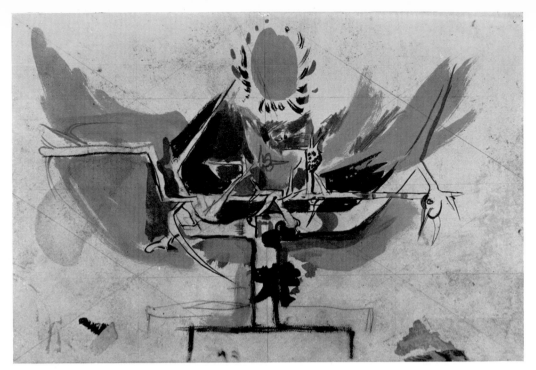

138a  **Thorn Cross and Sun**  1954  Ink and gouache  13 × 20½ in.

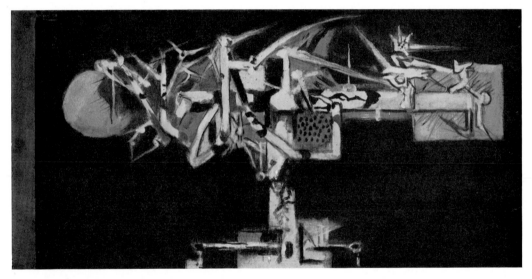

138b  **Thorn Cross**  1954  Oil on canvas  18½ × 36½ in.

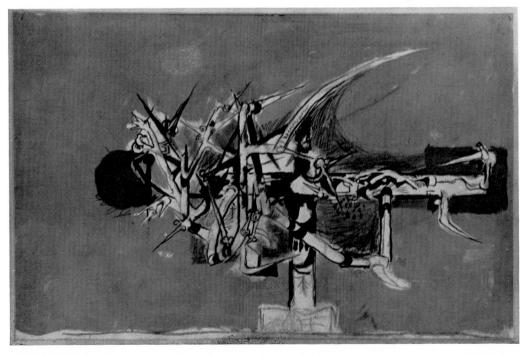

138c  **Study for 'Thorn Cross'**  1954  Oil, ink and chalk  13 × 20½ in.

139 **Monkey** 1955 Oil on canvas 30 × 25 in.

140    **Thorn Tree**    1954 Oil on canvas 53 × 24 in.

XII   **Monkey**   1953 Chalk and gouache $11\frac{1}{2} \times 8\frac{1}{2}$ in.

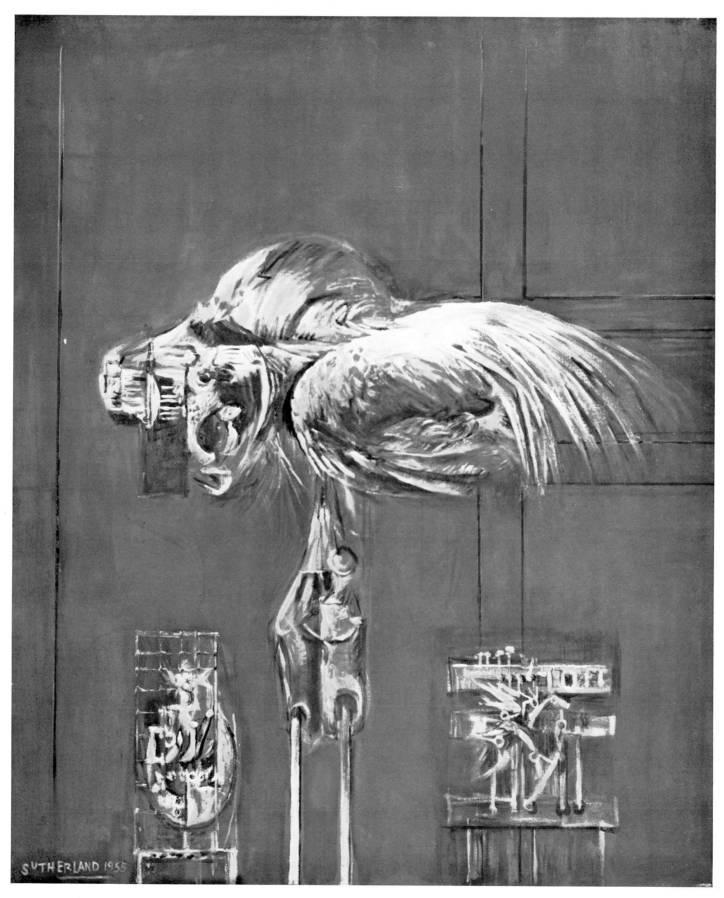

141    **La Petite Afrique III**   1955  Oil on canvas  56×48 in.

142　**Thorn Form**　1955　Oil on canvas　$44 \times 36\frac{1}{4}$ in.

143   **Study for Apple Tree**  1955  Oil on hardboard  13½ × 9½ in.

144    **Apple Bough**    1955  Oil on canvas  $21\frac{1}{2} \times 18$ in.

145a   **Study for Apple Tree**   1955   Oil on canvas   11 × 16¼ in.

145b   **Still Life with Apples**   1955   Oil on hardboard   6¾ × 14½ in.

146 **Cypress Cones** 1956 Oil on canvas 40×30 in.

147   **Palm Tree**   1957 Oil on canvas  $25\frac{3}{4} \times 21\frac{1}{4}$ in.

148    **Still Life with Apples and Scales**    1957 Oil on canvas $25\frac{3}{4} \times 21\frac{1}{4}$ in.

XIII    **Hanging Form over Water**    1955 Oil on canvas 43 × 34 in.

149    **Hanging Form over Water**    1957  Oil on canvas  $39\frac{1}{2} \times 31\frac{1}{2}$ in.

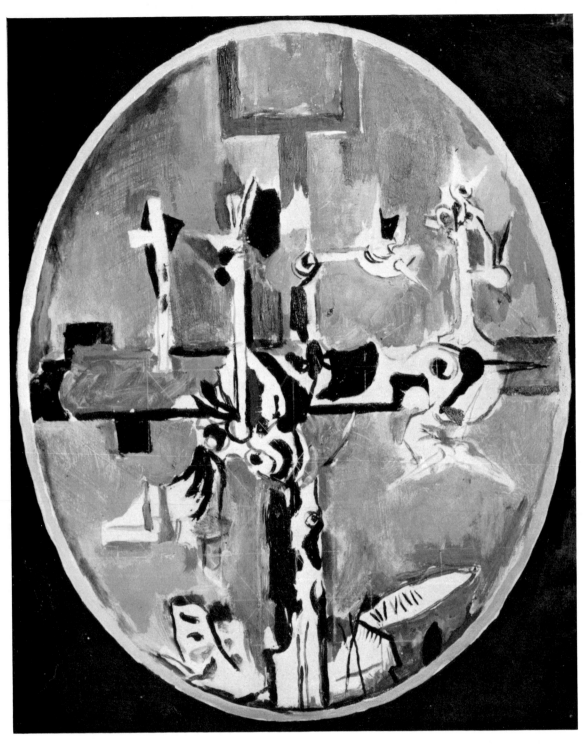

150    **Thorn Cross in Oval**    1959 Oil on canvas 25½ × 21½ in.

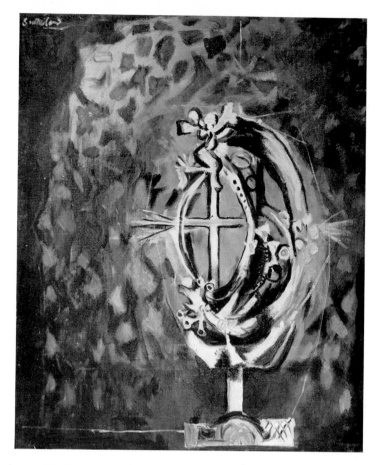

151a   **The Lamp**   1958 Oil on canvas 29 × 24 in.

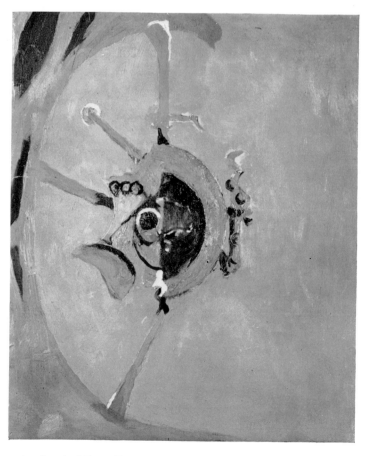

151b   **Attached Form: Root**   1959 Oil on canvas 25½ × 21½ in.

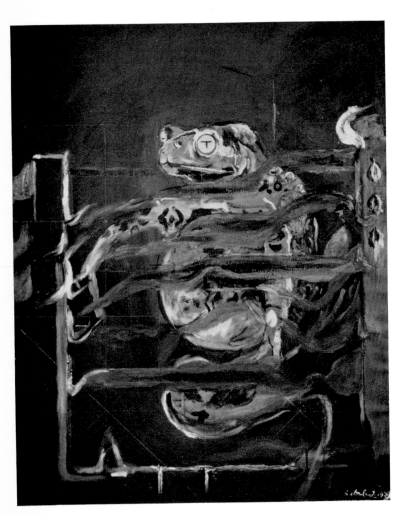

152a  **The Tank**  1959 Oil on canvas 39 × 31¾ in.

152b  **The Oracle**  1959 Oil on canvas 39 × 31¾ in.

XIV    **Toad II**    1958–59 Oil on canvas $50\frac{3}{4} \times 38\frac{1}{4}$ in.

153  **Dark Entrance**  1959 Oil on canvas 52 × 38¼ in.

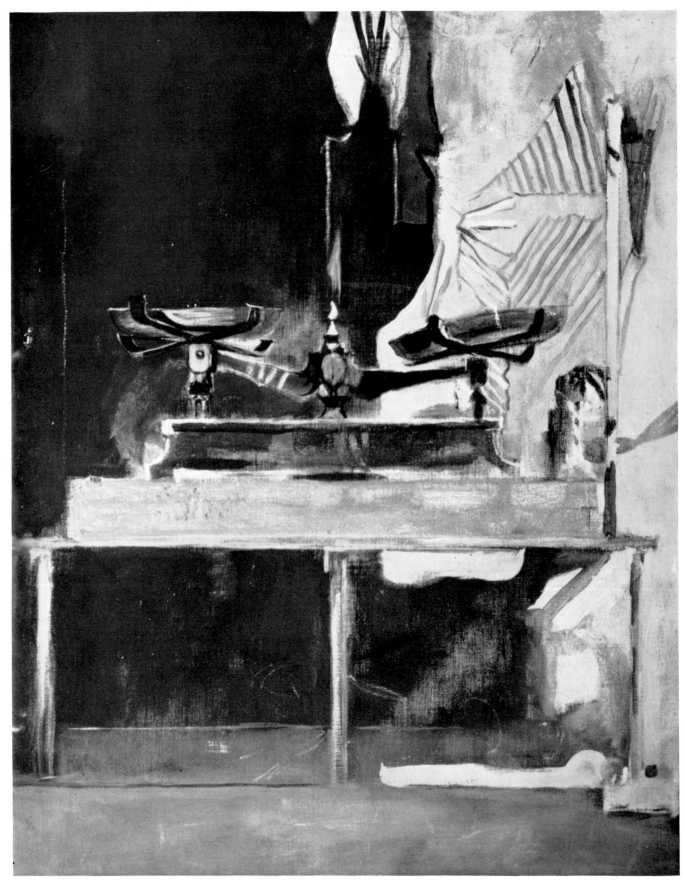

154 **The Scales** 1959 Oil on canvas 50×40 in.

155 **Path in Wood II** 1958 Oil on canvas 24 × 20 in.

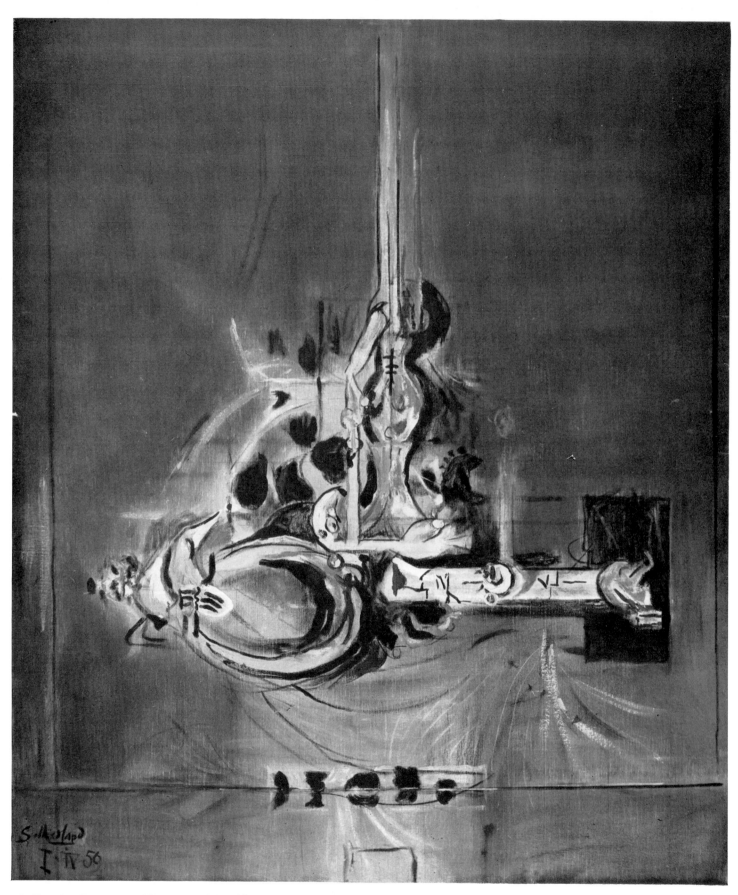

156  **Hanging Form**  1959 Oil on canvas 65¾ × 56 in.

157 **Chevaux de Frise** 1959 Oil on canvas 51×38 in.

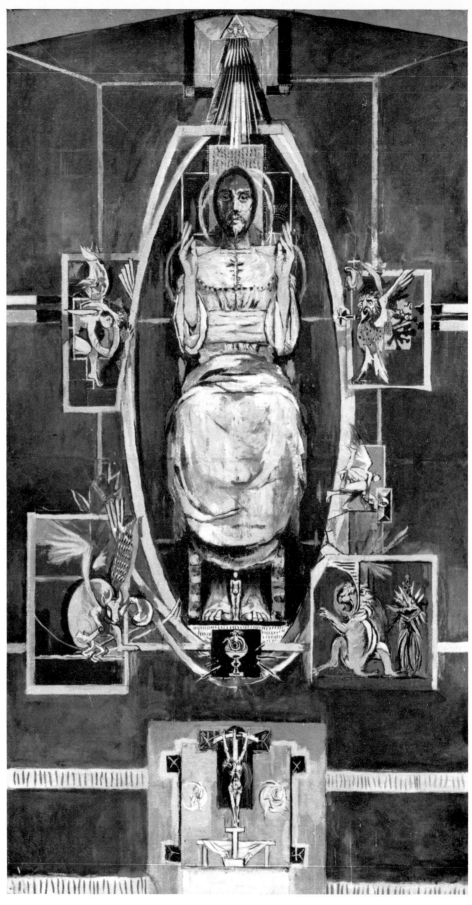

158 **Cartoon for the Coventry Tapestry 'Christ in Glory'** 1957
Oil on hardboard 74 × 40 in.

159 **The St John panel for the Coventry Tapestry** detail of plate 158

160   **Trial Woven Panel: St Matthew Symbol**   1958  Tapestry 10 × 6 ft.

# Figures and Portraits

Figures and Portraits

162 **Paraphrase of Figure with Key in Rembrandt's 'The Night Watch'** 1953 Oil on canvas 24 × 20 in.

163　**Laughing Woman**　1946　Oil on canvas　18 × 15 in.

164    **Study of Head for portrait of W. Somerset Maugham**    1949  Ink, charcoal and wash  9 × 6 in.

165    **Portrait of W. Somerset Maugham**   1949  Oil on canvas  $54 \times 25\frac{1}{2}$ in.

166   Detail of plate 167

167   **Portrait of Lord Beaverbrook**   1951  Oil on canvas  69 × 37 in.

168    **Study of Head for portrait of Sir Winston Churchill**    1954 Oil on canvas 24 × 20 in.

169b **Portrait of The Hon. Edward Sackville-West** 1954–59
Oil on canvas 24 × 24 in.

169a **Portrait of The Hon. Edward Sackville-West** 1953–54 Oil on canvas 66 × 33 in.

170   **Portrait of Arthur Jeffress**   1955–56 Oil on canvas 57 × 48 in.

171  **Detail of portrait of H. P. Juda**  1955  Oil on canvas  28 × 18 in.

172 **Portrait of Princess Gourielli** 1957 Oil on canvas 71 × 44 in.

173　**Portrait of Maja Sacher**　1957–58　Oil on canvas 44 × 26 in.

174    **Portrait of Paul Sacher**    1955–56 Oil on canvas 49½ × 40 in.

XV    **Portrait of Max Egon, Prince Fürstenberg**    1958-59 Oil on canvas 65 × 55 in.

# A Selective Bibliography on Graham Sutherland

by Bernard Karpel, Librarian of the Museum of Modern Art, New York

References are grouped as follows:

## Films

1 **Graham Sutherland.** Written and directed by John Read.
Produced by BBC Television Services. London, 1956.
No.8 in a series of half-hour documentaries: Art and Artists –
Great Britain. Includes interview with Sutherland, shows him in
England and France, reviews his paintings with a sequence on the
Northampton 'Crucifixion'.

2 **Out of Chaos.** Produced by Two Cities. London, 1945.
Wartime documentary, showing artists at work, including
Sutherland.
Briefly reviewed in *London Illustrated* 10 Feb. 1945.

## Books and Booklets

3 **Architects' Year Book: 3** pp.25, 31. London, 1949.
Essay by Patrick Heron: The visual arts. Also brief comment by
E. C. Gregory in *Year Book: 1*, pp.79, 82, 84 col. pl., 1945.

4 **Art for all.** London Transport posters, 1908–49. 39 pp. ill.
London, 1949.
Based on the exhibition at Victoria and Albert Museum (bibl.289).
Illustrates two Sutherland posters.

5 **Art since 1945.** London, New York, Paris, Cologne, 1958.
Chapter by Herbert Read: Great Britain; ill.

6 **Bertram, Anthony.** A Century of British Painting, 1851–1951.
pp.111–112. 2 ill. (1 col. pl.) London and New York, 1951.

7 **Brill, Reginald.** Modern Painting and Its Roots in the European
Tradition, p.27, pl.42. London, 1946.

8 **Busse, Jacques.** Graham Vivian Sutherland. *In* E. Bénézit:
Dictionnaire . . . des Peintres, Sculpteurs, Dessinateurs et Graveurs.
Nouv. ed. v.8, pp.187–188. Paris, 1955.

9 **Carrington, Noel and Harris, Muriel,** ed. British Achievement in
Design, pp.22, 24, 33. London, 1946.
Section on pottery, by Cecilia Sempill, illustrates designs by
Sutherland.

10 **Cassou, Jean.** Panorama des Arts Plastiques Contemporains, p.521.
Paris, 1960.

11 **Chamot, Mary.** Modern Painting in England, p.124. London and
New York, 1937.

12 **Clark, Kenneth.** Landscape into Art, pp.36, 109, 141. London,
1949. (Published as 'Landscape Painting', New York, 1949.)
Jacket designed by Sutherland.

13 **Courthion, Pierre.** L'Art Indépendant, p.245. Paris, 1958.

14 **Current Biography [Yearbook].** Edited by Marjorie D. Candee.
pp.589–591, ill. New York, 1955.
Incorporated into bibl.80.

15 **Damaz, Paul.** Art in European Architecture, pp.155, 176–177 ill.
New York, 1956.
Bilingual text: Synthèse des Arts.

16 **Digeon, Aurelien.** The English School of Painting, p.133 col. pl.
London, 1955.
A 'Pictura' series title also issued by Universe and Skira.

17 **Encyclopédie de l'Art International Contemporain,** pp.37–38 ill.
Paris, 1958.

18 **Evans, Myfanwy,** ed. The Painter's Object, pp.91–93 ill.
London, 1937.
Includes Sutherland's essay (bibl.133).

19 **Gascoyne, David.** Poems, 1937–42, 6 ill. (pt. col.) London, 1943.
Drawings by Sutherland, including coloured dustwrapper.

20 **Gray, Basil.** The English Print, pp.180, 211. London, 1937.

21  **Grohmann, Will.** Bildende Kunst und Architektur: (Zwischen den beiden Kriegen, Vol.III), ill. Berlin, 1953.

22  **Haskell, Arnold.** The Ballet Annual, v.1, p.79. London, 1947.
Includes Ayrton's article on Sadler's Wells' 'The Wanderer' (see bibl.75).

23  **Heron, Patrick.** The Changing Forms of Art, pp.31–32, 159–170, 244–245 (et passim). London, 1955.
Includes articles from *L'Age Nouveau* (Paris), *New Statesman and Nation* (London), BBC talks.

24  **Hodin, Joseph P.** The Dilemma of Modern Art, pp.120–127 ill. London, 1956.
'Graham Sutherland, the English and European aspects of his art' (see also bibl.96, 167).

25  **Hofmann, Werner.** Zeichen und Gestalt, p.123. Frankfurt-am-Main, 1957.

26  **Hsiao Chien,** ed. British Graphic Arts. Shanghai, n.d.; ill.

27  **Hubbard, Hesketh.** A Hundred Years of British Painting, 1851–1951, pp.266, 273, 278, 279 ill. London, New York, Toronto, 1951.

28  **Ironside, Robin.** Painting Since 1939, pp.28–30, 40. London, 1947.
Incorporated into bibl.62.

29  **Johnstone, William.** Creative Art in Britain, pl.207. London, 1950.

30  **Lake, Carlton and Maillard, Robert.** Dictionary of Modern Painting, pp.285–286 ill. New York, 1955.
Translation of Dictionnaire de la Peinture Moderne (Paris, 1955).
German edition: Knaurs Lexikon Moderner Kunst (Munich, 1955).

31  **La Littérature anglaise depuis la guerre,** pp.24–27 ill. (pt. col.)
Includes Peter Watson: Notes sur deux peintres anglais.

32  **Langui, Emile.** 50 Years of Modern Art, pp.179, 331 ill. London and New York, 1959.
Based on Brussels World Fair exhibit, 1958 (bibl.323).

33  **Lebel, Robert,** ed. Premier Bilan de l'Art Actuel, pp.13, 139, 321. Paris, 1953.
'Le Soleil Noir, nos.3–4: Positions.'

34  **Lewis, C. Day [and others].** Orion, v.3, pp.85–86, 89. London, 1946.
Includes Michael Ayrton: Some younger British contemporary painters, pp.84–89.

35  **London National Gallery.** War Pictures at the National Gallery. 2 ed., ill. London, 1944.

36  **McCurdy, Charles,** ed. Modern Art, a Pictorial Anthology, pp.45, 126 ill. New York, 1958.

37  **Man, Felix H.** Eight European Artists. London, Melbourne, Toronto [1954].
The eighth section, 'G. Sutherland', consists of 32 pages of trilingual text including drawings, facsimile MSS., colour plates, portraits and studio views.

38  **Marshall, H. G. Hayes.** British Textile Designers Today, p.320. Leigh-on-Sea, 1939.

39  **Melville, Robert.** Graham Sutherland. London, 1950, 2 ed. 1953.
'The imagery of Graham Sutherland', a 14-page introduction, also translated into French, Spanish, Portuguese. Includes 43 illustrations, 71 colour plates. Bibliography [by Henry Aronson], pp.[101–104]. Issued in edition of 2000; 25 copies with original lithograph. Thoroughly reviewed in *The Times Literary Supplement* (London) 9 Feb. 1951: 'A contemporary English artist'.
American reviews: *Art News* (New York) Apr. 1951 (50:12); *Magazine of Art* (New York) May 1951 (44:199).

40  **Mercer, F. A. and Gaunt, W.,** ed. Modern Publicity, 1934–5, p.47. London and New York [1935].
Colour illustration: Shell-Mex poster by Sutherland.

41  **Mills, Edward D.** The Modern Church, pp.131–133, 174, ill. London, 1956.

42  **Morton, J. B.** Blitz, p.63; pl.40–43. London, New York, Toronto, 1942.
No.2: War pictures by British artists.

43  **Myers, Bernard,** ed. Encyclopedia of Painting, p.463, ill. (col.) New York, 1955.
Also his Modern Art in the Making. 2 rev. ed. New York, 1959.

44  **Newton, Eric.** In My View, pp.85–87, 206–208. London, 1950.
'Graham Sutherland' text (dated Oct. 1938) supplemented by 'Symbolism of Sutherland's "Crucifixion"'.

45  **Newton, Eric.** War through Artists' Eyes, pp.6, 8, 11, 93–95, 5 ill. (2 col.) London, 1945.

46  **Picture Encyclopedia of Art,** pp. 68,224, 510 ill. London, 1958.
Original German edition: Westermann Verlag (Brunswick).

47  **Piper, David.** The English Face. London, 1957.

48  **Piper, John.** British Romantic Artists, pp.46–47 col. pl. London, 1942.

49  **Read, Herbert.** A Concise History of Modern Painting, pp.264, 276, 306 ill. London and New York, 1959.

50  **Read, Herbert.** Contemporary British Art, pp.23–26, 46 pl. (6 col.) London, 1951.

51  **Read, Herbert.** Great Britain *in* Art Since 1945.
(See bibl.5).

52  **Read, Herbert.** The Tenth Muse: Essays in Criticism, pp.310–313. London, 1957.

53  **Ritchie, Andrew C.** British Contemporary Artists, pp.14, 19, 33, 5 ill. Buffalo, 1946.

54  **Ritchie, Andrew C.** Masters of British Painting, pp.135–142, ill. New York, 1956.
Issued on the occasion of an exhibition at Museum of Modern Art; also shown at the City Art Museum of St Louis, the California Palace of the Legion of Honor, San Francisco. Bibliography.

55  **Rothenstein, John.** The Moderns and Their World, p.25, col. pl. 89. London and New York, 1958.

56  **Rothenstein, John.** The Tate Gallery, pp.110–111, ill. London and New York, 1958.

57  **Rothenstein, Michael.** Looking at Pictures, pp.36–37, 56, 61–62, col. pl.12. London, 1947.
Commentary, p.36, supplemented by Sutherland's text (from *The Listener* (London) no.670, 1941) and letters to Rothenstein.

58  **Russell, John.** From Sickert to 1948, pp.19, 41, 65, 68, 69, 71, 72, 73, 75, 77, 3 ill. (1 col.) London, 1948.

59  **Sackville-West, Edward.** Graham Sutherland. London, 1943 and 1955.
1955 edn. contains alterations in text and plates.
Includes 32 illustrations (16 in colour).
Reviewed in *Architectural Review* (London), July 1944 (96:28–29); *Museums Journal* (London), Jan. 1945 (44:168); *Royal Society of Arts Journal* (London), 16 Mar. 1945 (93:199–200).

60  **Shakespeare, William.** Henry VI, Part I. New York, 1940.
With illustration by Sutherland.

61 **Short, Ernest.** A History of British Painting, p.282. London, New York, Toronto, 1953.

62 **Since 1939,** pp.28–30, 40. London, 1948.
Incorporates Ironside (bibl.28); additional commentary on ballet-décor of 'The Wanderer'.

63 **Soby, James T.** Contemporary Painters, pp.134, 136, 138–139, ill. New York, 1948.
Chapter XV: Graham Sutherland.

64 **Soby, James T.** Modern Art and the New Past, pp.10, 12, 47, 130. Univ. of Oklahoma, 1957.

65 **Steuben Glass.** British Artists in Crystal. New York, 1954.
Plate 19: Sutherland's 'Mantis'. Booklet also used as exhibit catalogue.

66 **Sutherland, Monica.** La Fontaine: The Man and His Work. London, 1953.
Dustwrapper, in colour, by Sutherland.

67 **Thieme, Ulrich and Becker, Felix.** Allgemeines Lexikon der Bildenden Künstler, v.32, p.319. Leipzig, 1938.
Supplemented by Vollmer, 1958 (see also bibl.69).

68 **Trier, Eduard.** Zeichner des XX. Jahrhunderts, pp.133–134, ill. Berlin, 1956.

69 **Vollmer, Hans,** ed. Allgemeines Lexikon der Bildenden Künstler, v.4, pp.391–392. Leipzig, 1958.

70 **Wheeler, Monroe,** ed. Britain at War, pp.12, 36–37, 97, ill. New York, 1941. (See bibl.274).

71 **Wilenski, R. H.** The Modern Movement in Art, pp.28–29, 34, 38, 135. London and New York, 1956 et seq.

72 **World Biography,** p.4614. New York, 1948.

73 **Zahn, Leopold.** Kleine Geschichte der Modernen Kunst, pp.33, 158. Frankfurt-am-Main, 1956.

## Articles: English

74 **Art in our Time:** No.171 [Sutherland's Churchill].
*Courier* (London) pp.40 ff, 12 ill. (2 col.), July 1960.
With 4 pp. supplement of portrait sketches and drawings at the Beaverbrook Gallery in Canada.

75 **Ayrton, Michael.** The 'décor' of Sadler's Wells' ballets, 1939–46. (See bibl.22).

76 **Ayrton, Michael.** Some younger British contemporary painters. (See bibl.34).

77 **Barton, J. E.** Pictures in the schools. *Architectural Review* (London) 81, no.482: 2–4, pl.III, Jan. 1937.
Refers to portfolio published by Contemporary Lithographers, containing a reproduction in colour of Sutherland's 'The Sick Duck'.

78 **Boswell, James.** Recent trends in English illustration. *Graphis* (Zurich) 2 no.14: 186–188, ill., Mar.–Apr. 1946.
Also German and French text. Additional illustrations in other numbers (18:111; 26:127; etc.)

79 **British Painting** – A modern gallery. *Toledo Museum News,* no.146: 1–3, ill. 1953.

80 **Candee, Marjorie D.,** ed. Sutherland. *Current Biography* (New York) 16, no.1: 51–53, port., Jan. 1955: (See bibl.14).

81 **Churchill Portrait.** *Illustrated London News* 225:991, ill., 4 Dec. 1954.
Supplemental data in *Time* (New York) 64:78, 13 Dec. 1954 ('Force and Candor'); *Apollo* (London) 61:1, Jan. 1955 ('Problem of portraiture'); *Art News* (New York) 53:52, Jan. 1955 ('Monolithic presence'); *Studio* (London) 149: 124–125, Apr. 1955 ('London commentary').

82 **Clark, Kenneth.** The new romanticism in British painting. *Art News* (New York) 45:24, 25, 56–57, ill. (pt. col.), Feb. 1947.

83 **Clark, Kenneth.** A note on three illustrations to 'Wuthering Heights'. *Signature* (London) no.4: 12–17, ill., Nov. 1956.

84 **Clark, Kenneth.** War artists at the National Gallery. *Studio* (London) 123: 2–12, ill. (col.), Jan. 1942.

85 **Del Renzio, Toni.** Graham Sutherland's festival mural. *Art News and Review* (London) 4 no.23:4, 13 Dec. 1952.

86 **Denvir, Bernard.** Art collectors and their collections – 2: W. A. Evill. *Studio* (London) 137: 47, ill., Feb. 1949.

87 **Duval, Paul.** Accent on art: Churchill, artist and model, (3) pp. ill., *Toronto Telegram* 14 Jan. 1951.

88 **English Ballet in Wartime.** *Penguin New Writing* (London) no.13: 108–115, ill., Apr.–June 1942.
Comments on décor for 'The Wanderer'.

89 **Forge, Andrew.** [Introduction to 'romantic and abstract']. (See bibl.324).

90 **Gates, J. M.** British artists in crystal – designs for Steuben glass. *American Artist* (New York) 18: 50–55, ill., June 1954.

91 **Gaunt, William.** Profile: Graham Sutherland. *Art Digest* (New York) 27 no.15: 13, 25–26, ill., 1 May 1953.

92 **Gordon, J.** Art of the people at City Literary Institute, London. *Studio* (London) 123: 114, Apr. 1942.

93 **Graham Sutherland's 'Thorn Trees'** [acquisition]. *Gallery Notes* (Albright Gallery, Buffalo) 11: 25–26, July 1946.

94 **Grigson, Geoffrey.** Authentic and false in the new romanticism. *Horizon* (London) 17 no.99: 203–213, Mar. 1948.

95 **Hill, B. J. W.** [Reply to the Tate Gallery]. *New Statesman and Nation* (London) 48:506, 23 Oct. 1954.
Rebuttal to the Tate article, 48: 472, 16 Oct. 1954.

96 **Hodin, Joseph P.** Graham Sutherland: the English and European aspects of his art. *Numero* (Florence) 4 (ser.3) no.2: 4–5, 9, ill., Sept. 1952.
Incorporated into bibl.24.

97 **Hussey, Walter.** A churchman discusses art in the church. *Studio* (London) 138: 80–81, 95, ill., Sept. 1949.
Additional statement: 'Religion inspires a modern artist', *Picture Post*, (London) 33 no.12: 13, ill. 21 Dec. 1946. Includes text by John Piper.

98 **Johns, Ewart.** The artist and the scientific study of scenery. *Studio* (London) 149: 42–49, ill., 1955.

99 **Littlefield, Joan.** British movies teach art appreciation. *Design* (Columbus, Ohio) 46 no.7, ill., Mar. 1945.
Reviews 'Out of Chaos' (see bibl.2).

100 **Living Image: Art and Life, The.** *The Listener* (London) 26 no.670: 657–659, ill., 13 Nov. 1941.
Report of a discussion between Kenneth Clark, Henry Moore, V. S. Pritchett, Graham Sutherland.

101 **Melville, Robert.** Contemporary British tapestry. *Ambassador* (London) no.7: 126–129, ill. (pt. col.), 1949.
Two designs, including magazine cover in colour.

102 **Melville, Robert.** A panorama of modern art. *World Review* (London) pp.40–45, ill., Mar. 1949.

103 **Mortimer, Raymond.** Graham Sutherland's new paintings. *Harper's Bazaar* (London) 39 no.4: 44–47, 71, ill. (pt. col.), July 1948. Sketches in colour on magazine cover.

104 **Myerscough-Walker, R.** Modern art explained by modern artists. *Artist* (London) 27 no.1: 17–19, ill., Mar. 1949. An interview with Sutherland.

105 **New Ballet by Frederick Ashton.** *New Statesman and Nation* (London) 21 no.519: 110, 1 Feb. 1941. Sutherland's décor for 'The Wanderer'.

106 **Newton, Eric.** [Critic's choice, 1955 selection]. (See bibl.315).

107 **Newton, Eric.** English painting today. *Tomorrow* (New York) 1 no.2: 31–33, Oct. 1946.

108 **Newton, Eric.** Graham Sutherland. *Art News and Review* (London) 3 no.6: 2, 21 Apr. 1951.

109 **Newton, Eric.** New portrait of 'Bulldog and cherub'. *New York Times Magazine* pp.14, 38, 40, ill., 5 Dec. 1954.

110 **Newton, Eric.** Paintings of Graham Sutherland. *Canadian Art* (Ottawa) 9 no.3: 116–121, ill., 1952.

111 **Newton, Eric.** Religious art. *World Review* (London) pp.48–54, ill. (pt. col.), Dec. 1947.

112 **Nicolson, Benedict.** Graham Sutherland's 'Crucifixion'. *Magazine of Art* (New York) 40 no.7: 279–281, ill., Nov. 1947.

113 **Ogg, David.** Etchings of Graham Sutherland and Paul Drury. *Print Collector's Quarterly* (London) 16 no.1: 76–85, ill., Jan. 1929.

114 **Painting, Sculpture and the Architect.** *Architect and Building News* (London) 196 no.4213: 283–284, 16 Sept. 1949.

115 **Payoff** [the Maugham portrait]. *Time* (New York) 53 no.24: 51, ill., 13 June 1949.

116 **Pevsner, Nikolaus.** Can painters design fabrics? *Art in Industry* (Calcutta) 1 no.1: 11–17, ill., Dec. 1946.

117 **Picture or Painting.** *San Francisco Museum of Art Bulletin* pp.19–21, ill., May 1947.

118 **Piper, John.** An eternal subject. *Ambassador* (London) no.1: 67–69, ill., 1947.

119 **Piper, John.** Religion inspires a modern artist. (See bibl.97).

120 **Portraits at the Royal Academy.** *The Burlington Magazine* (London) 99: 24–27, 29, ill., Jan. 1957.

121 **Portraiture.** *Illustrated London News* 1: 1113, ill., 1955.

122 **River into Office.** *Art and Industry* (London) 24 no.143: 182, ill., May 1938. Sutherland's poster for the London Passenger Transport Board.

123 **Rothenstein, Elizabeth.** The Pre-Raphaelites and ourselves. *The Month* (London) (n.s.) 1 no.3: 180–198, Mar. 1949. Compares Sutherland's interpretation of nature with that of Gerard Manley Hopkins.

124 **Rothenstein, John.** War and the artists. *Apollo* (London) 37: 111–113, ill., May 1943.

125 **Sackville-West, Edward.** Art and the Christian church. *Vogue* (London) 103 no.3: 64–65, 114, 120, ill. (pt. col.), Mar. 1947. Also published in the New York *Vogue* (1 Mar. 1948) as 'Church art: new promise and past glory'.

126 **Salaman, Malcolm.** A gossip about prints. *Apollo* (London) 5 no.26: 82–86, ill., Feb. 1927.

127 **Schwarz, Heinrich.** The mirror in art. *Art Quarterly* (Detroit) 15 no.2: 116–118, ill., 1952.

128 **Sitwell, Sacheverell.** The arts in England. *Vogue* (London) 101 no.8: 32–33, 76, 82, Aug. 1945. Also published in the New York *Vogue* as 'The future of English arts' (106 no.6: 149 ff., ill. (pt. col.), 1 Oct. 1945).

129 **Soby, James T.** Art in England today. *Saturday Review of Literature* (New York) 29 no.49: 76, 7 Dec. 1946.

130 **Spender, Stephen.** English artists v. English painting. *Art News* (New York) 52 no.7: 47–48, ill., Nov. 1953. Supplemented by his 'English painting in the fifties'. *New Republic* (New York) 130: 16–17, 19 Apr. 1954.

131 **Sutherland, Graham.** [Correspondence with Curt Valentin]. 194?–195?. Letters written to his New York dealer, now on deposit in the Museum of Modern Art Library, New York.

132 **Sutherland, Graham.** English painting. *New Statesman and Nation* (London) 33 no.831: 74, 25 Jan. 1947. A reply to Nicolson's review in the *New Statesman* (see bibl.217).

133 **Sutherland, Graham.** An English stone landmark. *In* The Painter's Object, pp.91–92, ill. (pp.89, 93) London, 1937. (See bibl.18).

134 **Sutherland, Graham.** Graven images: line engraving and the illustrated book. *Signature* (London) no.6: 28–34, ill., July 1937.

135 **Sutherland, Graham.** Influence of Picasso. *New Statesman and Nation* (London) 29 no.740: 274, 28 Apr. 1945. Commentary on criticism by E. Sackville-West and M. Ayrton reported in the 31 Mar. and 14 Apr. numbers.

136 **Sutherland, Graham.** On painting: notes by the artist. *In* Arts Council of Great Britain. Paintings and drawings by Graham Sutherland. [3] pp. London, 1953. The first four paragraphs are taken from a letter to Sir Colin Anderson and published in *Horizon* (London) 5 no.28, April 1942. The rest, with the exception of the last six paragraphs, are from 'Thoughts on painting . . . a revised version'. Texts also partially published in French and German catalogues of the Council (see bibl. 179, 180).

137 **Sutherland, Graham.** Thoughts on painting. *The Listener* (London) 46 no.1175: 376, 6 Sept. 1951. Broadcast on the BBC Third Programme. Text frequently published elsewhere, or modified for partial quotation, e.g. bibl.238, 240, 242.

138 **Sutherland, Graham.** A trend in English draughtsmanship. *Signature* (London) no.3: 7–13, ill., July 1936.

139 **Sutherland, Graham.** Welsh sketchbook. *Horizon* (London) 5 no.28: 225–226, 230, 234–235, ill., Apr. 1942.

140 **Sutherland, Graham.** What is good design worth? *American Fabrics* (New York) no.48: 69–71, ill., Winter 1960.

141 **Sutherland, Graham.** [Discussion: The living image: art and life]. (See bibl.100).

142 **Sutherland, Graham.** [Interview: Modern art explained by modern artists]. (See bibl.104).

143 **Sutherland, Graham.** [Symposium: Painting, sculpture and the architect]. (See bibl.114).

144 **[Sutherland, Graham.]** Design in Steuben glass. *Illustrated London News* 227: 701, ill., 22 Oct. 1955 (see also bibl.226).

145 **[Sutherland, Graham.]** Graham Sutherland [in his studio]. *World Review* (London) Dec. 1949.

146 **[Sutherland, Graham.]** New forms at Easter. *Art News* (New York) 46 no.2: 21, ill., Apr. 1947.

147 **[Sutherland, Graham.]** Three lithographs by Graham Sutherland. *Poetry London* 2 no.9, 1943.
Illustrations from Quarles' 'Hieroglyphics'. Also magazine cover.

148 **Varga, Margaret.** Britain mobilizes her artists – What about America? *Magazine of Art* (New York) 34: 298–303, ill., June–July 1941.

149 **Walker, R. A.** [Chronological list of Sutherland's etchings and dry-points, 1922–38]. *Print Collector's Quarterly* (London) 16 no.1: 94–96, Jan. 1929.

150 **War Artists and the War.** *Penguin New Writing* (London) no.16: 108–117, ill., Jan.–Mar. 1943.

151 **Wardell, Michael.** The Beaverbrook Art Gallery. *The Atlantic Advocate* (Fredericton, N.B.) Sept. 1959; ill.

152 **Whiffen, Marcus.** Graham Sutherland's 'Crucifixion'. *Architectural Review* (London) 101 no.603: 105–106, 107, ill., Mar. 1947.
Rebuttal by E. Brandl, and rejoinder by Whiffen in Aug. 1947 (102:70 ff.)

## Articles: Foreign

153 **Alexander, A.** Ausstellung im Musée national d'art moderne, Paris: Graham Sutherland. *Das Kunstwerk* (Baden-Baden) no.6: 58, 1952.

154 **Alley, Ronald.** A obra de Graham Sutherland. *Habitat* (São Paulo) 5: 23, 42–43, ill., Aug. 1955.

155 **C.H.** [Hans Curjel?]. Graham Sutherland. *Werk* (Zürich) 40: 53–54 (supp.), ill., Apr. 1953.

156 **Clayeux, Louis-Gabriel.** La peinture. *Le Monde Français* (Paris) pp.314–315, Feb. 1946.

157 **D'Arcy, M. A.** L'art religieux en Angleterre. *Art d'Eglise* (Brussels) 23: 5–10, ill., 1955.

158 **Flemming, Hans T.** Moore und Sutherland. *Das Kunstwerk* (Baden-Baden) 1 nos.8–9: 49–52, ill. (pt. col.), 1946–7.

159 **Gasser, H. U.** Londoner Kunstchronik: Graham Sutherland. *Werk* (Zürich) 38 no.6: 82–83 (supp.), June 1951.

160 **Gasser, Manuel.** Graham Sutherland: méér dan uiterlijk. *Elseviers Weekblad* (Amsterdam) 5 no.16: 13, ill., 23 Apr. 1949.

161 **Gasser, Manuel.** Der Maler Sutherland. *Werk* (Zürich) 36 no.11: 376–379, ill., Nov. 1949.
Essay, similarly titled, also published in *Graphis* (Zürich) no.27: 359, 1949; *Die Neue Zeitung* (Berlin) 22 July 1949.

162 **Gasser, Manuel.** Northampton und die moderne Kirchenkunst. *Werk* (Zürich) 36 no.4:122–124, ill., Apr. 1949.

163 **Gibson, William.** Notes sur six artistes qui travaillent en Angleterre. *Choix* (London) 2 no.12:67–68, ill. (pt.col.), Jan. 1946.

164 **G. Sutherland.** [Text in Japanese]. *Bijutsu Techo* (Tokyo) no.83: 9–17, ill. (pt. col.), July 1954.

165 **Graham Sutherland . . .** *Emporium* (Bergamo) 116 no.696: 278–280, ill., Dec. 1952.

166 **Guilly, René.** Graham Sutherland. *Juin* (Paris) 17 Sept. 1946.

167 **Hodin, J. P.** Graham Sutherland: l'aspect anglais et européen de son art. *Arts Plastiques* (Brussels) 5 no.6: 434–440, ill., June 1952. Incorporated into bibl.24.

168 **Hodin, J. P.** Londoner Kunstchronik. *Werk* (Zürich) 36 no.2: 16–17 (supp.), ill., Feb. 1949.

169 **Nicolson, Benedict.** L'étonnante 'Crucifixion' de Graham Sutherland. *Vrai* (Brussels) 12 Oct. 1947.

170 **Pfefferhorn, Rudolf.** Rückkehr zu englischer Eigenart. *Das Kunstwerk* (Baden-Baden) 6 no.6: 37–45, ill., 1952.

171 **R . . . . , I . . . .** Spiel mit dem Abründigen. *Baukunst und Werkform* (Nuremberg) 10 no.5: 303–304, 1957.

172 **Read, Herbert.** L'Arte britannica alla XXVI biennale. *La Biennale* (Venice) no.9: 23–27, ill., 1952.

173 **Read, Herbert.** Beeldende Kunst in England. *Kroniek van Kunst en Kultur* (Amsterdam) 7 no.11: 327–352, ill., Nov. 1946.

174 **Read, Herbert.** Psychologie de l'art anglais jusqu'a la jeune peinture. *Art d'Aujourd'hui* (Paris) no.2: 3–6, ill., 1953.

175 **Read, Herbert.** Tendances récentes dans l'art anglais. *Arts Plastiques* (Brussels) nos.1–2: 31–33, ill., 1948.

176 **Savarus, Albert.** L'art de G. Sutherland. *Beaux-Arts* (Brussels) 15 no.537: 8, 8 June 1951.

177 **Soby, James T.** Notas sobre la pintura inglesa de neustros dias. *Revista Belga* (New York) 2 no.10: 29–38, ill., Oct. 1945. (See also bibl.278).

178 **Storey, Benjamin.** Sutherland e l'arte inglese d'avanguardia. *Emporium* (Bergamo) 116 nos.691–692: 57–64, ill., Aug. 1952.

179 **Sutherland, Graham.** Notes de l'artiste. [pp.10–11] Paris, 1951. (See note, bibl.136).

180 **Sutherland, Graham.** Über Malerei, Aufzeichnungen des Künstlers. [pp.3–4] Berlin, etc, 1954–5 (see note, bibl.136).

181 **Svensson, Georg.** Engelsk nutickonst. *Konstrevy* (Stockholm) 24 no.2: 87, ill., 1948.

182 **Watson, Peter.** Notes sur deux peintres anglais, 1945 (see bibl.31).

## Reviews

Exclusive of *foreign* references above.

183 **Alloway, Lawrence.** Charm. *Art News and Review* (London) 7 no.12: 7, 9 July 1955.

184 **Alloway, Lawrence.** A monumental phase: Graham Sutherland. *Art News and Review* (London) 3 no.11: 2, 30 June 1951.

185 **Alloway, Lawrence.** Sutherland and Moore. *Art News and Review* (London) 5 no.9: 4, ill., 30 May 1953.

186 **[Arb, Renée.]** Spotlight on Sutherland. *Art News* (New York) 47: 18, ill., Nov. 1948.

187 **Art for all** . . . poster art at Victoria and Albert Museum. *Illustrated London News* 214: 490–491, 9 Apr. 1949. Also reviewed in *Graphis* (Zürich) no.26, 1949; *Werk* (Winterthur) June 1949; *Art and Industry* (London) Apr.–June 1949; *Architectural Review* (London) May 1949; *Royal Institute of British Architects* (London) Apr.–June 1949.

188 **Art News of London.** *Art News* (New York) 37 no.3: 20, 15 Oct. 1938.

189 **Breuning, Margaret.** Modern English. *Art Digest* (New York) 20 no.11: 8, 1 Mar. 1946.

190 **Britain now: the chimeras of Sutherland.** *Art News* (New York) 45 no.1: 50, 2 col. pl., Mar. 1946.

191 **Britain's designers present** . . . *International Textiles* (London) no.5: 22–45 ill. (pt. col.), 1944.

192 **Burrows, Carlyle.** Art of the week: Graham Sutherland. *New York Herald-Tribune* section 5, p.7, 3 Mar. 1946.

193 **Clark, Kenneth.** War artists in the National Gallery. *Studio* (London) 123: 3–5, 8 ill. (pt. col.), Jan. 1942.

194 **Coates, Robert.** British, French and American. *New Yorker* (New York) 22 no.4: 74, 9 Mar. 1946.

195 **Curtis, J.** Graham Sutherland. *Studio* (London) 146: 48–51, ill. (pt. col.), Aug. 1953.

196 **Exhibition:** Graham Sutherland's works in Paris. *Manchester Guardian* 8 Nov. 1952.

197 **Feinstein, Sam.** On Sutherland's stage. *Art Digest* (New York) 27: 18, ill., 15 Mar. 1953.

198 **Fitzsimmons, James.** Art [reviews]. *Arts & Architecture* (Los Angeles) 70: 8, May 1953.

199 **Furst, Herbert.** Art news and notes: etchings and drawings by Graham Sutherland. *Apollo* (London) 8 no.47: 310, Nov. 1928.

200 **Greenberg, Clement.** [Art]. *Nation* (New York) 165 no.15: 389–390, 11 Oct. 1947.

201 **Hendy, Philip.** Graham Sutherland. *Britain Today* (London) no.148: 17–19, Aug. 1948.

202 **Heron, Patrick.** Graham Sutherland. *New Statesman and Nation* (London) 35 no.901: 477–478, 12 June 1948.

203 **Heron, Patrick.** The school of London. *New Statesman and Nation* (London) 37 no.944: 351, 9 Apr. 1949.

204 **Heron, Patrick.** Sutherland and Wood. *New Statesman and Nation* (London) 37 no.947: 432, 30 Apr. 1949.

205 **Hunter, Sam.** Chiefly abstract: paintings by Sutherland. *New York Times* section 2, p.9, 21 Nov. 1948.

206 **Ironside, R.** England's poets in paint. *Art News* (New York) 49: 20–23, ill., Oct. 1950. On the English-Speaking Union's touring exhibition. Also reviewed by B. Krasne (*Art Digest* (New York) 25: 7, 15 Oct. 1950), J. Bier (*St Louis Courier Journal Magazine* 7 Jan. 1951), etc.

207 **L. F., H.** [Henry LaFarge?] English drawing on American glass. *Art News* (New York) 53: 40, ill., May 1954. Review of Steuben show, including 5 illustrations of Sutherland's 'Mantis' design.

208 **Louchheim, Aline B.** Modern British paintings by Sutherland and sculpture by Moore in joint Boston show. *New York Times* 12 Apr. 1953.

209 **McBride, Henry.** Abstract report for April. *Art News* (New York) 52: 17, ill., Apr. 1953.

210 **Melville, Robert.** *Architectural Review* (London) 113: 133–134, ill., Feb. 1953. Also brief note on the Beaverbrook portrait at the Tate, Mar. 1952 (111: 207–208).

211 **Middleton, M. H.** Art. *Spectator* (London) no.6214: 141, 1 Aug. 1947.

212 **Middleton, M. H.** Art *Spectator* (London) no.6260: 734, 18 June 1948.

213 **Modern English.** *Newsweek* (New York) 27 no.10: 94–95, ill., 11 Mar. 1946.

214 **Mortimer, Raymond.** An arrival. *New Statesman and Nation* (London) 16 no.397: 490, 1 Oct. 1938.

215 **Mortimer, Raymond.** Notes on shows. *New Statesman and Nation* (London) 19 no.481: 615, 11 May 1940.

216 **Newton, Eric.** Current exhibitions. *Sunday Times* (London) 4 July 1948.

217 **Nicolson, Benedict.** [Review]. *New Statesman and Nation* (London) 32 no.826: 461, 21 Dec. 1946. A review to which Sutherland replied in bibl.132.

218 **Nicolson, Benedict.** Graham Sutherland. *New Statesman and Nation* (London) 14 no.1056: 446, 21 Apr. 1951.

219 **Piper, John.** Three painters. *Spectator* (London) no.5836: 626, 5 May 1940.

220 **Recent paintings at the Hanover Gallery.** *Apollo* (London) 54: 3, July 1951.

221 **Reichardt, Jasia.** Graham Sutherland. *Art News and Review* (London) 10 no.25: 3–4, ill., 3 Jan. 1959.

222 **Rouve, Pierre.** Sutherland – one, two and three. *Art News and Review* (London) 7 no.11: 6, 25 June 1955.

223 **Say it with Thorns.** *Time* (New York) 62: 46–57, ill. (col.), 3 Aug. 1953. Retrospective exhibition at the Tate Gallery. Also reviewed in *Art News* (New York) 52: 60, June 1953; *Apollo* (London) 58:3, July 1953.

224 **Seckler, Dorothy G.** Graham Sutherland. *Art News* (New York) 52: 37, Mar. 1953.

225 **Thomas, Trevor.** Moore-Piper-Sutherland exhibition. *Museums Journal* (London) 41 no.11: 260, ill., Feb. 1942.

226 **Wakefield, Hugh.** British artists decorate Steuben glass. *Studio* (London) 149: 148–151, ill., 1955. Supplemented by bibl.144.

227 **Year of the Vegetable.** *Time* (New York) 61: 74, 13 Apr. 1953.

## Catalogues and Exhibitions: Individual Exhibitions

228 **Twenty One Gallery.** Catalogue of Etchings by Graham Sutherland, A.R.E. 14 pp. 20 ill. London, 1928. Brief foreword; quotes reviews; held 27 Sept.–13 Oct. Sutherland exhibited here in 1925 (see also bibl.264,265).

229 **Rosenberg and Helft Galleries.** Recent works of Graham
Sutherland. 8 pp. London, 1938.
Show held 20 Sept.–8 Oct.; lists 25 works; introduction by
Kenneth Clark. First exhibition of Sutherland's painting.

230 **Buchholz Gallery [Curt Valentin].** Graham Sutherland.
8 pp. ill. New York, 1946.
First New York showing, 26 Feb.–23 Mar.; lists 35 works.

231 **Lefevre Galleries.** Preliminary paintings for 'The Northampton
Crucifixion' by Graham Sutherland. 16 pp. London, 1947.
Show held 1–31 July.

232 **Hanover Gallery.** Paintings by Graham Sutherland. 5 pp.
London, 1948.
Show held 2 June–11 July; lists 39 works.

233 **Buchholz Gallery [Curt Valentin].** Graham Sutherland. 8 pp. ill.
New York, 1948.
Show held 16 Nov.–4 Dec.; lists 38 works; introduction by
R. Mortimer.

234 **Institute of Contemporary Arts.** Graham Sutherland, a
retrospective selection, 1938–51. London, 1951.
Show held 10 Apr.–5 May; ill.

235 **Hanover Gallery.** Recent paintings – Graham Sutherland.
London, 1951.
Show held 20 June–4 Aug.

236 **Biennale di Venezia.** [Works by Sutherland.] Venice, 1952.
Show arranged by the British Council, shown later, with
modifications, at Paris, Amsterdam, Zurich.

237 **Musée National d'Art Moderne.** Exposition Graham Sutherland.
18 pp. 7 ill. (3 col.) Paris, 1952.
Exhibited 7 Nov.–14 Dec.; preface by H. Read; catalogue of 71
works; Notes de l'artiste, 1951.

238 **Valentin [Curt] Gallery.** Graham Sutherland. 16 pp. 13 ill.
New York, 1953.
Show held 10–28 Mar.; nos.1–14 (oils), nos.15–29 (gouaches);
preface by H. Read, pp. [2, 3–4, 6]; Sutherland's 'Thoughts on
painting' (BBC programme, Sept. 1951, bibl.137), pp. [7–8, 10–11].

239 **Institute of Contemporary Art.** [Sutherland: 50th Birthday
Retrospective]. Boston, 1953.

240 **Arts Council of Great Britain.** An exhibition of paintings and
drawings by Graham Sutherland. 16 pp. 20 pl. (4 col.)
London, 1953.
Show held May–9 Aug.; lists 77 works; additional items exhibited.
Arranged by the Arts Council and the Tate Gallery. Foreword by
P. James; Introductions by K. Clark pp. [3–4] and H. Read pp. [5–6];
biographical notes (1903–53). 'On painting: notes by the artist'
pp. [7–9].

241 **Stedelijk Museum (Amsterdam).** Graham Sutherland. 22 pp. 7 ill.
Amsterdam, 1953.
Show opened 3 Jan. Lists 63 works. Organized by the British
Council (see bibl.240).

242 **Kunsthaus (Zurich).** Graham Sutherland. 16 pp. 8 ill. Zürich, 1953.
Show held 1 Mar.–6 Apr.; lists 63 works (see bibl.240).

243 **Akademie der bildenden Künste.** Graham Sutherland. 7 pp. 8 ill.
Vienna, 1954.
Organized by the Arts Council and the Albertina; included gouaches,
watercolours and drawings; also shown at Innsbruck. Preface by
K. Clark, H. Read, and the artist: 'Über Malerei'; lists 59 works.
Similar folding catalogue (with variant list of 57 works) issued for
'Ausstellung von Gemälden und Zeichnungen' circulated to Berlin,
Cologne, Stuttgart, Mannheim, Hamburg (1954–5).

244 **Museu de Arte Moderna (São Paulo).** Obras de Sutherland.
6 pp. ill. São Paulo, 1955.
Organized by the British Council for the third biennial; lists 19 oils,
8 gouaches, 1 tapestry. Preface by H. Read.

245 **Frankfurter Kunstkabinett.** Graham Sutherland: Oelgemälde,
Gouaches, Graphiken. 16 pp. 7 ill. Frankfurt, 1957.
Show held 2 Apr.–1 May. Prefaces; lists 75 works; chronology.

246 **Hoffman Galerie.** Graham Sutherland: Gemälde, Aquarelle, Graphik.
Hamburg, 1957.
Exhibited July.

247 **Jeffress Gallery.** Graham Sutherland, a collection 1939–58. 11 pp. ill.
London, 1959.
Exhibited 13 Jan.–6 Feb.

248 **Rosenberg & Co.** Recent paintings by Graham Sutherland.
New York, 1959.
Show held 9 Nov.–5 Dec. 1959; lists 22 works; 11 ill.
Reviewed *Art News* (New York) 58:17, Nov. 1959; *Arts* (New
York) 34: 57, Nov. 1959; *Apollo* (London) 71: 26, Jan. 1960.

249 **Galleria Galatea (Turin).** Graham Sutherland. 4 pp. and cover. 3 ill.
(1 col.) Turin, 1961.
Show held 13 Jan.–2 Feb.; lists 20 works

## Group Exhibitions

250 **Leicester Galleries.** Catalogue . . . of paintings by Walter Goetz
. . . and Graham Sutherland. 8 pp. London, 1940.
Show held 1–31 May; biographical note; lists 50 works.

251 **Temple Newsam (Leeds).** Exhibition of works by Henry Moore,
John Piper, Graham Sutherland. 23 pp. Leeds, 1941.
Nos.130–163 by Sutherland; foreword by P. Hendy, pp.2–5.

251a **British Institute of Adult Education.** 3 British artists: Henry
Moore, John Piper, Graham Sutherland, 14 pp. London, 1942.

252 **Redfern Gallery.** Paul Nash, Henry Moore, John Piper, Graham
Sutherland. 5 pp. London, 1944.
Show held 6–29 Jan.; 6 works by Sutherland.

253 **Lefevre Galleries.** Recent paintings by Bacon . . . Hodgkins . . .
Moore . . . Smith . . . Sutherland. 8 pp. London, 1945.
Show held 1–30 Apr.; 11 works by Sutherland.

254 **British Council (London).** Quelques contemporains anglais.
Paris, 1945–6.
Shown at '28 Ave. des Champs Elysées'. Nine artists, including
Sutherland.

255 **Lefevre Galleries.** Recent paintings by eight British artists. 4 pp.
and cover. London, 1946.
Show held Feb. 1946. Nos. 12, 13 by Sutherland.

256 **Redfern Gallery.** Sutherland . . . Adler . . . Mayersohn . . . Ubac
. . . Bachmann. 8 pp. London, 1946.
'19 landscape studies by Sutherland'; shown 31 Oct.–23 Mar.

257 **Hanover Gallery.** Chagall and Sutherland: Watercolours.
London, 1950.
Exhibited 17 Jan.–18 Feb.

258 **Redfern Gallery.** Graham Sutherland – Keith Vaughan.
London, 1952.
Show held 27 Nov.–27 Dec. Included Sutherland's 'Ideas and studies
for the Festival painting – "The origins of the land"'.

259 **Institute of Contemporary Art (Boston).** Graham Sutherland –
Henry Moore. Boston, 1953.
Show held 2–26 Apr.; toured Canada and the United States until
spring 1954.

260 **Redfern Gallery.** Ayrton – Sutherland – Rothenstein – Wynter. London, 1953.
Show of gouaches held 6–31 Oct.

261 **Phillips Gallery.** Paintings by Graham Sutherland and sculpture by Henry Moore. Washington, D.C., 1954.
Show held 7 Mar.–6 Apr. Terminus of Boston 1953 show.

262 **Jeffress Gallery.** Five English painters. London, 1957.
Show held 9 July–2 Aug.: Kinley-Piper-Reynolds-Sutherland (nos.17–23)-Vaughan.

263 **Roland, Browse and Delbanco.** Wishaw and Sutherland. London, 1960.
Exhibit of gouaches 'around 1944'; noted *Art News and Review* (London) 12 no.2: 3, 13–27 Feb. 1960.

## Collective Exhibitions

264 **Royal Academy of Arts (London).** Catalogues of annual exhibits for 1923–30; etchings only.

265 **Royal Society of Painter-Etchers and Engravers (London).** Catalogues of annual exhibits for 1925–27 and 1930; etchings only.

266 **Musée des Arts Décoratifs.** Exposition de la gravure moderne anglaise. Paris, 1927.
Shown 20 Oct.–24 Dec.; 2 etchings.

267 **New Burlington Galleries.** International surrealist exhibition. 31 pp. London, 1936.
Show held 11 June–4 July; two paintings.

268 **Franklin Institute.** New poster. 20 pp. ill. Philadelphia, 1937.
Illustrates Sutherland's Shell-Mex poster 'Doctors prefer Shell'.

269 **Storran Gallery.** Exhibition of paraphrases (free copies). London, 1939.
Show held 15 Feb.–11 Mar. No.24 by Sutherland: Detail from 'Agony in the Garden' after El Greco.

270 **British Council.** Contemporary British art. London, 1939.
Nos.143–145 by Sutherland, ill.

271 **British Pavilion, World's Fair.** Contemporary British art. New York, 1939.
Nos.143–145 by Sutherland, ill. Also shown at the Boston Museum of Fine Arts (1940) and elsewhere.

272 **National Gallery (London).** [First exhibition of war artists]. London, July 1940.

273 **Notanda Gallery.** England today: exhibition of modern British art. Sydney, 1940.
Also exhibited at Melbourne. No.55 by Sutherland; biographical note; preface by C. Plate.

274 **Museum of Modern Art.** Britain at War, ill. New York, 1941.
6 works by Sutherland (see bibl.70).

275 **Museum of Art (Toledo).** Contemporary British art. Toledo, 1943.
Organized by the British Council; circulated by the Museum. Biographical note; nos.105–108 by Sutherland. Foreword by B. M. Godwin; introduction by J. Rothenstein. Probably same exhibition shown at the Institute Cultural Anglo-Uruguayo (Montevideo, 12–31 Aug. 1943) and America del Sur (1943).

276 **Arts Council of Great Britain.** British painters: 1939 to 1945. [London, 1945?]
Nos.63–70 by Sutherland.

277 **Suffolk Galleries.** Exhibition of historical and British wallpapers. London, 1945.
Includes Sutherland designs; preface by S. Sitwell.

278 **Buchholz Gallery [Curt Valentin].** Contemporary British artists. 5 pp. ill. New York, 1945.
Nos.26–28 by Sutherland. Catalogue also issued for show at Arts Club of Chicago (4–31 May 1945).
Introduction by J. T. Soby; reprinted in bibl.177.

279 **British Council (London).** Tableaux britanniques modernes appartenant à la Tate gallery, pp.7, 22. Paris, 1946.
Shown at the Musée de Jeu de Paume. Catalogues issued for exhibition circulated to Athens, Berne, Brussels, Rome, Stockholm, Vienna. Introduction by J. Rothenstein; nos.108–112 by Sutherland.

280 **Institute of Modern Art (Boston).** Modern British artists. Boston, 1946.
Shown 17 Apr.–26 May.

281 **Musée d'Art Moderne (Paris).** Exposition internationale d'art moderne. Paris, 1946.
Show held 18 Nov.–28 Dec.; nos.55–57 by Sutherland.

282 **Manor House (New York).** Painting by five of the younger British artists. New York, 1946.
Shown 19 Nov.–31 Dec. 'in a living room designed for a collector'; note by M. H. Middleton; no.8 by Sutherland.

283 **Albright Art Gallery.** British contemporary painters. Buffalo, 1946.
Nos.50–54 by Sutherland; text by A. C. Ritchie. Also shown at the Metropolitan Museum, 19 Sept.–31 Oct., New York, 1947.

284 **Roland, Browse and Delbanco.** British paintings of the past 50 years. London, 1947.
Show held Nov.–Dec.; no.32 by Sutherland.

285 **Studio d'Arte (Palma).** Quindici pittori inglesi. 18 pp. ill. Rome, 1947.
Shown December; nos.46–49 by Sutherland.

286 **Drouin, René, Galerie.** La jeune peinture en Grand-Bretagne. Paris, 1948.
Shown 23 Jan.–21 Feb.; organized by the British Council, also shown at the Brussels Musée d'art moderne. Nos.46–49 by Sutherland; 2 illustrations. Text by H. Read, C. Estienne, R. Guilly.

287 **Arts Council of Great Britain.** Selection of paintings and drawings acquired by the Contemporary Art Society. London, 1948.
Preface by C. Anderson; nos.59–62 by Sutherland.

288 **Lefevre Gallery.** Contemporary British painters. London, 1949.
Shown August; nos.59–60 by Sutherland.

289 **Victoria and Albert Museum.** Art for all: London Transport posters, 1908–49. London, 1949.
Shown spring, 1949; published in bibl.4.

290 **New Burlington Galleries.** Contemporary British art from the collections of the Arts Council and the British Council. London, 1949.
Nos.39–41 by Sutherland; ill.

291 **Institute of Contemporary Arts.** 40,000 years of modern art. London, 1949.
No.169 by Sutherland.

292 **Stedelijk Museum (Amsterdam).** Twaalf Britse schilders. Amsterdam, 1949.
Organized by the British Council; shown February. Nos.42–51 by Sutherland, 2 ill.; preface by H. Read.

293 **English-Speaking Union of the United States.** Last fifty years of British art, 1900–50, pp.7–8, 15. New York, 1950–1.
Included Sutherland. Preface by K. Clark.

294 **British Council.** Moderne Englische Zeichnungen und Aquarelle. 'Veranstaltet von dem British Council. Deutschland, 1950–1.'
Preface by G. Grigson. Nos.37–40 by Sutherland; ill.

295 **Pennsylvania Academy of Fine Arts.** Contemporary British painting, 1925–50. Philadelphia, 1950–1.
Show held 9 Dec. 1950–7 Jan. 1951; foreword by G. E. Dix, Jr. nos.70–74 by Sutherland.

296 **Arts Council of Great Britain.** Three centuries of British water-colours and drawings. London, 1951.
Nos.180–182 by Sutherland, introduction by B. Ford.

297 **Bristol Art Gallery.** Contemporary British painting. Bristol, 1951.
Show held 11 May–8 June; preface by J. Wood Palmer; nos.72–73 by Sutherland.

298 **Institute of Contemporary Arts.** Ten decades: a review of British taste, 1851–1951. London, 1951.
Introduction by G. Grigson. Nos.229, 251 by Sutherland.

299 **New Burlington Galleries.** British painting, 1925–50.
London, 1951.
Preface by D. Baxandall; nos.96–101 by Sutherland.

300 **Vancouver Art Gallery.** 21 modern British painters.
Vancouver, 1951.
Introduction by D. Shadbolt; nos.34–35 by Sutherland.
Organized by the British Council; circulated to Seattle, San José, San Francisco, Salt Lake City, Portland.

301 **Museu de Arte Moderna ( São Paulo).** I Bienal. São Paulo, 1951.
Shown Oct.–Dec.; nos.82–84 by Sutherland; preface to English section by R. Adam.

302 **Arts Council of Great Britain.** Three young collectors: [Banks, May, Meyer]. London, 1952.
Preface by J. Wood Palmer; 2 works by Sutherland; ill.

303 **Venice. Exposizione Biennale Internazionale d'Arte, XXVI.**
Catalogo, pp.298–304. Venice, 1952.
Also separate catalogue: 'The British pavilion exhibition of works by Sutherland, Wadsworth [and others] organized by the British Council'; preface by K. Clark; lists 68 works.

304 **Carnegie Institute.** International exhibition of contemporary painting. Pittsburgh, 1952.
Show held 16 Oct.–14 Dec.; no.266 by Sutherland.

305 **Arts Council of Great Britain.** British contemporary paintings from southern and midland galleries. London (?), 1953.
No.18 is by Sutherland.

306 **Cardiff Museum.** British romantic painting. Cardiff, 1953.
Show held 27 July–22 Aug.; also shown at the National Library of Wales (29 Aug.–19 Sept.), and the Glynn Vivian Gallery, Swansea (26 Sept.–24 Oct.).
Nos.55–57 by Sutherland.

307 **Redfern Gallery.** Coronation exhibition: Contemporary British paintings. London, 1953.
Nos.6–9 by Sutherland; 2 ill. (1 col. pl.).

308 **Arts Council of Great Britain.** Recent British painting.
London, 1954.
Foreword by J. Commander; no.55 by Sutherland.

309 **Yale University Art Gallery.** Object and image in modern art and poetry. New Haven, 1954.
Show held 30 Apr.–14 June; introduction by G. H. Hamilton; no.33 by Sutherland (ill.).

310 **Steuben glass.** British artists in crystal. New York, 1954.
Shown May (?); included 'Mantis' design by Sutherland.

311 **Walker Art Center.** Reality and fantasy, 1900–54. Minneapolis, 1954.
Show held 23 May–2 July; introduction by H. Arnason; no.160 by Sutherland.

312 **Motte Galerie.** Aspects de la peinture anglaise contemporaine.
Geneva, 1954.
Show held 28 May–18 June; 2 works by Sutherland; preface by A. Kalman.

313 **Valentin [Curt] Gallery.** In memory of Curt Valentin. New York, 1954.
Show held 5–30 Oct.; no.30 (ill.) by Sutherland.
Also included in 'Closing exhibition', 8 June 1955 (nos.173–176).

314 **Museum Fridericianum.** Documenta: Kunst des XX.
Jahrhunderts, p.61, pl.90. Kassel, 1955.
Show held 15 July–18 Sept.; nos.607–610 by Sutherland.
Introduction by W. Haftmann.

315 **Tooth, Arthur, & Sons.** Critic's choice: 1955 – Eric Newton.
London, 1955.
Show held 14 Sept.–8 Oct. 6 works by Sutherland.

316 **British Council.** British water-colours and drawings of the twentieth century – Canadian tour. Ontario, Winnipeg, Vancouver, 1955–7.
Introduction by G. Grigson; nos.55–58 by Sutherland, cover ill.

317 **Arizona Art Foundation.** Art in Britain today. Scottsdale, Arizona, 1956.
Show held 19 Mar.–14 Apr.; no.9 by Sutherland.

318 **Yale University Art Gallery.** Pictures collected by Yale alumni.
New Haven, 1956.
Show held 8 May–18 June; no.240 by Sutherland (ill.); forewords by L. Moore, T. Sizer.

319 **Silberman Galleries.** Contemporary British art. New York, 1956.
Show held 12 Oct.–10 Nov.; nos.28–33 by Sutherland; 2 ill.; foreword by J. Rothenstein.

320 **Museum of Modern Art.** Masters of British painting, 1800–1950.
9 ill. (1 col. pl.) New York, 1956.
Shown 2 Oct.–2 Dec.; nos.100–108 by Sutherland. Also shown at St Louis (10 Jan.–2 Mar. 1957), and San Francisco (28 Mar.–12 May 1957).

321 **Kunstnernes Hus.** British natidskunst: malerei, skulptur, grafikk.
Oslo, 1956.
Catalogue 175; shown 12 May–10 June. Nos.86–90, 207 by Sutherland; col. pl. (cover).

322 **Walker Art Center.** Contemporary British art. Minneapolis, 1957.
Show held 26 May–23 June.

323 **Brussels International Exhibition.** 50 ans d'art moderne.
Brussels, 1958 (see bibl.32).

324 **Arts Council.** The Arts Council Collection of paintings and drawings: [part 3] romantic and abstract. 1958–9.
Circulating show: 25 Jan. 1958–3 Jan. 1959. Preface by P. James; introduction by A. Forge; nos.42–46 by Sutherland.

# Index

DATE DUE

| JE 01 '79 | | | |
|---|---|---|---|
| | | | |
| | | | |
| | | | |
| | | | |
| | | | |
| | | | |
| | | | |
| | | | |
| | | | |
| | | | |
| | | | |
| | | | |
| | | | |
| | | | |
| | | | |